DIANA
THE LAST DAYS

DIANA
THE LAST DAYS

Martyn Gregory

This updated edition published in 2004 by
Virgin Books Ltd
Thames Wharf Studios
Rainville Road
London W6 9HA

First published in Great Britain in 1999 by
Virgin Publishing Ltd

A catalogue record for this book is available from the British Library.

ISBN 1 85227 220 1

Typeset by TW Typesetting, Plymouth, Devon
Printed and bound in Great Britain by
Mackays of Chatham PLC

CONTENTS

*This edition of the book is dedicated
to my godchildren
Laura Burden, Sam Hollamby,
Jasmine Gregory and Sebastien Delanney*

AUTHOR'S NOTE

Some of the key witnesses to the events of 30/31 August in Paris have made important contributions to this book and, where appropriate, these have been acknowledged. Some witnesses have extracted money from the media for their stories; no witness quoted in this book has received any money at all from myself or my publisher.

In attempting to piece together Princess Diana's last days I have obtained information about statements made by some witnesses to Judge Stéphan's enquiry into the Alma tunnel crash that killed Diana, Princess of Wales. France's severe legal and medical secrecy laws are designed to prevent this from being done. In practice, documents emerge unofficially, and many of them have informed this book. Readers can be sure that all factual references and quotations relating to the investigation are reliably sourced, but none can be acknowledged in my footnotes. I would like to thank those who have made this possible, and particularly those whom I am unable to identify.

Jean-Marie Pontaut and Jérôme Dupuis' excellent book *Enquête sur la mort de Diana* (Éditions Stock, Paris, 1998) makes liberal use of statements made by witnesses to the events of 30/31 August in Paris, and extracts from their book are acknowledged in the footnotes. *Death of a Princess* was painstakingly, if very rapidly, researched by *Time* magazine journalists, Thomas Sancton and Scott MacLeod and was published less than six months after the crash. Their book, too, had good access to the early months of Stéphan's investigation, and some excellent French sources. I interpret events around the crash in a different way to the two Americans, but I would like to acknowledge the value of their book's contribution to understanding how Fayed worked after the crash, and for its detailed study of the technical aspects of the crash itself.

Mohamed Fayed refused my requests to speak to him or any of his staff in Paris or in London. I am, therefore, particularly grateful to his past and present associates and employees who did speak to me. Their insights, and their information about what happened both before and after Princess Diana's death, have been invaluable. Where appropriate, their contributions are identified in the footnotes. Two of Fayed's key security personnel, Kez Wingfield and Ben Murrell, were both generous with the time they devoted to lengthy conversations with me. I am particularly grateful to them for helping me to understand what really happened during Princess Diana's last days in the Fayed family's care. Lawyers in France and Britain, who must remain anonymous, have given me valuable assistance with documents, guidance and insight.

I lent Tom Bower the interview files from my *Dispatches* investigation while he wrote his first-class, unauthorised biography of Mohamed Fayed which has already become the standard work on the Egyptian. I would like to thank him for his generous response in allowing me access to the invaluable notes he took of interviews he was permitted to conduct with Fayed's staff in Paris and London in the week after the crash.

Dr Murray Mackay, professor emeritus of Transport Safety at Birmingham University, is one of the world's leading analysts of car crashes, and he helped me to interpret the findings of the French investigation. Professor Peter Vanezis, Regius professor of Forensic Medicine and Science at Glasgow University, was kind enough to discuss his analysis of the autopsy conducted on Henri Paul.

Some of Princess Diana's closest friends have helped me both off and on the record. The personal devastation they experienced when she died has only been exacerbated by the fantasists who have feasted on her memory. This motivated many of them to speak to me; I am deeply grateful to all of them. Any mistakes I might have made are entirely my own responsibility.

Martyn Gregory
June 2004

FOREWORD

Like most people I know, I remember vividly where I was when I learnt the awful news that Princess Diana was dead. I woke at 04.00 on 31 August in a hotel room in the north of England. The television was on, showing 24-hour news – I think I must have rolled on to the remote control in my sleep. The screen showed a static shot of the entrance to the Alma tunnel. The rear of a black Mercedes was visible in a scene that was bathed in an eerie orange light and the studio presenter's voice informed me that 'Dodi Fayed is dead, and Princess Diana has been rushed to hospital . . .' I watched in stunned dismay until the Princess's coffin emerged from the Pitié Salpêtrière hospital many hours later.

From a personal point of view, the timing of the tragedy could not have been more hideously inappropriate. The previous day my brother, the Reverend Clive Gregory, had married Jenny Hyde in the village of Tetney. Some of our family's happiest moments had been celebrated that afternoon in the Lincolnshire wolds. On the morning that Princess Diana died, I made my way back to London with my other brother, Adrian, his wife Lisa and their baby daughter, Holly, listening in virtual silence to the blanket coverage of the tragedy on every radio station we tuned in to.

Princess Diana's life and death became the most ploughed furrow in world journalism in the months that followed the crash. I started my own investigation at the invitation of Channel 4's *Dispatches* programme in 1998. On the day the film was broadcast, 4 June 1998, I was the first journalist to meet with Princess Diana's bodyguard from the night she died – Alexander 'Kez' Wingfield – since he had left his post with Mohamed Fayed less than 48 hours earlier. He told me what he had witnessed that night. I could not report what Wingfield said in my film that evening, but he confirmed what I had long suspected – despite the unprecedented coverage, the real story of Princess Diana's last days, and how she came to die, had not been told. This book is my attempt to rectify that state of affairs.

Martyn Gregory
June 2004

LIST OF ILLUSTRATIONS

Part of the family: Mohamed, Dodi and Diana (Rex Features)

Princess Diana talked to friends all over the world from the *Jonikal* (Rex Features)

Dr Hasnat Khan (Rex Features)

Kelly Fisher (Rex Features)

Diana and Dodi being piloted in Saint-Tropez (Rex Features)

Diana and Dodi enter the Ritz separately (Alpha)

Diana enters the Ritz followed by Kez Wingfield (Popperfoto)

Dodi and his 'model employee', Henri Paul (BIG Pictures)

Henri Paul, Diana, Dodi and Trevor Rees-Jones (Popperfoto)

French Interior Minister Jean-Pierre Chevènement announces the death of the Princess of Wales (Popperfoto)

Mohamed Fayed arrives at the hospital (Rex Features)

Paul Handley-Greaves at the Harrods press conference. Diana was said to be pregnant with Dodi's child (BIG Pictures)

Mohamed Fayed emerges from the Palais de Justice surrounded by his security team (Popperfoto)

Michael Cole and John Macnamara (PA News)

Former British spy Richard Tomlinson (Rex Features)

François Levi/Levistre (Rex Features)

X-Ray of Trevor Rees-Jones's skull and injuries (Rex Features/Sipa)

Trevor Rees-Jones returns to Paris to give a statement to the French investigation (Associated Press)

Commander Mulès, Judges Hervé Stéphan and Marie-Christine Devidal (Getty Images)

Coroner Michael Burgess, Martine Monteil and Commissioner John Stevens (PA News)

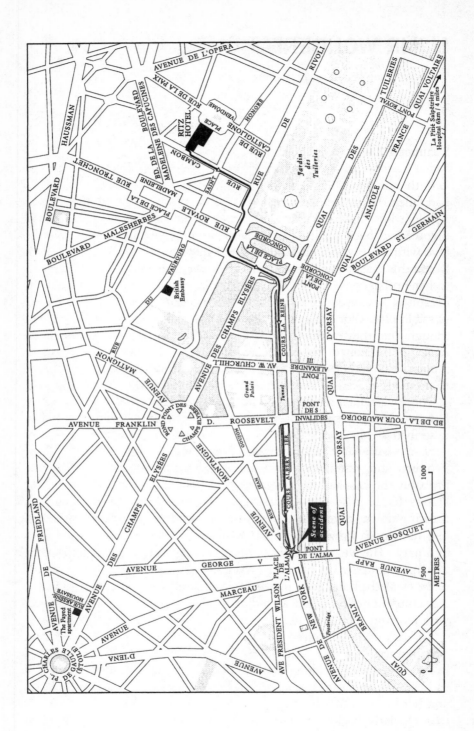

1. 'MR WONDERFUL'

'I'm never going to date an Englishman again, they're such inadequates.'
Diana, Princess of Wales

Summer 1997

Less than a year after her divorce from Prince Charles, Princess Diana had fallen deeply in love. She knew she had to hide her feelings from a public whose interest in her romantic liaisons had soared since the divorce had been finalised in August 1996. The man she had fallen in love with, and whom she called 'Mr Wonderful', was a Muslim. Diana feared that because of this he would be unacceptable to certain elements in her British constituency. Privately, however, she told friends that she dreamt of having his children. She had even asked friends to scout out possible places for the two of them to live after they had married. She thought that they might settle in Nelson Mandela's apartheid-free South Africa, or possibly on the west coast of the USA. Diana longed to become a plain 'Mrs' rather than a Princess, and she had even travelled abroad to meet her new man's extended family.

The lovers had shared nights together in Kensington Palace. Only Diana's closest friends and her butler, Paul Burrell, whom she once described as her 'rock', knew of her new romance, and her secret was very safe with him. In London the couple loved the West End, taking in clubs and restaurants in Soho and Camden. Because Diana was probably the best-known face in the world, she wore wigs, scarves and glasses to disguise her appearance. Dressing up, or more accurately dressing down, gave Diana an enormous thrill. A close friend who saw her in her dark wig said that it succeeded in making Diana look 'ordinary'. The wig enabled her to do everyday things, such as shopping in supermarkets and queuing, without being recognised. She would place excited phone calls to friends from the queue for Ronnie Scott's jazz club in London. She was 'hiding in plain sight', as one of her friends who received such calls put it.

The risk of the disguised Princess being detected on such expeditions was reduced by her companion's appearance. He was a slightly overweight, chain-smoking, dark-skinned foreigner. Rather than use one of her own limousines or expensive and powerful run-arounds, Diana and her lover would drive into the West End in his clapped-out old car that regularly backfired. The Princess was more worried about being rumbled by a policeman stopping the car than being recognised by anyone in the street. She called her companion on these trips 'Mr Wonderful'. He called himself Dr Hasnat Khan.[1]

'Isn't he drop-dead gorgeous!' Princess Diana remarked immediately after she met Dr Khan for the first time at the Royal Brompton hospital in 1995. The surgeon had chatted with Diana in blood-spattered surgical boots for a few minutes after she had dropped into the hospital to visit a friend. The talented Pakistani had arrived in England to work under the internationally renowned heart surgeon, Professor Sir Magdi Yacoub. His life's ambition was to become a consultant, and working under Yacoub represented an enormous step in that direction.

Diana took the initiative by inviting Khan to dinner at Kensington Palace in the autumn of 1995, after meeting him casually several times at the hospital. The couple enjoyed weekends in the Stratford-upon-Avon home of Khan's relatives. They would spend some nights together in the luxury of Kensington Palace, others in the more spartan accommodation of Hasnat's on-call quarters at the Royal Brompton. Sometimes a bewigged Diana would steal into the hospital. On other occasions she would visit patients before slipping into Hasnat's rooms.

Khan insisted that their relationship remain private and thus they were obliged to embark upon a series of deceits to ensure that it stayed that way. Even though Khan's name was occasionally mentioned in the papers as being a 'friend' of Diana's, he was not prepared to countenance the publicity that would engulf an announcement of their true relationship.

Diana was prepared to feed disinformation to the media to keep the illusion that her friendship with Khan was simply a professional one. To do this she ruthlessly exploited her media contacts. In November 1996, for example, the *Sunday Mirror* splashed the story of her romance with Hasnat Khan while Diana was in Australia. Knowing that such exposure could be fatal to her relationship with the publicity-shy doctor, she briefed the *Daily Mail*'s Richard Kay with information to defuse the *Mirror* story. Kay was probably closer to Diana than any other journalist, and Diana knew a story under his byline would be influential as other journalists were aware of their friendship. Kay was also in Australia at the time, and his 4 November story appeared to demolish the *Sunday Mirror*'s scoop. He wrote, 'Princess Diana succinctly described a report that she was in love with a doctor as b******t.' An 'aide' was then

---

[1] Details of Khan romance from *Diana: The Secret Years*, Simone Simmons, *Sunday People* 29 November 1998, and briefings from Diana's friends. The best account of Diana's relationship with Hasnat Khan is Kate Snell's *Diana: Her Last Love* (Granada Media/Andre Deutsch, 2000).

quoted as rubbishing the report, claiming, 'It is no secret the two are friends, but in an entirely professional way. Mr Khan is one of many doctors that the Princess knows at the Brompton and Harefield hospitals in London. That is all there is to it.'

The previous year Diana had been caught by a photographer from the *News of the World* as she left the hospital after visiting Khan. To prevent her romance being exposed, she gave the reporters a sensational reason for her presence at the hospital. That Sunday's front page featured a 'World Exclusive' on how the Princess had been secretly visiting patients at the hospital late at night, in order to spare them the inevitable press attention that followed her everywhere.[2]

Another celebrated public sighting of Diana disguised a Hasnat-related mission, and illustrated her determination to keep her friendship with him out of the papers. Diana was famously photographed in April 1996 observing an operation at the Royal Brompton in the *News of the World*. The pictures, showing her heavily mascaraed doe eyes peeping out from over a surgical mask, were widely seen as part of her bid to achieve her objective of becoming, as she herself later put it, 'Queen of people's hearts'.[3]

On another occasion when the *News of the World* was preparing an exposé of her relationship with Khan, Diana asked one of her friends, Simone Simmons, to phone and tell the *News of the World* that she was still seeing Oliver Hoare.[4] Hoare was a former 'friend' of Diana's – an art dealer who had come into the public eye over a series of late-night nuisance phone calls which Diana was accused of making.

Experienced by now in manipulating the press, Diana was able to keep the lid on the story of her romance, but she found Hasnat's reticence to go public both alluring and frustrating. She loved being with a talented man who was so dedicated to his work and who was not the least bit impressed with her status. Friends said that he was drawn to Diana's caring and her compassion. He feared that a public relationship with Diana would prevent him carrying on with his own work. Khan's family welcomed her into their midst with a lack of pretence that deeply impressed her. One friend summed it up succinctly: 'Diana had spent years meeting a selection of complete arseholes, aristos and people always trying to impress her but she was completely unimpressable. She said, "I'm never going to date an Englishman again, they're such inadequates." '[5]

---

[2] Mark Honigsbaum, *Spectator*, 27 September 1997.
[3] Panorama interview with Martin Bashir, 20th November 1996.
[4] *Diana: The Secret Years*, Simone Simmons.
[5] *Sunday People*, 29 November 1998.

A sign of Diana's commitment to Hasnat was that she introduced him to her sons, William and Harry, on several occasions. According to Diana's friends, the two boys approved of him. The Princess was determined that William and Harry should learn about her loves first-hand rather than reading about them in the papers.

Diana's well-publicised and much photographed visit to Pakistan to see Jemima Goldsmith and her husband Imran Khan, also involved a degree of subterfuge. Her main reason for being in the country was to visit Hasnat's mother, Mrs Naheed Khan, in the hope that she could convince her that she would make a suitable wife for her son. According to Diana's friends, Naheed Khan was not convinced. Mrs Khan wanted her son to marry a woman from the family's own, aristocratic Pathan clan. She felt that Diana was not 'dignified' enough, despite the Princess's strong desire to fit into a Muslim family with loving and supportive bonds. Maternal objection to Diana weighed heavily with Hasnat, and was one factor in the relationship's foundering in the early summer of 1997. According to very close friends, Diana was at a loss to think how she would be able to overcome Mrs Khan's reservations. Playing on Hasnat's jealousy might flush out his true feelings.

In early June, Diana was seen nightclubbing for the first time since her divorce from Prince Charles. Her companion was Gulu Lavani, an extremely wealthy businessman, also a Pakistani. According to her closest friend she had a major row with Hasnat after a description of how the couple danced until well after midnight in Annabel's nightclub was reported in the papers.

As she danced with Lavani, Diana was trying to decide whether to accept his offer to holiday with him at his luxury beach house in Thailand, which would surely have made Hasnat even more angry, or another offer she had received from Mohamed Fayed and his family. She had known the Egyptian billionaire for some time as he was a friend of her late father, Johnnie Spencer. Diana's father had been one of Harrods' most loyal customers. His widow, Raine Spencer, had subsequently accepted Fayed's invitation to become a member of the board of Harrods. Diana had declined Fayed's invitation to follow in her stepmother's footsteps. However, she thought fondly of the controversial Egyptian businessman and his family. He had invited the Princess to holiday with him in the past but she had always refused. Diana knew that successive governments had refused to grant him British citizenship. Because Diana was divorced, she was free to holiday where she wished; however, she required permission from Her Majesty the Queen if she wanted her sons, the heirs to the throne, to accompany her on holiday.

As Prince Charles had expressed no objection to the idea, Diana did not imagine there would be a problem.

Diana was primarily concerned that William and Harry should have a really good holiday in the first summer since her divorce. She also wanted to enjoy her summer. She told the designer, Lana Marks, that she did not intend to spend it staring at the walls in Kensington Palace.[6]

Friends she discussed her holiday dilemma with in private expressed little enthusiasm for the idea of her going away with the Fayeds. One close friend, Rosa Monckton, strongly advised Diana not to go on the holiday.

Rosa Monckton is the wife of Dominic Lawson, the editor of the Conservative-supporting *Sunday Telegraph*, and Princess Diana would not necessarily have expected her to think favourably of Fayed after he had been involved in discrediting John Major's Conservative government in the Cash for Questions scandal.[7] However, Diana was also godmother to Monckton's daughter, Domenica, and Rosa insists her concern for Diana was personal and not political. The two women had forged their strong friendship while Diana's marriage to Prince Charles was disintegrating. Princess Diana regularly sought Rosa Monckton's friendship and guidance as she parted from the Prince. Over the years neighbours had frequently spotted the Princess calling in at Monckton's West London house which was close to Kensington Palace.

Close friends in the media warned Princess Diana that there would be an almighty outcry if she were to be seen anywhere near Fayed and his family, particularly with her sons. Anti-Fayed newspapers and media outlets, of which there were many, would not miss the chance to criticise Diana's choice of her first holiday host since her divorce. Some media friends told Diana they would ensure they were on holiday so their editors would not be able to ask them to cover the story if she decided to accept Fayed's invitation. Diana replied that she 'couldn't understand' what they were making a fuss about. The Princess told them that Fayed 'seemed so charming'.[8]

Diana had an ability that many friends had noted to close her ears to advice she did not wish to hear. Some of those who had advised the Princess against the Fayed holiday did not hear anything from Diana until they saw her picture on the front pages of the newspapers with the

---

[6] Author's interview with Lana Marks.

[7] Conservative politicians that had been caught up in what became known as the 'Cash for Questions' scandal had been ousted in the May 1997 general election as their government fell. However, Fayed's own role in the affair had been unsavoury.

[8] Author's interview with Henry Porter for *Dispatches*.

Fayeds in the middle of July. A key factor in Diana's decision to accept the Fayed family's invitation had been her feeling that William and Harry would enjoy themselves with other children of their own age: she hoped that her two sons would get along with the four young Fayed children – Karim, Jasmine, Camilla and Omar. Fayed had promised the Princess that the privacy she craved would be guaranteed by his own security around the villa in which they would be staying. In correspondence with Fayed's office Diana was assured, 'If we handle this thing properly, nobody will ever even know that you've gone. The idea is that you have a quiet family holiday.'[9]

Everyone in the Fayed family circle was aware how much the Princess's decision to bring the two princes to the South of France would mean to Mohamed. In June, shortly after Diana had told him she would accept his invitation, Mohamed led a family expedition to Pisa in Italy to inspect a luxury yacht he was thinking of buying to entertain the royal party. The *Jonikal* was a fifty-five-metre long, 873-tonne pleasure yacht he thought might be suitable for the holiday. He brought an interior designer to give him professional advice. Fayed's eldest son by his first marriage, 41-year-old Dodi, joined his father on his Italian jaunt. Dodi was accompanied by his girlfriend, Kelly Fisher, the Calvin Klein model he had been dating for nearly a year.

Fayed was keen to ensure that everything was in place for the royal party, and he wanted the yacht's decor to be appropriate. As Kelly toured the boat with Mohamed, he asked for her opinion.

'We went over some pictures that Mohamed wanted to hang around the boat, and he asked me if I liked them. They were posters so I said, no I didn't like them. I didn't think he should put posters up on a multimillion dollar yacht.'[10]

Despite such light-hearted disagreements over decor, Kelly enjoyed the trip to Pisa. She knew how excited Mohamed was at the prospect of welcoming royal visitors and how he craved acceptance. Earlier in the year he had invited Kelly to meet the Queen at the Royal Windsor Horse Show. Her modelling commitments prohibited her from taking up the invitation.

On 11 June, shortly after the family returned from Pisa, Princess Diana wrote to accept Fayed's holiday invitation, on behalf of herself and Princes William and Harry. The following day Mohamed bought the yacht for twenty million US dollars from its Italian owners. It was

[9] Michael Cole letter to Diana in *Death of a Princess*, p. 96.
[10] Author's interview with Kelly Fisher.

registered in the name of his Bermuda based company, Mohafa (an acronym of Mohamed Al Fayed) Shipping Co. Ltd, twelve days later on 24 June.[11] Mohamed Fayed was ready to receive the Princess of Wales and her two sons.

Few people were in a better position to understand Fayed than Adnan Khashoggi, who knew the Italian textile manufacturers from whom Fayed bought the *Jonikal*. One of the best-known arms dealers in the world, Khashoggi had known Fayed for over forty years. Once his inspiration, mentor and business partner, the Saudi Arabian had also become his brother-in-law when Fayed married his sister Samira Khashoggi in 1954. The two men later fell out very badly after Fayed's adultery led to Samira divorcing him, a year after the birth of their son, Dodi. Khashoggi terminated his business relationship with Fayed in 1958.

Khashoggi remained an acute observer of Fayed's business career which had prospered in the shadow of his own, and had an interesting observation about the royal visit:

> As a Middle Easterner, if you have a VIP visiting you, you make a special effort. But I think in this case the special effort to get a boat for $20 million had other meanings than the high seas. To over-impress Princess Diana. I think basically he wanted to get closeness to the British Royal Family, to the British government . . . we say when an opportunity knocks on your door either you open the door and take advantage of it or you don't answer it. Well, Mohamed is the type that would open the door. That's what he was doing in Saint-Tropez.[12]

Someone else who could have been expected to be acutely aware of the opportunities that the royal visit could present for his boss, was Fayed's 54-year-old spokesman, Michael Cole. The former BBC news reporter had developed a second career after joining Harrods as Director of Public Affairs in 1988. He was well placed to manage the PR side of the royal visit as he had been the BBC's court correspondent until shortly before he left the corporation. He thus had firsthand experience and knowledge of royal protocol, and had got to know Princess Diana professionally while at the BBC. Indeed, it was while making a BBC film about the Duke and Duchess of Windsor, a film which I directed, that Michael Cole first met Mohamed Fayed.

---

[11] Details from the transcript of register.
[12] Author's interview with Khashoggi.

As Michael Cole prepared for the royal visit to the Fayeds' villa in the South of France he was in his element. Ever since he had taken over as Fayed's spokesman, Cole had spent much of his career on the defensive. A DTI inquiry into Mohamed Fayed's acquisition of Harrods had indelibly blemished his boss's reputation, and cast a major shadow over his extensive philanthropic and charitable work. It had also overshadowed his success in turning Harrods into his British power base. Fayed's longstanding bid for a British passport showed no signs of being resolved in his favour, despite a new government being elected. His four children by Heini, his second wife, of Finnish descent, were British by virtue of being born in the UK, but their father was still denied citizenship.

In the summer of 1997, Cole knew that Fayed faced at least two further serious threats to his standing. The first was a libel case which Fayed had launched against the society magazine, *Vanity Fair*, over an article about him two years earlier. Although mild in comparison with much that has subsequently been written about him, Fayed instructed his lawyers to sue the magazine. The case was showing ominous signs of backfiring. The lawyers representing *Vanity Fair*'s owners, Condé Nast, had proved resilient and the magazine's London editor, Henry Porter, had also become a considerable thorn in Fayed's side.

The second threat came from 'Tiny' Rowland, whose ten-year feud with Fayed, ostensibly resolved in 1993, had started to become a nuisance again. By the summer of 1997 Rowland was claiming that Fayed had personally supervised a break-in to a safety deposit box in Harrods, which the former Lonhro chief had forgotten he owned until it was brought to his attention by Fayed's disaffected former head of security, Bob Loftus. Rowland was incensed by the break-in, and his allegations against Fayed were also being investigated by Scotland Yard. It was possible that the Yard's investigation might result in criminal charges being levelled against the Harrods boss and several of his senior staff.

This police investigation into Fayed was ongoing as Princess Diana and her sons prepared for the South of France. For Cole the royal visit was a PR gamble it would be difficult to lose. He had written to Princess Diana saying that he hoped that her holiday with the Fayeds would pass unnoticed. It would have been optimistic, to put it mildly, to believe that Princess Diana and her sons were going to enjoy an undetected holiday, but if the most likely outcome occurred, and the holiday became a media jamboree, Fayed couldn't lose either. He would be seen relaxing informally with royalty.

The press, however, had different ideas. When the story broke in the middle of July, a picture of a casually clad Mohamed Fayed with his arm around the Princess's waist on board the *Jonikal* appeared all over the British press, and prompted an angry response.

Diana's holiday companion was identified as a SLEAZE ROW TYCOON on the front page of the *News of the World*, while the *Sunday Mirror* ran with the more succinct DI'S FREEBIE. Inside the paper quoted Harold Brookes-Baker, editor of *Burke's Peerage*, the directory of the British aristocracy, spluttering, 'This is totally irresponsible of the Princess'. The *Daily Telegraph* summed up a lot of people's feelings with their headline PRINCESS AND HARRODS BOSS SAIL INTO NEW CONTROVERSY.

Abroad, the press speculated about the holidaymakers' relationship in more lurid terms. *Paris Match* compared young divorcee Diana with Jackie Kennedy, widow of the murdered American President, who embarked upon a second marriage with the considerably older Aristotle Onassis, the Greek oil tycoon, during a holiday on his yacht. The magazine was forced, however, to admit that such an outcome was unlikely given the presence of Mohamed's wife, Heini, on the *Jonikal*.

Michael Cole was quick to brush off criticism in the press as spiteful and unfair, huffily pointing out to journalists that 'this is a private holiday. It is a private matter for the Princess and her children and their father.'[13]

The publicist, Max Clifford, gave his own opinion to journalists. Clifford had forged a strong personal link with Fayed during the Cash for Questions scandal, and he had also developed a rapport with Cole. Clifford says he accepted no money, as he told the *Times*:

'The Princess will have gone into this with her eyes wide open . . . One of the reasons why she is the most popular member of the Royal Family is because she mixes with all sorts of people and understands how most of us think'.[14]

There was no comment from Buckingham Palace.

In the London *Evening Standard*, Henry Porter reacted furiously to the pictures of Princess Diana being handled by Fayed on board his yacht: 'The judgement of the Princess of Wales – normally so acute about her public profile – plainly suffered a lapse when the idea of spending a holiday with Mohamed Al Fayed was raised. To expose herself to this tubby social climber's hospitality would be bad enough, but suggests that she has succumbed to the old allure of a yacht in the sun . . . which the Royal Family past and present has found hard to resist.'

---

[13] *Daily Telegraph*, 14 July 1997.
[14] *The Times*, 14 July 1997.

Porter reminded his readers of the Duchess of York's reputation as a 'freeloader' and 'gift seeker'. In an article derisively entitled 'A graduate of the royal school of junketing', Porter derided Princess Diana's decision to take her sons on holiday with the Fayed family. He conjured up the spectacle of Fayed's involvement in the Cash for Questions scandal.

'We expect better these days ... it is inconsistent to accept money from the public purse, or in the case of Diana, a large divorce settlement from her husband, at the same time as benefiting from the largesse of a man like Mohamed Al Fayed. We pay them to keep their distance, just as we paid Neil Hamilton and his wife not to accept Al Fayed's hospitality at the Ritz hotel.'[15] Porter could not have known when he wrote his article that the Fayeds would entertain Princess Diana herself at the Ritz hotel before the month was out.

Readers of the *Evening Standard* would not necessarily have known that the author was involved in a bitter legal battle with Fayed at the time. When Diana was pictured on the *Jonikal*, the libel case was scheduled to be heard in the High Court in London in October 1997. As editor, Porter was at the helm of *Vanity Fair*'s defence.

Having discovered in the course of preparing their defence, information about Fayed's attitude towards women, the pictures of him cavorting with a scantily clad Diana particularly appalled Porter. Diana was now, literally, in his hands.

Porter was worried chiefly about the potential danger to Diana's reputation. It would be uncharacteristic if Fayed did not seek to exploit his freshly forged royal link with the Princess and her two sons to his own advantage in the libel case. Fayed had instructed George Carman QC, the most feared libel lawyer in Britain, to prosecute *Vanity Fair*.

In addition to Porter's proprietorial concern induced by Diana consorting with his sworn enemy, Porter was concerned for Diana on a personal level. Though he did not himself enjoy a personal friendship with the Princess, he had met her socially on a couple of occasions, and was delighted when his daughter had presented Diana with a bouquet when she was the guest of honour at the *Vanity Fair* summer party in 1996.

Porter resolved as soon as he saw the pictures of Diana with Fayed that he should warn her of the danger she could be placing herself in. Through intermediaries he sent urgent warnings to the Princess. He was disturbed when both intermediaries informed him that his warnings had not been well received: 'I think she felt she could handle it all, I think

---

[15] *Evening Standard*, 14 July 1997.

she felt that he was sometimes a "rogue" – she put it in that mild way – but that he was no threat to her. Frankly she took no notice whatsoever.'[16]

Porter also knew about Fayed's dubious, yet perfectly legal, practice of bugging his staff and colleagues' telephones, as well as those in his private residences, such as the villa in Saint-Tropez where Diana and the princes were staying with the Fayed family. On the basis of what he had learnt about Fayed's past activities, Porter was concerned that Fayed might take a secret recording of the Princess while she was in his family's care. *Vanity Fair*'s lawyers had come across very substantial evidence of what Porter describes as Fayed's

almost obsessive use of eavesdropping equipment. All sorts of things have appeared from former employees demonstrating that he made a great habit of taping telephone calls, bugging rooms, filming people and so forth. And this we felt was quite dangerous for her, for obvious reasons: she was the most famous woman in the world and she could easily have been taped; she'd already had trouble with taped conversations in her life [the 'Squidgy tapes' of a private conversation with a boyfriend which had been leaked to the press] and she could easily have been taped talking, unawares that she was being listened to.[17]

Porter knew from Fayed's former director of security, Bob Loftus, that Fayed had already used his sophisticated security setup to track the Princess when she had visited Harrods. A former major in the Royal Military Police, Loftus had worked for Fayed for nine years before he was dismissed in 1996. He had become *Vanity Fair*'s most important witness as it constructed its defence against Fayed's libel writ. He had retained nearly 300 hours of tapes that Fayed had instructed him to record while he worked for him. Included amongst these were several which revealed how Fayed had monitored Princess Diana's progress around Harrods before appearing to bump into her by chance.

Whenever Diana appeared in the store, security assistants stationed at every door were expected to report the fact to the control centre. Loftus would then be advised – and so would Fayed's private secretary, Mark Griffiths, or his personal assistant. They would also be told where she was heading.

---

[16] Author's interview with Henry Porter for *Dispatches*.
[17] Author's interview with Henry Porter for *Dispatches*.

Often, especially after her separation and divorce, she would have no personal-protection officer with her, unless one of the princes was accompanying her. She would be uninhibited as she walked around the store, often stopping to talk to people.

Once Fayed had been notified (assuming he was in the store) he would find out from store detectives exactly where she was, and then go down to the shop floor – with his own personal-protection team – to greet her, making the whole thing look like a chance meeting.

Porter feared that the Princess, enjoying her first summer since her divorce from Prince Charles, was a vulnerable target for what he saw as Fayed's wiles. She had not much to do that summer, and she needed somewhere to entertain her children when they broke up from school: 'he was a rich man with an apparently jolly nature, with immense generosity, offering her a boat and every possible enjoyment on her holiday, and she was really a sitting duck.'[18]

The pithy one-liner that perhaps best sums up the nature of the beast that Porter believed Mohamed Fayed represented, was minted by the CIA more than thirty years earlier. As they monitored Fayed's activities in Haiti, they reported that he was at once 'friendly and evil'.[19]

Fayed's colourful past had made him obsessed with his personal safety, and that of his family. In the intervening three decades, as Fayed's wealth and his empire had grown, he had built one of the most extensive personal security setups in Europe. The long, dirty wars with Tiny Rowland had further heightened his paranoia over his own security, and that of his young and growing second family.

Former employees, headed by Bob Loftus, had given detailed accounts of Fayed's extraordinary obsession with his personal security, details which could only have comforted Princess Diana as she flew with her sons to the South of France in the Gulfstream jet provided by her host. She could not have failed to notice how Fayed's team supplemented the security provided by the Royal and Diplomatic Protection squad.

In charge of Fayed's personal close-protection team was a large, bespectacled former British soldier, 32-year-old Paul Handley-Greaves. Michael Cole had liaised with Kensington Palace over the details of Diana's holiday and Handley-Greaves would be responsible for the close protection that would be required. Handley-Greaves had served in the Middle East, guarding the British Ambassador in Beirut at one stage in his career, before joining Fayed in 1996. Fayed had been particularly

---

[18] Author's interview with Henry Porter for *Dispatches*.
[19] Quoted by Bower, *Fayed*, p. 22.

pleased to hire Handley-Greaves, as he had obtained the distinction of winning the 'sword of honour' when he was at Sandhurst.

Fayed's own bodyguards – usually referred to by him and his family as 'donkeys', or even, to the knowledge and disgust of the guards, as 'dickheads' – were trained in Close Protection to guidelines developed by the Royal Military Police. These had been devised by the RMP to protect members of the British government and the Royal Family. The guidelines prescribe that, 'Each company in overseas theatres is to maintain a five man team for tasks within the theatre'.[20] For his own family, Fayed insisted on even more rigorous measures – undercover bodyguards were inserted into his children's schools, and car patrols cruised through the area to spot potential kidnappers when they were away from home.

The Fayed team's quasi-military bearing and communications were impressive. The whole family were allocated secret codewords that the bodyguards used when they spoke to each other on shortwave radios, or muttered into mobile phones. Fayed himself was known as 'Condor', his Finnish wife, Heini, as 'Dove'. Three of Fayed's children were known by the codewords 'Hawk', 'Kestrel' and 'Raven'. Fayed's bulletproof car that he uses in London is known as 'Lion', and his gold jet ranger helicopter is codenamed 'Greyhound'. The epicentre of Fayed's empire, Harrods, is known as 'Snowdon', and his favoured London heliport at Battersea as 'Sparrow'. Fayed's head of security in Paris, Ben Murrell, remembered how close protection personnel waiting for Fayed to land at 'Sparrow' were required to communicate: 'If you are waiting at the heliport, instead of saying "Mohamed is two minutes away", we used the word "Moon" which meant that he was two minutes away from landing.'

When questioned over the Princess's security in Saint-Tropez by journalists concerned about the arrangements that had been made for Diana and the two princes, Fayed was able to boast, 'she has superb security, both Scotland Yard and my own 24-hour bodyguards, who are ex-British army, either SAS or the marines. There are always four security men wherever she and the children go.'[21]

Even though the team around the royal party was one short of the RMP textbook requirements, and only half the number who routinely surround Fayed whenever he emerges in public himself, the presence of the princes' two Royal and Diplomatic Protection Squad officers compensated for the shortfall.

---

[20] Royal Military Police Training Instruction, Close Protection Course Manual.
[21] *Mail on Sunday*, 20 July 1997.

Princess Diana and her two sons struck up a good rapport with the Fayed guards during the holiday. Diana was particularly struck by the performance of a former royal marine, Alexander 'Kez' Wingfield, and made a point of writing to him personally when she returned to Britain. Wingfield had worked for Fayed for five years since leaving the marines, and he was the leader of the close-protection team Handley-Greaves assigned to Princess Diana. As a marine corporal Wingfield had completed the Royal Military Police Close Protection course, and he had served at NATO HQ at Northwood, where he was stationed.

Dodi Fayed did not join his father in the South of France for the start of the royal visit. He was enjoying a break with his girlfriend Kelly Fisher in Paris. Kelly had a modelling assignment in Nice in the week that Princess Diana was to spend with the Fayeds, and she hoped they would meet the Princess later in the week. Dodi had been presented to the Princess on a couple of occasions in the past, but Kelly had never met her. As France celebrated Bastille Day on Monday, 14 July, the couple paid a visit to Mohamed's villa Windsor, in the Bois de Boulogne on the outskirts of Paris. They both knew it would be their last visit to see the villa in its current state because Mohamed had decided to auction its entire contents in two months' time. What neither knew as they played with their pet dog, Bear, in the villa's spacious grounds was that they would never again visit the villa as a couple.[22]

The villa had been the Duchess of Windsor's home until her death in 1986, and Mohamed Fayed had rented it from the city of Paris since that time. The then Mayor of Paris, Jacques Chirac, had allowed Fayed to take over the property at a nominal rent, as the Egyptian had promised to restore the shabby house to the standard that the former King Edward VIII and his wife had maintained. Fayed's restoration of the Paris Ritz in the 1980s had greatly impressed Chirac, and in recognition of the millions he had spent on the hotel, he was awarded France's 'Chevalier de la Légion d'Honneur' in 1986. In 1993 he was promoted to the rank of 'Officier'.

The villa's main rooms and the Windsors' living quarters on the first floor had been faithfully restored, and kept as a private museum, while the top floor was an apartment for the Fayed family's private use. Gregorio Martin, a Spaniard who had been the Windsors' chauffeur still lived there, more than thirty years after he had started working at the villa. He had been retained as a caretaker and general factotum.

---

[22] Author's interview with Kelly Fisher.

Mohamed Fayed had, however, tired of the expense of maintaining the villa, and had decided to sell all its contents at auction. Sotheby's had commissioned a shipping firm to start packing 40,000 items from the villa later in the month, and take them to its New York auction house. Because this would be Dodi and Kelly's last visit before the New York auction, Kelly brought along her video camera so she could capture a few memories. Ben Murrell watched the couple tour the villa and play with their dog. A former marine commando, Murrell lived there with his wife, Rebecca. The Murrells remember Dodi and Kelly looking happy together as they played with Bear in the garden and wandered around the house.

Kelly might have been one of America's top models, but as a camera operator she was a cheerful amateur. The wobbly pictures she took were intended only for private viewing and were strictly for fun. The tape shows the couple fooling around in the Duchess's bedroom, and the footage she took included a famous 1939 portrait of the Duchess of Windsor painted by Gerald Brockhurst, with Kelly and her camera visible in the mirror. The Duchess's famous pug-dog cushions are much in evidence on the tape, and the couple can be heard chatting fondly to each other.

'We should do this in our house, baby!' cried Kelly to Dodi at one point on the video. The house Kelly was referring to was the luxury, multimillion-dollar mansion that Mohamed had bought for Dodi in Malibu, California. It was the house the couple were planning to share.

Later in the day, back at the Fayed apartment just off the Champs-Elysées, Dodi received a call from his father that would change both his and Kelly's lives for ever. Knowing how obedient Dodi always was to his father's wishes, Kelly was not particularly surprised when Dodi came off the phone and announced that his father required his presence in London. Dodi told Kelly that they would rendezvous in Saint-Tropez when he returned. This fitted in with their holiday plans, and Kelly's modelling assignment in Nice the following week. Kelly had been dating Dodi for ten months and she knew how the Fayed family worked well enough not to object to Dodi's sudden disappearance.

Dodi was born not long before his parents' divorce in 1956. In his name at least the child was devoutly Muslim – he was given the name 'Emad', which means 'Pillar of Faith' – but, just as he would be known throughout his life by the pet name of Dodi, religion would not play a significant part in his life. Under Egyptian law his father took custody of Dodi after his divorce from Samira, but his burgeoning business interests meant that Mohamed was away from the family home in

Alexandria for lengthy periods of time. The boy spent much of his childhood in the care of his uncle Salah and his wife, Adriana. He is remembered as a solitary and shy child, very backward in his studies and barely literate at the age of ten.[23] Deprived of his mother, whom the angry Mohamed had tried to block completely from his life, he was racked with anxiety and often screamed and cried in his sleep. When his father was at home he was tormented by the sounds of his son's misery, and, as he has told journalists, he often took Dodi into his own bed for comfort.[24] He attempted to make up for the shortcomings in his son's emotional life by spoiling him materially; indeed, his rapid success in international commerce made conspicuous consumption possible. As a boy Dodi was showered with toys; as a teenager he was relocated to London, given a luxury apartment of his own in his father's block in Park Lane, and granted the services of a chauffeur and his own Rolls-Royce.

In adolescence Dodi remained academically ungifted, lasting less than a year at the Institut Le Rosey in Switzerland,[25] and begging to leave after only a few weeks at the Sandhurst military academy. Unfit, and unused to discipline and early rising, the seventeen-year-old enjoyed only one aspect of his short career there – playing polo. Indeed, it was at a polo tournament sponsored by his father that he first met the Princess of Wales in 1986.[26]

Mohamed was often frustrated by his son, who seemed to many to lack the drive and passion that spurred on his ambitious father. As a young man, Dodi seemed happy to drift through life, funded by his now multimillionaire father. His monthly allowance (rumoured to be around £100,000–150,000) was largely squandered on meals in expensive restaurants, visits to exclusive nightclubs, parties for glamorous friends and high living. Although his father loved him dearly – he even named one of his fleet of boats after him – he was sometimes enraged when confronted with the bills for Dodi's escapades.

The cocaine habit his son acquired in the 1980s did not help him to find a purpose in life.[27] Several times his father cut off his allowance and refused to pay his huge credit card bills, but Dodi became adept at

---

[23] All information on Dodi's early life taken from Bower unless otherwise stated.

[24] Reported in several UK newspapers, 31 August 1997.

[25] *Death of a Princess*, p. 55.

[26] *Death of a Princess*, p. 48.

[27] Dodi's cocaine habit is widely referred to in all sources that do not rely on the testimony of his father or his employees. In his book, Dodi's butler René Delorm explicitly denies that he ever saw evidence of drug taking when employed by Dodi.

playing on the family enmities he had lived with as a child. He knew he was always welcome with his mother's side of the family, the Khashoggis, whom Mohamed despised, and whose lifestyle was perhaps even more glamorous than his own. When father and son suffered their biggest schism in the early 1980s Dodi spent much of his time with his uncle's family, and did not even inform his father of his first engagement, to an Iranian girlfriend, in 1983. It was later broken off. When father and son were reconciled, it was on the condition that Dodi have nothing further to do with his mother's side of the family. When Samira died in 1986 Dodi was devastated, but he agreed not to attend her funeral.

At times, however, father and son were a close and loving duo. Dodi was responsible for two of Mohamed's luckiest breaks – he introduced him both to his second wife, Heini Wathen, 34 years his junior, and to the Sultan of Brunei, the richest man in the world, whom Dodi met at a party thrown by Adnan Khashoggi. The Sultan was later widely held to be the source of the funds the Fayeds used to purchase House of Fraser and Harrods, although both parties have always denied this.

Mohamed also funded Dodi's dream career in the film industry, although his success in this sphere was varied. Inspired by his invitation to the screening of a James Bond film in 1971,[28] Dodi spent most of that decade trying to persuade his father to branch out into films. He got his way in 1979 when Mohamed invested £90 million in a new company, Allied Stars, and appointed Dodi as its chief executive. Perhaps because of the unstable nature of his childhood or his inexperience in the world of work, however, Dodi took little interest in the day-to-day running of the company, and it was his father who ended up making most of the decisions about which projects to get involved with. On occasions his frustration with his son would spill over into rage, and Dodi received a very public dressing down from his father in at least one business meeting.

The company had a shaky start, losing £50,000 on its first film, *Breaking Glass*, but followed with an outstanding success in the Oscar-winning *Chariots of Fire*. Allied Stars had a 25 per cent stake in the film, and Dodi, as executive producer, attended the shoot on several occasions. Unfortunately, the producer, David Puttnam, had to throw Dodi off set on one occasion when he was caught offering cocaine to the cast, but happier events were to follow, not least his presentation to the Queen at the film's London premiere.

---

[28] *Death of a Princess*. Dodi was a friend of Barbara Broccoli, the daughter of 'Cubby' Broccoli, the producer of the Bond films, and they visited the set of *Live and Let Die*.

Later Allied Stars productions failed to live up to that film's success, although Stephen Spielberg's *Hook* in 1991 was something of a return to form commercially. This was not enough to save Dodi's venture, by then operating at an enormous loss, and in 1993 Allied Stars was taken over by a Liberian company, the British wing closing down the following year.[29] It was at *Hook*'s premiere that Dodi was to have his second meeting with the Princess of Wales.

Although he led the life of the archetypal playboy, friends of Dodi testify to his generosity, his courteousness and his pleasant and friendly nature. He was in many ways not changed from the damaged little boy who had suffered such nightmares in Alexandria. In his Park Lane apartment he had a room devoted to his collection of baseball caps, and he loved his fleet of fast cars and speedboats. His life was in many ways a fantasy, an imitation of the glamour he sought in the films he was so desperate to make. He dressed in military uniforms, drove a powerful 1,100cc motorbike, and, on occasion, piloted his father's helicopter. Even when drunk, he often insisted on driving himself in his Mercedes, his Lagonda or one of his two Aston Martins. He would spend a fortune on entertaining glamorous showbiz companions such as Bruce Willis, Koo Stark and Brooke Shields.[30]

However, there was another side to his character. In 1986 he married Suzanne Gregard, a model, without informing his family. That marriage ended in an amicable divorce ten months later. Gregard, and many of the other women Dodi dated, testify to his vulnerability and, in particular, his talent for sympathetic listening. His adult personality seems inextricably linked to his spoilt and unstable childhood, and he remained entirely dependent on his father for the whole of his life. Allied Stars, although nominally his company, was entirely funded by Mohamed.

He was also offered a two-day-a-week job at Harrods, where he was appointed a board member. However, he was uncommitted to the job, and when he was dismissed after three weeks for nonattendance, it was marked down as another in a series of half-hearted ventures doomed to failure. His uncle, Ali, commented, 'He's missed the boat. We offered him Harrods, Turnbull and Asser, and lots more. He's screwed it.'

His excesses – the cocaine use, the evenings when he had to be carried back to his apartment paralytic after boozing sessions – all of them hinted at the aimlessness that had so frustrated his driven father.

---

[29] 'Slicker' column, *Private Eye*, 19 September 1997.

[30] *Death of a Princess*. The tabloids also romantically linked him to Winona Ryder, who would have been fourteen at the time it was claimed they had a relationship.

Dodi's careless attitude to money was a legacy of a youth both misspent and overspent upon. Given all that he could require in the way of material goods from birth, Dodi grew up, perhaps not surprisingly, with no appreciation of the value of anything. His lack of interest even in his own finances was coming back to haunt him in the mid-nineties: his years of 'brat-pack' behaviour in Hollywood[31] were terminated when ten suits were filed against him for the recovery of massive debts in the US. The distributors of the last film project he was involved in – *The Scarlet Letter*, which flopped at the box office – joined American Express and a string of landlords in seeking payment of Dodi's debts through the courts.

Mohamed recalled his son to London, and once again attempted to involve him in Harrods. He hoped to provide him with a purpose in his life as well as keeping an eye on him. It was the latest of many such attempts – previously Mohamed had paid for sessions with a psychiatrist he hoped might be able to straighten his son out and rid him of his cocaine habit.[32]

By the summer of 1997 it seemed to many observers and friends that Dodi, at 41, had finally begun to grow up and sort himself out. His relationship with Kelly Fisher had lasted nearly as long as his abortive first marriage, and he was preparing to marry her. Mohamed had bought a five-acre estate in Malibu, where the couple planned to live. Richard Gere and Barbra Streisand would be neighbours. His close friend Barbara Broccoli remembers him waxing lyrical on his 41st birthday that April: '. . . he would talk about how he wanted to have kids and a proper relationship'.[33] On the business side, Dodi was seeking funding for several new film projects.

Then came the phone call from his father, summoning him to the fateful holiday in Saint-Tropez as he celebrated Bastille Day with Kelly Fisher in Paris.

That evening, Kelly phoned Dodi's London apartment in Park Lane. No one had seen him there or heard that he was due. Mohamed was not in London either. Kelly eventually tracked Dodi down in the early hours of the following morning on his mobile phone. He was in the South of France. The two had what Kelly described as 'quite a brawl' over Dodi's 'white lie'. He apologised profusely and dispatched one of

---

[31] The *Mirror* of 9 August 1997 claimed he was part of a notorious pack of British expats commonly known as 'The Viles'.
[32] Bower, p. 254. Dodi was 24 at the time.
[33] *Death of a Princess*, p. 71.

Mohamed's private jets to fetch her from Paris the following day. At the time Kelly played down the incident: 'I just thought, it's something with his father, and I knew that was important so I didn't want to come in between.'[34]

In fact Dodi had been ordered to Saint-Tropez by Mohamed so he could introduce him to the Princess of Wales, who had arrived there with Princes William and Harry on Friday 11 July. Dodi could not have known as he flew down on Monday 14 July that, according to many who knew her well, Diana was a woman searching for love that had been missing from the later years of her marriage. He would not have known either the Princess's unhappiness and frustration at the state of her secretive two-year relationship with Hasnat Khan. When Dodi arrived anonymously in the South of France he could not have imagined the opportunity that awaited him.

Earlier that day, Diana had held an impromptu press conference at sea for the British press at which she attempted to deal with the explosion of interest in her holiday. The news that she had arrived with her two sons at the Fayeds' Saint-Tropez compound had remained a secret for less than 24 hours. Michael Cole in London said, 'there was no point in denying it [that the royal party was present]. By Saturday afternoon, twenty hours after they arrived, the cat was out of the bag.'[35]

Over the weekend the British press had been full of pictures of the Princess, apparently relaxing in a one-piece swimsuit. In fact Diana was disturbed, not on her own behalf, but principally for William and Harry, who, she told the journalists, had been 'freaked out' by the intrusive coverage. Apparently naively, she asked the British journalists and photographers how long they would be staying, before tantalising them with a parting thought, 'You will have a big surprise coming soon, at the next thing I do.'

The very next thing Diana did was to put on an extraordinary solo show for a boat full of French photographers. After Fayed's security had persuaded the French coastguards to order the British press boat from the area, Diana posed for the French snappers in a tigerskin-patterned, one-piece bathing suit.

Dodi Fayed could not have been the 'big surprise' that Princess Diana was referring to. He slipped quietly into the Fayed compound in the evening of 14 July, after Diana's afternoon performances. That evening they had their fateful meeting. The veteran *Mirror* newspaper royal

---

[34] All Kelly Fisher quotes from author's interview.
[35] *Death of a Princess*, p. 100.

correspondent, James Whitaker, who trailed the Princess throughout the Saint-Tropez holiday, had no idea that Dodi was even in the South of France. He was virtually unknown to the press pack, apart from the most avid Fayed watchers of whom there were few in the pack hunting Diana. When Whitaker's photographer later took a picture of Dodi on the *Jonikal*, 'everyone thought he was a sailor'.

Fayed's staff particularly enjoyed looking after William and Harry. The two princes appeared unaffected and very open, sometimes coming below deck on the *Jonikal* to chat to the staff. The two boys were not afraid to poke fun at their mother over what they considered to be the rather obvious moves that Dodi was making towards her. According to the bodyguards, the princes thought Dodi was a bit of a poser, and saw how he was trying to impress her. The guards soon picked up the princes' mood and, as the banter grew, they got the impression that Diana had sized Dodi up pretty accurately. On one occasion while Dodi was walking ahead of Diana with his large sunglasses characteristically perched on his head, and with his permanently present mobile phone clasped to his ear, one of the guards asked Diana why she was hanging out with 'someone like Dodi'. Diana said nothing but gave the guard a knowing smile, which caused both of the princes to fall about laughing.

From Diana's point of view, despite the unwelcome press furore, the trip must have seemed a resounding success. She'd found another apparently suitable distraction from the foundering romance with Hasnat Khan, and her boys had had the chance of a good holiday.

Many in the Fayed holiday party in the South of France had noticed how well Dodi and Diana had got on with each other, and how they appeared to be talking endlessly to each other whenever they were together. The bodyguards also knew that Kelly Fisher had come to Saint-Tropez with Dodi, and they imagined that Dodi was simply helping his father to entertain the Princess.

When she arrived in the South of France on 16 July, however, Kelly was disturbed by the Fayeds' behaviour as soon as their driver picked her up from the airport. She was taken to other boats in the Fayed's fleet, first the *Sakara*, and then the *Cujo*, where she was to spend the next two nights with Dodi. She felt there was something strange going on as Dodi spent large parts of the day at the family's villa, Castel Saint Hélène, but asked her to stay on the boat. Dodi was doing his best to keep the two women apart, and his plans would have been upset by the striking American being introduced as his partner. The *Cujo* was moored only yards away from the Fayed villa, 'I could have thrown a rock and hit it,' remembers Kelly.

'Dodi would say, "I'm going to the house and I'll be back in half an hour." And he'd come back three or four hours later. I was furious. I'm sitting on the boat, stuck. And he was having lunch with everyone. So he had me in my little boat cage, and I now know he was seducing Diana. So he had me, and then he would go and try and seduce her, and then he'd come back and the next day it would happen again.'

'I was livid by this point, and I just didn't understand what was going on. When he was with me he was so wonderful. He said he loved me, and we talked to my mother, and we were talking about moving into the house in California.'

At the time, Fisher accepted Dodi's excuses for slipping off to see 'father', as he invariably referred to Mohamed, 'I just thought they maybe didn't want a commoner around the Princess.'

Dodi was sleeping with Kelly at night and was courting Diana by day. His deception was assisted by Kelly Fisher's modelling assignment on 18–20 July in Nice. The Fayeds were happy to lend her the *Cujo* and its crew for three days to take her there. By the time she returned the royal party had left.

Dodi rejoined Kelly for the last two days of her holiday before they flew back to Paris together on Wednesday 23 July. The model left for Los Angeles the following day, unaware that the friendship between Dodi and Diana had started under her nose.

Although Kelly Fisher and Dodi spoke frequently on the phone in the two weeks after their strained Saint-Tropez holiday, she would never see Dodi again. She learnt about Diana's romance with Dodi only after the news broke in August.

When Diana was back in Britain, she wrote to Mohamed Fayed to thank him warmly for the holiday. Dodi started sending bouquets of pink roses to Kensington Palace. By the weekend Diana had returned to Paris to spend two days with Dodi at the Ritz hotel.[36]

---

[36] René Delorm, *Diana and Dodi: A Love Story*, p. 52.

2. KISS CHASE

'The establishment are absolutely going to hate it, it's a relationship born out of hell as far as they are concerned.'

Max Clifford

'The kiss' provided confirmation of Princess Diana's love affair with Dodi Fayed to the world on 10 August. 'LOCKED IN HER LOVER'S ARMS, THE PRINCESS FINDS HAPPINESS AT LAST' ran the *Sunday Mirror* headline describing 'THE KISS'.

The photo itself, which dominated the front page, was a fuzzy image of Diana and Dodi embracing on the *Jonikal*. It had been taken by Mario Brenna, an Italian photographer, on 4 August. Brenna had snapped the couple with a telephoto lens from a distance of several hundred yards. The *Sunday Mirror* had triumphed in one of the most fierce bidding wars in newspaper history. It paid £250,000 for the right to use the pictures first, and Mario Brenna made an estimated $2 million in total.[1] The *Mirror* had originally broken the news of Diana and Dodi's relationship on Thursday 7 August. The front page story, DI'S NEW MAN IS AL FAYED'S SON, was written by the paper's royal correspondent, James Whitaker, who later won awards for the scoop.

For the previous two weeks, Diana and Dodi had been conducting their romance in secret. Remarkably, the relationship had not been revealed beyond their immediate families and staff. Dodi had followed up the bouquets of pink roses he sent Diana after her Saint-Tropez holiday with a surprise weekend in Paris. It was the couple's first private weekend together. There was absolutely no media coverage of this trip at the time.

By Sunday 27 July, Diana and Dodi had returned to London, and the world was none the wiser about their weekend in Paris. Four days later, on 31 July, the couple were back in the South of France for an intimate cruise by themselves. They had flown to Nice in one of Mohamed Fayed's executive jets. From there, the couple were taken to the *Jonikal* which was moored just off Saint-Laurent-du-Var.

Many of Mohamed Fayed's own Park Lane security operatives had been unaware of the Ritz trip until after it had taken place. When the couple arrived in the South of France, even the crew of the *Jonikal* was unaware they were coming until they saw them being brought from the shore to the yacht in a small tender.

---

[1] *Death of a Princess*, p. 113.

Diana was pleased to see that Mohamed Fayed had once again nominated Kez Wingfield to manage security on the *Jonikal*. A second bodyguard whom she had not met before, Trevor Rees-Jones, was also present. The 29-year-old former paratrooper has wrongly been described as 'Dodi's shadow'. He was, however, regularly detailed to guard Dodi who felt comfortable with the big Welsh bodyguard around him and Dodi had previously trusted Rees-Jones to mind Kelly Fisher on trips to London and Paris. Mohamed Fayed wanted his son's cruise on the *Jonikal* with the Princess to be 'low key', preferably secret. Although the Princess and her sons had been accompanied by officers from the Royal Protection Squad when she had been in Saint-Tropez in July, she had made it clear after her divorce from Prince Charles that she did not want such protection when she travelled alone. She suspected that information about her private life was leaking back to Buckingham Palace. As a result of her decision, her safety would be placed in the hands of Mohamed's personal security organisation.

The secrecy surrounding the couple's second holiday suited both Diana and Dodi who were both still embroiled in relationships. Diana had still not completely lost hope of rekindling her romance with 'Mr Wonderful', Hasnat Khan,[2] and, during her first holiday with the Fayeds, she had continued to speak to him on her mobile phone from the *Jonikal*. Dodi was also still in touch with Kelly Fisher on a regular basis. She still had no idea that he was starting a relationship with Princess Diana. When she spoke to Dodi he told her that he was partying with Princess Diana and the singers, George Michael and Elton John. In one phone call, on 6 August, Fisher says Dodi told her he would be in LA to see her in a couple of days.[3]

On the first day of the cruise, the *Jonikal* headed east from Saint-Tropez towards Monaco where Diana and Dodi went ashore in Monte Carlo. It was Dodi's habit to shower his lady friends with jewellery, and he wanted to buy Diana a ring. The couple sought out Alberto Repossi's shop in Monaco, and cast their eyes over several examples of the master jeweller's work. A range of jewels called 'Dis Moi Oui' (Tell Me Yes) displayed in the window, caught Diana's eye. Repossi was not actually present when Diana and Dodi visited but his staff briefed him on the couple's requirements. Repossi set about designing a special ring for Diana that he says was based on the ideas in the 'Dis Moi Oui' range, but inspired by the Princess herself. Although the

---

[2] *Sunday People*, 29 November 1998 and Simone Simmons.
[3] Author's interview with Kelly Fisher.

original came from the 'Dis Moi Oui' range, neither Diana nor Dodi had given any indication that the ring was intended as an engagement ring.

Repossi promised that he would have the specially designed ring ready for Dodi to collect in Paris on 30 August. In the hope that Princess Diana might personally visit his Paris boutique, Repossi started to sketch some ideas for an entire range of jewellery, including necklaces, earrings and bracelets, as well as the ring he had been commissioned to create.[4]

As Dodi was courting Diana in Paris and on the *Jonikal*, Mohamed Fayed had begun making preparations for the day when inevitably the news would break that his son and the Princess of Wales were lovers. He had spoken privately to the publicist, Max Clifford, to prepare the ground: 'Mohamed and Michael Cole contacted me and told me what was going on, this is in the early days of the relationship . . . between Dodi and Diana which became a romance. He asked if I would be able to talk to Dodi and give him a little bit of advice because of what was possibly going to be happening. Obviously there would be huge media interest worldwide. I said I was happy to, and I spoke to Dodi a few times over the weeks.'[5]

Clifford advised Dodi as his father had asked him to. The publicist remembers warning him, 'You realise there's going to be an awful lot of criticism of you because of the fact you are Mohamed's son. He's going to come in for an awful lot of flack over it. The establishment are absolutely going to hate it, its a relationship born out of hell as far as they are concerned.'

The choice of Clifford to publicise the romance was significant. Harvey Thomas, the international public relations consultant, formerly an adviser to Prime Minister Margaret Thatcher, thinks the decision was revealing: 'I don't think he considers himself in public relations, he considers himself a publicist and he's very good at getting publicity. And if you want to enhance the reputation of your son and a princess, you don't go to Max Clifford. If you just want a lot of publicity in the papers then you might go to Max Clifford, who will stage a series of gimmicks and events to titivate the tabloid press and get a lot of coverage.'[6]

Certainly Clifford has not enjoyed the same low profile as most PR experts. Exclusives such as Antonia De Sancha's 'Kiss and Tell' affair with government minister David Mellor, Mandy Alwood's octuplets and OJ Simpson's protestations of innocence, have ensured a lasting fame for

---

[4] Author's interview with Repossi.
[5] Author's taped interview with Max Clifford.
[6] Author's interview with Harvey Thomas.

Clifford. In the nineties, his name has become almost synonymous with a certain kind of tabloid chequebook journalism.

Clifford had given Dodi his holiday number in Spain. He was soon alerted to the purchase of the ring, and to the couple's intention to collect it in Paris.

During the course of the cruise on the *Jonikal*, Dodi also phoned his Los Angeles press agent, Pat Kingsley, to tell her that he had started a relationship with Princess Diana. He told her that he thought that they might already have been photographed, but that he could not be sure.[7] Both Clifford and Kingsley were in place on either side of the Atlantic in preparation for the story breaking. The two press agents supplemented the work of Michael Cole's office in Harrods.

The news appeared the day before Diana flew to Bosnia to further her humanitarian work, and her campaign against landmines. The timing of the news about Diana's new relationship could not have been worse from the point of view of the campaigning groups that Diana had flown to Bosnia to support. Although the Princess was officially described as 'relaxed' about the news of her new romance being made public, she was also concerned that the media's obsession with her private life was now obscuring the important messages she was trying to communicate from Bosnia.

By Sunday 10 August, no British tabloid believed it could be without 'THE KISS' pictures. Having been beaten in the auction for the pictures, the *News of the World* featured a picture of Dodi cuddling his former wife, Suzanne Gregard, touched up to look like the Princess. The headline ran, 'My love for Diana', and many readers on first sight would have been mistaken as to the blonde's identity.

With the publication of 'THE KISS' pictures, the *Sunday Mirror* predicted that Princess Diana and Dodi Fayed were on the brink of becoming engaged. Dodi was said to be hunting for an engagement ring in Los Angeles, and members of Princess Diana's 'inner circle' had told the *Mirror* that Diana had said, 'The next time I see him, I am expecting an engagement ring.' The paper also claimed to have interviewed Dr Hasnat Khan who was quoted as saying 'I wish them every happiness'. Dr Khan's mother, Naheed Khan, told the paper, 'What a relief. I was worried about the effect this relationship was having on my son. Of course the news is sad because Diana is one of the family. But I am sure that Diana and Hasnat will stay friends'.

Fayed had to tread very carefully after the big news had broken. He tried to help what he judged to be a 'friendly' paper which had lost out

---

[7] *Death of a Princess*, p. 101.

in the picture auction of 'THE KISS'. Dodi's romance with Diana was potentially the most positive story to emerge concerning the Fayed family since Mohamed and his brothers had shocked the City of London by unexpectedly winning the battle for Harrods and the House of Fraser.

Details of the couple's previously 'secret' weekend in Paris were leaked to the *Mail on Sunday*. The paper compensated for its failure to buy 'THE KISS' pictures by running a two-page article the same day about 'Diana's secret night at the Ritz'. The heading, 'Suntanned and happy, the glowing Princess was escorted through a side entrance to the finest suite Al Fayed could provide, with a vast bed just like Marie-Antoinette's' typified the tone of the article. 'Sources close to the Al Fayed family' revealed to the authors that Dodi was 'in the hotel at the time'.

The information had not been supplied to Diana's close friend on the paper, Richard Kay, but to Chester Stern who had written favourable pieces about Fayed. Stern's colleague, Sarah Oliver, had been to Paris to write the Ritz story. She was given access to Ritz staff ranging from the hotel's president, Frank Klein, to chambermaids who had serviced the Imperial Suite which, Oliver reported, had apparently 'enchanted' Diana. Fayed had entirely revamped the Imperial Suite after he bought the Ritz. It had been redecorated in the style favoured by the Duke and Duchess of Windsor. The former King Edward VIII and his wife stayed in an apartment in the Ritz from before World War II until they acquired their villa in the Bois de Boulogne in the outskirts of Paris in 1953.

On a day when the *Mirror* had clearly beaten all its rivals by buying 'THE KISS', the *Mail on Sunday* considered its Ritz scoop to be the 'best of the rest' of the Di and Dodi coverage. However, a second double-page spread on DODI'S UNPAID BILLS, detailing his various financial problems offset the romantic gloss of Stern and Oliver's report of his 'romantic tryst' with Diana.

While the Fayeds might have relished the prospect of annoying what they perceived to be 'the establishment' by revealing Dodi's romance with Diana, they would have been naturally concerned about how Kelly Fisher would react. Clifford advised them to treat her, and any of Dodi's other former girlfriends who might emerge after the news broke, as 'bimbos'. Dodi should be portrayed as the victim of a 'bimbo eruption', not the boat-hopping, bed-hopping playboy that Kelly would be bound to see him as. Clifford had helped Dodi to make his calculations before the news of his romance with Diana broke.[8]

---

[8] Author's taped interview with Max Clifford, May 1998.

Kelly Fisher was stunned when she saw the pictures of Princess Diana and Dodi kissing each other. A friend had faxed her the *Mirror* pictures in the middle of the night. Kelly claims she had thought until that moment that she was going to marry Dodi. She says she was planning to move into a luxurious new mansion in Paradise Cove in Malibu with Dodi, and that Mohamed Fayed had bought it as a gift for the couple.[9] The distraught American immediately phoned Fayed's Park Lane HQ in London, unable to believe the news she had just heard. Dodi was not present but she spoke to Mohamed who left her in no doubt that her relationship with his son was over. 'He told me never to call back again . . . and just disappear.'

Whether or not Kelly Fisher was actually engaged to Dodi became a matter of fierce dispute. Dodi was sufficiently concerned to take Concorde to New York and then a private jet to Los Angeles, to try and deal with her. Nevertheless, Kelly Fisher decided to share her distress with the media. With her lawyer, Gloria Allred, seated beside her, Fisher held a press conference in Los Angeles on 14 August to announce that she would sue Dodi Fayed for breach of contract. Allred claimed that Kelly had been promised $200,000 by Dodi in compensation for curtailing her modelling career at his request in order to marry him. Dodi's first cheque had bounced, but a later cheque for $60,000 had cleared. Allred also claimed that Dodi had asked Kelly's parents for permission to marry her. A $200,000 sapphire and diamond engagement ring that Kelly claimed Dodi had given her was tearfully displayed at the press conference.

Crucially for the Fayeds, Princess Diana did not appear to be upset over the newspaper revelations about Kelly Fisher's relationship with Dodi. Unsurprisingly, Diana did not take up Fisher's offer to meet 'anywhere in the world' for a briefing about Dodi and the Fayeds. Clifford felt that Dodi's jilted girlfriend had played into his hands.[10]

When she learnt that Clifford was operating on behalf of the Fayeds, Fisher had mistakenly thought that no one would believe Dodi's story: 'The guy had represented OJ Simpson so I assumed that no one would believe anything he said'.

Clifford claimed that he helped Michael Cole's press office shoulder the burden of the enormous, worldwide interest in Dodi's romance with Diana. Although he insists he was not paid by the Fayeds during the summer of 1997, Clifford was much sought after by journalists seeking guidance in early August.

---

[9] Author's interview with Kelly Fisher.
[10] Author's taped interview with Max Clifford.

The main point I was getting across to anybody and everybody who wanted to call me and discuss the subject, was that in my view this was a genuine romance. They were falling in love; they were very happy together, and I believed that he would make her very happy. That's what I honestly felt and that's what I honestly saw and that's what I honestly believed, so that was the main message.[11]

When Diana returned from Bosnia on 11 August, her every move was tracked by hoards of journalists and photographers. Emerging late one night from Dodi's Park Lane apartment, she was greeted by over fifty photographers.

Diana was due to take a long-planned break in the Greek islands with her close friend, Rosa Monckton. By now large sections of the world's media had become obsessed with her new romance, and any hopes the two friends entertained of slipping away quietly had vanished.

Diana phoned Rosa Monckton to tell her that Dodi had persuaded her that they should travel in one of Mohamed's private jets from Heathrow. When Rosa Monckton arrived at Kensington Palace on 15 August, the Princess informed her that the travel plans had changed again: Fayed's jet would fly them from Stansted.

This did not go unnoticed, and news of their departure was reported on the front page of the *Daily Telegraph* the following morning. Dominic Lawson, editor of the *Sunday Telegraph* and husband of Rosa Monckton, was surprised to learn of the late change in plans. He had no idea that his wife and the Princess had flown from Stansted until he read about it in the *Daily Telegraph*.

Even the Fayeds did not know exactly where the two friends had disappeared to, although Dodi spoke to Diana on her mobile phone several times while she was away. Diana feared that after the worldwide coverage of her affair with Dodi, her relationship with Hasnat was effectively over. As soon as 'THE KISS' photographs appeared, the British tabloids virtually married Diana off to Dodi.

In Greece, Rosa Monckton heard a different version. When she discussed Dodi, Rosa could see Diana was clearly besotted with him, but reservations surfaced in a conversation about his preoccupation with material things: 'While we were on our little boat in Greece she said of Dodi Fayed to me: "He's given me a bracelet. He's given me a watch. I know that the next thing will be a ring." Then she laughed and said: "Rosa, that's going firmly on the fourth finger of my right hand." '[12]

---

[11] Author's taped interview with Max Clifford.
[12] *Sunday Telegraph*, 15 February 1998.

Diana said that she really appreciated being with someone who would be there for her 24 hours a day. After ducking, diving and disguising to be with Hasnat Khan for nearly two years, it was a refreshing change for Diana to be with someone who had no qualms about being seen in public with her. Dodi's family appeared to relish the publicity she brought to their lives and, unlike Hasnat Khan's mother in Pakistan, the whole Fayed family had welcomed her unreservedly amongst them.

Diana also felt confident that Dodi could stand the heat that anyone she became involved with would have to cope with. After the intensity of the press's interest in her love life, and the shadow it had cast over her trip to Bosnia, Diana's Greek holiday gave her a chance to reflect on the turbulence of her romantic affairs, and the impact these were having upon the rest of her life.

When the sun fell in the Aegean sky, the Princess would pore over maps with the Greek skipper, plotting the boat's course for the next day. According to Rosa Monckton, Diana appeared to enjoy the sense of adventure and the atmosphere of the hunt engendered by the invisible threat of the paparazzi. Rosa was flabbergasted by the intensity of the paparazzi's interest which had reached new heights in the wake of 'THE KISS' photographs being sold around the world. However, she noted that Diana herself maintained her sense of humour, as she and the Greek skipper successfully managed to plot a course to avoid the long lenses. Fellow Greek skippers and harbour masters spoke to the captain of the Princess's boat on short-wave radio to help him outmanoeuvre the hoards of paparazzi who were on Diana's trail. Local television reported that hundreds of journalists and photographers were scouring the islands for a glimpse of the Princess. Local reporting of the hunt for the two women was wildly inaccurate, with sightings being registered throughout the Greek archipelago, and a veritable armada of boats and planes being cited as their means of transport. In fact the two friends were sailing around Hydra, hundreds of miles away from most of the islands on which they had allegedly been sighted.

Sometimes they went ashore to shop. The only picture of Diana that appeared in the press during this period was taken by a tourist when they ventured ashore. As soon as she realised that a happy snapper had taken her picture, Diana turned to Rosa and said, 'That'll be in the British papers tomorrow'. She was right. The enterprising tourist had sold it to the *Sun*, and it duly appeared on the front page.

When Diana and Rosa arrived back in Britain at midday on 20 August, they took a helicopter to Battersea heliport. They were met by Mohamed Fayed's security which had provided a limousine. Also waiting was a photographer with a long lens from the *Daily Mail*'s Nigel Dempster column. He snapped the two women darting out of their helicopter. The Fayed security was not needed and the two returned to west London in one of Diana's cars.

The following day, on 21 August, Diana flew to the South of France to start her third Mediterranean holiday in five weeks. Before she left she visited the Man Fong Mei clinic in Camden, north London. There she saw Dr Lily Hua Yu, a Chinese GP whom she had been seeing since February 1996. Most recently Dr Lily had been treating the Princess for premenstrual tension. Dr Lily remembered how happy her patient appeared to be: 'She told me she had never felt so physically well in all her life.'[13] Before she left, she booked an appointment for a fortnight later, 4 September. She flew from London to Nice in a Harrods jet, and would spend two nights at Mohamed Fayed's Saint-Tropez compound where she had been in July. As the Princess flew to the South of France, the *Jonikal* slipped its moorings at Saint-Laurent-du-Var and headed towards Saint-Tropez.

Dodi joined Diana from the Fayeds' Malibu mansion in California. He had spent a few, somewhat unsuccessful days in Los Angeles. As he attempted to sort out the trouble that Kelly Fisher had caused with her performance with Gloria Allred on 14 August, Dodi found himself doggedly and aggressively pursued by the media.

Accompanying Dodi from Malibu was the Reverend Myriah Daniels, a self-styled 'Missionary of Natural Spiritualism'. Her business card declares that she is a missionary, 'Specializing in Wholistic Healing for Musician's Injuries & Caring for the Well Be-ing of People' (sic). Dodi had met the Revd Daniels in California where she worked in Hollywood, and he had known her for six years. She was Dodi's personal masseuse. The Revd Daniels would spend the whole of the holiday with the couple. The *Jonikal*'s chief stewardess would once again be New Zealander, Debbie Gribble, and Dodi's butler from Los Angeles, René Delorm, would again wait upon the couple. Security would be handled by Kez Wingfield, who would look after Diana for the third time that summer, and Trevor Rees-Jones who joined the *Jonikal* for the second time.

Kez Wingfield knew he would require additional security back-up when it became clear in Saint-Tropez that Dodi was proposing to take Diana on another cruise on the *Jonikal*. Their romance had become the hottest media story in the world since 'THE KISS' photographs had

---

[13] *Mirror*, 23 February 1998, confirmed via Professor Man Fong Mei, 16 April 1999.

appeared two weeks earlier. Everyone in the Fayed party was aware that hundreds of photographers were scouring the beaches of the French Riviera for a sighting of Diana with Dodi. At one point, on 23 August, a helicopter rented by *Paris Match* photographers buzzed Fayed's Saint-Tropez compound as well as the *Jonikal*.[14]

The intensified hunt for pictures of Princess Diana and her new lover increased the anxiety of Fayed's security team. For the bodyguards charged with looking after the couple, the security equation had changed completely. Whereas the cruise at the beginning of the month had successfully been completed before anyone knew that Dodi and Diana were lovers, the one they were about to embark upon would present the challenge of being observed and hunted by the world's media. Kez Wingfield discussed the challenge confronting himself and Trevor Rees-Jones with Mohamed Fayed on the beach in Saint-Tropez, and asked him to authorise the extra security he was sure would be necessary. Fayed himself always has a minimum of eight bodyguards looking after him in Saint-Tropez. Fayed replied that the proposed cruise was to be another 'low key' affair, like the previous, secret cruise. Fayed decided that Wingfield and Trevor Rees-Jones should be capable of handling security for the cruise by themselves.

Wingfield knew that Fayed had much to think about with the dramatic escalation in media interest in the Fayed family in August. However, because he was still concerned about the security cover proposed, he raised the matter with his immediate boss, Paul Handley-Greaves. Handley-Greaves was developing a very hands-on role during Diana's third trip to Saint-Tropez. He was photographed by the press in T-shirt, baseball cap and baggy shorts, piloting a small craft from which Diana and Dodi jet-skied. Handley-Greaves was seen to be leading his close protection team by example, and so Wingfield shared his concerns with him. Sensitive to Fayed's priorities, the enormous security chief refused Wingfield's request for more support. Wingfield and Rees-Jones would be left in sole charge of security for the final cruise.

Fayed's press operation, by contrast, did receive some supplementary support at this time. Max Clifford was taking some of the enormous strain that the romance had placed upon Michael Cole's office. Informed by bulletins from Dodi himself on board the *Jonikal*, Max Clifford was able to steer photographers and journalists in the right direction as the

---

[14] Although there was no reaction at the time, ten days after the crash in Paris an infuriated Mohamed Fayed brought a successful legal action against the magazine under France's strict privacy laws.

yacht made its way around the Mediterranean coast. He will not reveal precisely which media he tipped off, but Clifford claims he acted as a 'signpost' for selected members of the pack of journalists and photographers who were hunting the couple, 'It was a bit more specific than saying they'll be in Saint-Tropez or wherever. I was dealing with media from all over the world all the time, and there were some people out there who I would be inclined to help.'[15] He also gave Dodi advice on how he should react to the fevered press attention.

Having ordered the ring in Monte Carlo, Dodi continued to shower Diana with gifts in the way that Diana had described to Rosa Monckton while they were in Greece. On one occasion while the *Jonikal* was anchored off Porto Cervo in Sardinia, Diana and Dodi went shopping. Debbie Gribble, the *Jonikal*'s chief stewardess, recalled, 'She came back with armfuls of cashmere sweaters. When she said she liked one, Dodi bought her every colour they had. He also bought her pairs and pairs of shoes from JP Todd's at £300 a pair. She only had to look at a thing and he'd get it'.[16]

Although Diana had told Rosa Monckton that she found such conspicuous consumption off-putting, she ended her last conversation with her friend by saying that she was happy. When Rosa asked her, 'Tell me, is it bliss?' Diana replied, 'Yes, it's bliss.'

Diana had called Rosa Monckton for the last time on Wednesday 27 August, from the *Jonikal*. She had been in a state about an interview that had appeared that morning in the French newspaper *Le Monde*. The interview had plunged Diana into controversy she neither foresaw nor desired. The following paragraph in the article about her humanitarian work was the cause of the row: 'She didn't hide her pleasure at the immediate decision by the Labour government to campaign for a total abolition of landmines. "Its position on this subject has always been clear. It is going to do good work. The last government drove me to such despair. I hope we will be able to persuade the USA to sign the charter banning landmines in Ottawa in December." '[17]

Diana had given the interview to the leading French journalist, Annick Cojean, in early June. Cojean had been to Kensington Palace to interview the Princess, and had invited her to choose a photograph of herself to illustrate the profile. Significantly, Diana had chosen a picture in which she is seen cuddling a blind Pakistani boy in Lahore. She had met the child during her visit to Pakistan to meet Hasnat Khan's family.

---

[15] Author's taped interview with Max Clifford.
[16] *News of the World*, 7 December 1997.
[17] *Le Monde*, 27 August 1997.

Diana's eyes are closed in the picture and the image exudes compassion. At the time she chose the photo, Diana had not lost sight of her dream of bearing Khan's children. By the time it was published she had become involved with Dodi Fayed.

When it was published nearly three months after the interview had taken place, the article created a storm.

DIANA SHOULD KEEP QUIET, was the *Express* newspaper's front page headline on Thursday 28 August. A statement was issued on Diana's behalf denying that she had made the comments attributed to her, as Conservative MPs lined up to tell Diana to 'stay out of politics'. Her critics in the press asked, 'Has she gone too far?'

Finding herself once again in the middle of a media row, and a long way from home, Diana phoned close friends, including Rosa Monckton, to seek comfort and guidance, and said she was furious with Cojean and *Le Monde*. She knew very well that in her position she could not make any comments that would be interpreted as party political, and these comments in the way they were reported came into that category. Annick Cojean defended herself robustly saying that she was astonished by the reaction. She described her interview with the Princess as cool and relaxed and put down her swift denial to the pressure that had been put on her after the article appeared.[18] The row over the interview upset Diana, and close friends who spoke to her at the time say that the furore the interview caused in Britain was a factor in Diana's decision to linger longer in the Mediterranean than she had originally planned.

Meanwhile, Fayed was working hard to establish further royal links. With the independent TV producer, the late Desmond Wilcox, he was preparing a documentary, *Edward and Mrs Simpson: Going, going, gone*, about the villa Windsor in Paris. Initially the project took the form of a corporate video, sponsored by Fayed himself. By the time the BBC had expressed an interest in making a documentary about the auction of the villa's contents in New York, Wilcox's team had already filmed extensively in the villa including footage of the contents being packed for shipment to the USA. As a result of the BBC's interest, Wilcox produced the film as an independent producer for the BBC. The corporation agreed that copyright would be vested in Dodi's production company, Allied Stars.[19]

Wilcox's film featured a jovial and benevolent Fayed explaining how he had restored the villa because of his love of his adopted country. The

---

[18] Author's interview with Annick Cojean.
[19] Author's interviews with Desmond Wilcox and the BBC.

film featured Fayed and Michael Cole hosting a small dinner party in the villa Windsor, with celebrity friends of Mohamed Fayed such as Esther Rantzen, Desmond Wilcox's wife; Hugo Vickers, the royal historian; Diana's stepmother, Raine Spencer; and Ingrid Seward, a writer on the British Royal Family.

On the day the BBC documentary was transmitted, the *New York Times* ran a large feature on Fayed, which represented the apotheosis of his summer's efforts. The US press has, inevitably and historically, been far less critical of Fayed's activities than the British. The *New York Times* article, running as it did on the same day as the Fayed-sponsored BBC documentary on the other side of the Atlantic, was probably the peak of Cole's stewardship of Fayed's PR. Allowing a rare interview with Fayed, Cole sat in on the interview with the paper's Alan Riding. All the familiar criticisms of Fayed were omitted or (in the case of the DTI report) glossed over. The US broadsheet savoured the jovial, extrovert and pugnacious Fayed's contentious relationship with the 'British establishment'. The paper ran unchallenged Fayed's contention that he was '70 or 80 per cent' responsible for the Conservative government's humiliation at the polls less than four months earlier. His victory, Fayed claimed, had led him to enjoy the support of the 'ordinary people – that's why I'm still here. It's still my country. I'm not leaving'.[20] He was in his element.

The article was laced with the inevitable royal references and Fayed's comparisons between his son's romance with Diana and that of Edward VIII and Wallis Simpson. Fayed had little difficulty comparing Diana and Dodi's month-long romance with the relationship which had changed the history of the British Royal Family. 'They [Edward VIII and Mrs Simpson] were driven out of London, and to preserve their love nest, they chose Paris', Fayed informed the paper, inviting obvious parallels with his own dreams for his son's future.

Fayed had been very disappointed not to acquire the Duchess of Windsor's jewels after she died in 1986. Her executors insisted that her will be respected and that the jewels should be auctioned for charity in aid of the Institut Pasteur. The auction in Geneva raised £31 million. Fayed had offered £6 million to buy them before they were auctioned.

Seeking to impress his American audience with his loyalty to the British crown, and his philanthropy ('What you can spare, you share') he assured readers that he would be prepared to buy back any items of interest to the Royal Family. The article was timed very carefully. It ran

---

[20] All *New York Times* quotes from 28 August 1998.

on 28 August, the first anniversary of Princess Diana's divorce from Prince Charles. The following day, as Diana and Dodi prepared to leave Sardinia, the *Express* reran the *New York Times* interview in the UK, demonstrating how Fayed liked to see close parallels with the Windsors.

'Like the Duke of Windsor met this American woman and fell in love, it's just life – destiny. Nothing is organised.'[21]

To complete Fayed's dream of Diana and Dodi emulating the Windsors, the couple had to visit the villa Windsor. Such a visit would also be helpful in promoting the Sotheby's auction of the villa's contents which was to take place only two weeks later. The couple's stopover in Paris, two days after the article appeared, would provide the opportunity.

Close friends who spoke to Diana in the last week of her life say she was very much looking forward to coming home to see her boys. She had been planning to return before the weekend so she could spend time with them before they went back to school. Trevor Rees-Jones and Kez Wingfield were certainly hoping the holiday would end soon. The two bodyguards were very weary, having embarked upon what they were told would be a three to four day tour of duty on 20 August. The cruise had turned into a prolonged game of cat and mouse with the media off the Mediterranean coast and both men were exhausted. One of them had to be on duty at all times to ensure that a round-the-clock watch was maintained on deck. The guards noted down the names of every boat they spotted, particularly those they knew were bearing paparazzi. Trevor Rees-Jones had grown particularly vexed with Dodi, who he thought was ignoring his advice on security and making plans without consulting him at all.

On the evening of Thursday 28 August Diana celebrated the first anniversary of her divorce from Prince Charles on a secluded Sardinian beach with Dodi Fayed. Diana had toasted the occasion in champagne with Dodi on board the *Jonikal* before going ashore to share a barbecue. According to René Delorm, the couple ate caviar followed by barbecued chicken burgers, pork and smoked sausages prepared by the *Jonikal*'s cook, Christiano. Delorm was dressed in an evening suit and a bow tie. According to his account, that night was one of the most romantic evenings of the holiday, and the staff left them cuddling on the beach by the fire while they returned to the boat. Trevor Rees-Jones was obliged to stay near to the couple on the beach, hovering discreetly in the shadows.[22]

---

[21] *Express*, 29 August 1997.

The crew of the *Jonikal* were used to the fact that plans might be changed at the last minute. On the evening of 29 August, a rumour passed amongst the crew that Dodi was planning to take the Princess home via Paris, but nothing was formally confirmed. It was not until the next morning that the bodyguards were informed that Dodi did, indeed, intend to take the Princess to Paris. Kez Wingfield had not had any chance to make security arrangements for the arrival in Paris, so he immediately phoned his operations desk in Park Lane.

Park Lane informed the head of Fayed's Paris security setup, Ben Murrell. He was told that Dodi and the Princess would be arriving in Paris in the afternoon at Le Bourget airport, and that they would drop into the villa Windsor on the way into Paris. Arrangements would be made to meet the party at Le Bourget when they landed.

After breakfast, Princess Diana and Dodi Fayed left the *Jonikal* and made for the tiny Sardinian airport at Olbia. Mohamed Fayed's Gulfstream IV executive jet was waiting on the tarmac to fly them to Paris.

[22] Delorm, p. 139.

3. PARIS – THE LAST DAY

'The plan has been okayed by Mohamed.'

Henri Paul, 30 August 1997

Princess Diana's party swept through the vast gates of the villa Windsor in the Bois de Boulogne just outside Paris at around 15.45 on 30 August. The Princess and Dodi Fayed were travelling with Trevor Rees-Jones in a black Mercedes driven by Dodi's Paris chauffeur, Philippe Dourneau.

The villa's security chief, Ben Murrell, watched the Mercedes on the closed-circuit security cameras which survey the entrance. Then he made his way to the villa's doors to welcome his boss's son and his famous new girlfriend. It was the first time Diana had been to the villa, and only the second time Dodi had visited in the eighteen months that Murrell had been living and working there. The only other time Murrell had seen Dodi at the villa was on 14 July when he came to visit with Kelly Fisher. Kez Wingfield had phoned Murrell on his mobile to say that they were being chased by photographers.

When Diana and Dodi arrived at Le Bourget they had been greeted by a dozen photographers who were in position when they touched down. To the exasperation of the bodyguards, cameras started whirring as the party stepped from Mohamed Fayed's executive jet and they were then chased from the airport. According to Wingfield, 'We never knew where we were going from hour to hour, but the paparazzi were certainly being told by someone'.

Once Princess Diana had been sighted at Le Bourget the news travelled very quickly. Some of the paparazzi had initially been tipped off by their Mediterranean colleagues who watched the party board the jet in Sardinia. Others had spoken to air traffic control in Sardinia to establish where the plane was flying to.

Wingfield knew that Dave Moody, who was in charge back at the 'Ops Room' in Park Lane, would contact Ben Murrell in Paris, and he had assumed that Paul Handley-Greaves would organise full security back-up. The Princess and Dodi were transferring from a boat anchored off a Sardinian coastal resort to the French capital, and the security equation had changed to one that the Fayed team were more familiar with. On Mohamed Fayed's trips to Paris he is routinely transported from Le Bourget in a bullet-proof Mercedes and a back-up car equipped with full medical facilities. He travels with a retinue of eight bodyguards at all times.

For Princess Diana's visit to Paris, however, the skeletal security that had accompanied Diana and Dodi in the South of France was only partially increased. At Le Bourget, the party was met by Philippe Dourneau and Henri Paul, Fayed's acting Head of Security at the Ritz, in a Mercedes and a Range Rover. The presence of the paparazzi convinced both Wingfield and Rees-Jones that they needed more support to stand a chance of deflecting their attentions. Their work over the previous ten days had been further complicated by Dodi's tendency to make plans on the hoof. Dodi often told the bodyguards only at the very last minute what the couple planned to do next. Their arrival in Paris that afternoon was a case in point.

The security cameras surveying the entrance to the villa showed Murrell that Dourneau had managed to shake the press off. However, Princess Diana appeared flushed as she jumped out of the Mercedes without waiting for the door to be opened for her and darted through the doors of the villa Windsor. Murrell recalls:

'Diana looked flustered and her face was red. She didn't look happy. Dodi was still sitting in the car by the time Diana walked into the house. It was obvious something had occurred during the journey but you can't ask questions. Diana looked shaken.'

Murrell asked Diana and Dodi if they needed anything. They replied that they did not. The couple made straight for the office on the ground floor and closed the door behind them, hardly speaking to Murrell.

As Diana and Dodi composed themselves, Murrell caught up with Trevor Rees-Jones and Philippe Dourneau who were stretching their legs outside the villa. The 35-year-old Dourneau had been Dodi's chauffeur for three years, driving him mostly in Paris which Dodi would visit once or twice a month, at the Fayed estate in Gstaad in Switzerland and sometimes in London. Dourneau had chauffeured Dodi and Princess Diana in Paris during their 'secret weekend' at the end of July. He had picked the couple up when they touched down in Mohamed Fayed's helicopter, and driven them everywhere they wished to go until they returned to London on the Sunday morning. The relaxed tone of that weekend was in marked contrast to the white-knuckled ride the couple had just experienced from Le Bourget. According to Dourneau the paparazzi had made Dodi very nervous and he had instructed him to speed up and, 'lose the paparazzi'.[1] At one stage that day Princess Diana screamed at Dourneau to 'slow down', as she was very worried that there would be a collision with one of the paparazzi motorbikes that were

---

[1] Bower (unpublished) interview with Dourneau, September 1997.

chasing them. Dourneau apparently executed a deft manoeuvre on the périphérique (the Paris ring road) and lost the paparazzi at the Porte Maillot exit, which pleased the Princess enormously.

The Princess placed her hand on Dodi's knee and whispered into his ear. Dourneau could not hear everything that she said to him, but he did hear her trying to soothe him, 'Don't worry Dodi'.

As he waited outside the villa Windsor, Trevor Rees-Jones was in a foul mood according to Murrell:

'He said that Dodi wasn't listening to his advice. It was Trevor's job to advise on security, but Dodi kept on coming up with his own plans, and not telling Trevor what he was going to do.'

Murrell says he was told that Mohamed had ordered Dodi to show Diana around the villa. Murrell returned to his position and monitored the visit on the closed-circuit TV. After emerging from the office, the couple went upstairs and looked at the empty rooms that used to be the Duke and Duchess's boudoir and bedrooms for a few minutes. There was much less for Princess Diana to see than there was when Dodi had brought Kelly Fisher the previous month. Since that visit the entire contents of the villa had been shipped to New York to be exhibited by Sotheby's in advance of the September auction. Murrell tracked the couple's progress. It appeared to him that Diana was not particularly interested and that she was keen to get the visit over as quickly as possible.

While Diana and Dodi were in the villa, Murrell spotted Kez Wingfield on his monitors arriving in the black Range Rover. The vehicle was driven by Henri Paul who had collected Kez, René Delorm, Debbie Gribble and Myriah Daniels from Le Bourget and taken them to the Fayed apartment just off the Champs-Elysées. The apartment is a stone's throw from the Arc de Triomphe on the rue Arsène-Houssaye. Having dropped them at the apartment, Paul had driven Kez Wingfield to the villa Windsor.

A tubby, round-faced man, Henri Paul, as the acting head of security at the Ritz hotel, would always play a key role in supervising security when the Fayeds were in Paris. The balding, forty-one year old had worked in the Ritz hotel's security since it was established in 1986. Highly valued by the Fayeds for his loyalty and his discretion, Paul had been in charge of the hotel's security for the past three months since the retirement of his predecessor, Jean Hocquet. Although he had been passed over for Hocquet's job in 1993, Paul was hopeful that he would now succeed his departed boss. The hotel management described Paul as 'a model employee' and he was known to be particularly close to the

President of the Ritz, Frank Klein. Staff at the Ritz referred to him behind his back as '*les yeux et les oreilles de Klein*', the 'eyes and ears' of the boss.[2]

Earlier in the day, Dodi's chauffeur, Philippe Dourneau, had been surprised to discover that, due to the size of the group arriving at Le Bourget, Paul would be one of the drivers of Dodi's party. Dourneau had never seen Paul drive before and he had been obliged to familiarise him with the Range Rover's controls.[3] Dourneau normally used the Range Rover to chauffeur Dodi. Kez Wingfield, who had never met Henri Paul before, saw nothing in Paul's performance to trouble him during the journey from Le Bourget.

Ben Murrell, however, was struck by Henri Paul's behaviour when he arrived at the villa. He knew Paul quite well and he thought he seemed to be over-excited, and possibly drunk, when he encountered him at the villa Windsor.

> I went down to the gate to let Paul in. As he pulled alongside he opened the window. He suddenly pulled me towards him and said 'Yeah, Ben, you good.' His breath smelt. It was the sort of smell I recognise from someone who has had a good lunch with wine. It was quite overpowering . . . I stood there quite shocked by his actions. To grab me was so out of character. He seemed so excited. I'm sure he'd had a drink.

By now Diana and Dodi were ready to leave. They got into Dourneau's Mercedes with Trevor Rees-Jones, while Kez Wingfield followed in the Range Rover driven by Henri Paul. As the two cars left the villa's grounds, Murrell phoned Fayed's Park Lane HQ and reported that the couple had left the villa. He noted down the times of their arrival – 15.47 – and departure – 16.18 – in the log he was required to keep of every visitor. When he returned to his living quarters in the villa, Murrell mentioned to his wife, Rebecca, how strangely Henri Paul had behaved.

Diana and Dodi made straight for the Ritz hotel after visiting the villa Windsor. Having started the day on the *Jonikal* in Sardinia, the couple were looking forward to relaxing in the Fayed family's hotel. They were both tired, and because the paparazzi were buzzing around, Diana abandoned thoughts of shopping for presents for her boys on the Champs-Elysées. Diana was keen to have her hair done in the hotel's

---

[2] *Death of a Princess*, chapter 10.
[3] Bower interview with Dourneau, September 1997.

salon after several days at sea on the *Jonikal*. Dodi was already late for the appointment he had made with jeweller, Alberto Repossi, in the place Vendôme. However, Dodi was confident that Repossi would wait for him.

At the rue Cambon entrance at the back of the Ritz, Diana and Dodi were greeted by Claude Roulet, the 46-year-old assistant to the president of the Ritz. Roulet was standing in for his boss Frank Klein who was on holiday. The urbane Roulet is a French Swiss national who had worked for the hotel for 17 years. As the hotel's archivist and historian he was in the process of writing a history of the hotel, *Ritz, Une histoire plus belle que la légende*, to be published in 1998, the centenary of the hotel's foundation by César Ritz. Roulet had not met Diana when she spent her secret weekend in the Ritz a month earlier. The hotelier asked the woman who everybody in France refers to as 'Lady Di' (Laddy Dee) how he should address her. The Princess put her hand on his arm and answered, 'Just call me Di'.

Roulet showed the couple to the Imperial Suite where the Princess had stayed in July. At last Diana and Dodi could relax in privacy.

Preoccupied as he was by his own security since the arrival in Paris, Dodi Fayed insisted on being driven by Philippe Dourneau to Alberto Repossi's showroom, less than 100 yards from the Ritz. Alberto Repossi had brought the ring from Monaco himself and he had waited for Dodi to arrive, even though he was over three hours late for their rendezvous. Repossi had privately hoped that Princess Diana would accompany Dodi but he was disappointed.

Dodi was accompanied by Trevor Rees-Jones. The bodyguard waited in the Mercedes while Dodi went to inspect the ring. Claude Roulet and Kez Wingfield had walked from the Ritz and they were waiting for Dodi to arrive. He was shown downstairs to the small reception room in the basement of Repossi's shop. The suave Italian proudly showed Dodi the ring which he had created. Fashioned from white gold, it had a hexagonal emerald as its central stone, bordered by four triangular diamonds. The band was covered in smaller diamonds.[4]

Repossi says that Dodi was delighted with the ring he had created. Repossi also gave Dodi a second ring to show Diana. This second ring was to be the model for the new line of jewellery Repossi was hoping to create for Diana. Dodi was also shown Repossi's sketches for a bracelet, a watch and earrings which he proposed to create if Diana approved of them.

---

[4] Author's interview with Repossi.

Repossi's security cameras recorded the whole of Dodi's visit which lasted only five minutes. Dodi departed in the Mercedes with Rees-Jones and he left Roulet, accompanied by Wingfield, to bring the rings to the Ritz. Roulet also made arrangements for payment as Mohamed Fayed was to pick up the bill. According to one report, Fayed paid a 'special price' of £12,000 for the ring.[5] The price for a similar ring in the 'Dis Moi Oui' range which inspired the ring that Repossi created for Princess Diana would have been between £120–130,000. Alberto Repossi will not be drawn on how much Mohamed Fayed actually paid for it.

While Dodi was at Repossi's, Diana phoned friends in London, including Richard Kay, from the Ritz. The *Daily Mail*'s royal correspondent wrote about his last conversation the day after the tragedy.[6] Like Rosa Monckton, Kay recalled Diana saying she was 'blissfully happy'. Indeed, Kay concluded his article with his opinion that 'On Saturday evening, Diana was as happy as I have ever known her. For the first time in years, all was well with her world'.

At 18.30 Roulet knocked on the door of the Imperial Suite with the jewels he had brought back from Repossi. Dodi opened the door, examined the rings and pocketed the one he had commissioned Repossi to design for him. He instructed Roulet to return the other one.[7]

Although Princess Diana appeared relaxed and happy during that afternoon to those who spoke to her, the media pressure on the couple had increased noticeably since their arrival in Paris. After ten days of being hunted from a distance by long lenses mounted on boats, helicopters and static positions on the coasts of the South of France and Sardinia, it was clear that they would now have to deal with the prospect of lenses being thrust in their faces in the French capital.

During their secret weekend at the Ritz in July, when there had been no security provided at all, Diana and Dodi had successfully used the Ritz's rear exit in the rue Cambon to escape attention.[8] As they now left at 19.00 by the same exit, there were photographers waiting but the atmosphere was cordial. Wingfield and Rees-Jones followed the couple's Mercedes to the Fayeds' Arsène-Houssaye apartment in the Range Rover. Henri Paul had clocked off and he had been replaced behind the wheel by Jean-François Musa, one of the bosses of Etoile Limousine and a fully qualified chauffeur. 'We decided to give them a little privacy', Rees-Jones

---

[5] Bower, p. 426.

[6] *Daily Mail*, 1 September 1997.

[7] Bower interview with Roulet.

[8] *Death of a Princess* and the testimony of various Fayed employees (Dourneau, Delorm, etc.) They are in fact the only sources we have that the couple were in Paris that weekend.

recalled. 'We were followed very closely by the journalists. At one point they overtook us. But there were no incidents. We asked the photographers not to take photos during the journey, particularly at crossroads and traffic lights.'[9]

Outside the Fayeds' apartment the security situation deteriorated very quickly as Diana and Dodi got out of the Mercedes just after 19.00. Wingfield and Rees-Jones had to physically push the paparazzi out of the way as they hurled themselves at the couple. Diana and Dodi spent the next two hours in Dodi's apartment but their chaotic arrival had increased the pressure they were under. The group of paparazzi who had met the party at the airport and had snapped them at the Ritz had now been supplemented by others. The Angéli agency had already put the first pictures of Diana and Dodi's arrival in Paris on the wires, and this had alerted all the picture agencies and news desks with offices in the French capital. Wingfield recalled the couple's reaction to the noisy assault by the photographers outside the Arsène-Houssaye apartment. 'This really upset the Princess, even though she was used to it. The paparazzi were shouting, which made them even more threatening. Dodi was particularly annoyed by their behaviour. He wasn't used to it, and he asked me what could be done to get rid of them. I told him it was impossible to escape from them just like that.'

One of Dodi's French security staff at the apartment, Didier Gamblin, became particularly rattled by the paparazzi onslaught, so much so that he telephoned Henri Paul on his mobile for instructions. Paul told him to let the paparazzi take their photos, as long as they did not get too close to the cars. After the fraught arrival, the two British bodyguards wandered casually out of the apartment while Diana and Dodi prepared for their evening on the town. They tried to cool the temperature, and made a point of talking to Romuald Rat, a burly photographer who they had identified as one of the more aggressive characters. Rat had been with the chasing group since Le Bourget. Some of the photographers had already left to get their latest pictures developed and offer them for sale to the following morning's papers.

The scenes outside the Fayeds' apartment when Diana and Dodi left for dinner that night at 21.45 were to determine their fate. They left in the black Mercedes driven by Philippe Dourneau, with the two bodyguards following in the black Range Rover driven by Musa. Dodi

---

[9] All witnesses quoted in the rest of this chapter made statements to the French investigation. They are recorded in Pontaut and Dupuis, *Enquête sur la mort de Diana*, chapters 2 and 3, unless otherwise stated.

had made a late decision to eat at Chez Benoît, a trendy but discreet restaurant popular with celebrities visiting Paris. The bodyguards had not been given the opportunity to reconnoitre the route or even 'sweep' it, as their normal procedure would require.[10] In fact, the bodyguards had no idea where they were going according to Trevor Rees-Jones. 'As we left the apartment, the butler [René Delorm] told us that the couple were going to a restaurant, but he didn't tell us which one . . . only Dodi knew our destination.'

Dodi had only decided where he wanted to take Diana shortly before they left. He had informed Claude Roulet, and the Ritz official had been despatched to Chez Benoît to ensure that everything was ready for their arrival. A table had been reserved in Roulet's name.

Myriah Daniels and Didier Gamblin watched the party leave. Gamblin remembers the scene vividly, 'Despite the agreement made with the paparazzi, they didn't respect anything we had asked them to do . . . as soon as the couple's car moved off they behaved like real devils. They called their bikes and sped off like fools, trying to stick to the car. They could have knocked over pedestrians. People flattened themselves against walls as the paparazzi's bikes mounted the pavements and sped past.'

Dodi was shaken by the paparazzi surrounding the Mercedes. According to Dourneau, Dodi was infuriated by them and cried out, 'It's too much! It's crazy all these paparazzi!'

Dourneau described the scene, 'They were all around us, at the sides, in front, behind. They were everywhere. Some were scouts, going ahead of us to find out where we were going. I think that was what really made Dodi nervous. On the way to Chez Benoît, Dodi asked me to warn Roulet, who was already at the restaurant, that he wanted to eat at the Ritz where he would be protected from the photographers.'

Dourneau phoned Roulet as he changed course. Roulet immediately phoned his duty night security manager, 43-year-old François Tendil. By the time Roulet got through to Tendil, the couple had already arrived and the night manager was under pressure. He told his boss: 'It's already happened and it's a bloody mess! I'm alone here and the paparazzi are trying to get into the hotel.'[11]

Wingfield and Rees-Jones had jumped out of the Range Rover when it stopped behind Dourneau's Mercedes in front of the Ritz having had no chance to prepare for the arrival (the 'de-bus' in bodyguard-speak) at the Ritz. Diana got out of the Mercedes first and Dodi followed a few

---

[10] RMP guidelines.
[11] Bower interview with Claude Roulet.

seconds later when he had finished a phone call. Diana was casually dressed in tight white trousers and a black blazer and top. Dodi wore blue jeans, cowboy boots and a loose-fitting brown dear-skin jacket over a grey shirt. As Diana approached the swing doors at the entrance to the hotel, the security camera captured two photographers taking her picture. Dodi's slightly delayed exit from the car thwarted their attempts to capture the couple entering the Ritz together.

The hotel video recorded a grim-faced Princess entering the hotel followed by Wingfield, then a tight-jawed Dodi and finally Rees-Jones. Fayed's son was embarrassed that the bodyguards had allowed the paparazzi so near to Diana. He immediately vented his anger, describing the entry into the hotel as a 'fuck-up'. The distressed Princess wept quietly in the Espadon restaurant a few minutes later.

The bodyguards' patience had been stretched by Dodi's chaotic planning and decision-making since the beginning of the holiday. Now Wingfield replied bluntly to their boss's son, telling him that his sudden decision to change destination en route to the Ritz had robbed them of the opportunity to prepare properly. Dodi soon backed down, apparently not wanting a full-scale row with Wingfield. Although Dodi chastised Wingfield, Rees-Jones was even more wound up. The Yorkshireman had to calm down 'the big fella' as he calls his Welsh friend and colleague. Wingfield felt that Rees-Jones could have been on the point of resigning.

After a few minutes, Diana and Dodi made their way upstairs to the Imperial Suite. They felt they were attracting too much attention in the restaurant. Dodi's plans for a quiet romantic meal were in ruins.

The mildly chaotic arrival of Diana and Dodi at the Ritz also prompted the return to the hotel of Henri Paul. The security chief had left the Ritz shortly after 19.00, telling one of his night security officers, François Tendil, to phone him if Diana and Dodi returned to the hotel.[12] When they appeared at the Ritz unexpectedly at 21.50, Tendil followed his boss's instructions.

Tendil noticed that when Henri Paul returned, he was dressed in the same clothes that he had been wearing throughout the day. Ritz video cameras reveal that Paul appeared to have some difficulty parking his Mini in a large vacant space outside the hotel. Paul paced around restlessly when he returned to the Ritz, and he made at least a dozen return trips to the first floor where Diana and Dodi were eating their meal in the Imperial Suite.

---

[12] Bower (unpublished) interview with François Tendil.

Kez Wingfield and Trevor Rees-Jones were eating a meal in the bar Vendôme. Henri Paul joined them and ordered a drink. The three made small talk as they waited for their 'principals' to finish their meal in the Imperial Suite. According to statements they later made to the police, neither bodyguard had any idea that Paul was drinking alcohol. He did not appear to either of them to be drunk. Tendil made a similar sworn statement on the basis of what he saw of Paul. Paul's drinks appeared to be of no significance to the bodyguards, or any Ritz staff, at the time as he was not due to drive anybody other than himself that evening. Dodi's chauffeur, Philippe Dourneau, was waiting outside to drive the principals away from the Ritz, as he had done since they touched down in Paris earlier in the day. The bodyguards' bar Vendôme bill included two Ricard, a brand of pastis.

Rees-Jones did not warm to Paul who he had met on previous trips to Paris. Paul was also puffing on small cigars while the bodyguards ate which the two nonsmokers found unpleasant. When they had finished their snacks they made their way upstairs to wait outside the Imperial Suite so they could talk privately and await the departure.

At 23.10 Claude Roulet made a call to François Tendil's office to check that he had the situation under control. Roulet had gone home after his trip to Chez Benoît, and he was concerned because Tendil had sounded so rattled when he spoke to him earlier. To his surprise, Henri Paul picked up the phone in the security manager's office. Roulet had thought that Paul was off duty when he left the hotel at 19.00. Paul told Roulet that there were lots of people outside because Princess Diana had returned, but that there was no need for him to worry, 'I have the situation in hand'.[13]

Paul had made several sorties outside the front of the hotel to check on how the situation was developing. A large crowd had gathered in the place Vendôme, attracted by the photographers. According to several of the photographers, Paul addressed them at least three times, winding them up with promises that the Princess and Dodi would be emerging within minutes.

At 23.37 Paul walked up the stairs again and went into the Imperial Suite. The bodyguards were waiting outside the room. While they had been sitting there Kez Wingfield heard sounds of laughter and joking inside. Despite all the pressures of the day since they left Sardinia, and the row he had had with Dodi as they entered the Ritz, Wingfield felt Diana and Dodi were contented, 'I think that evening was the happiest I ever remember them being.'

---

[13] Bower interview with Roulet.

Several minutes later, Henri Paul emerged with an announcement. He said that Dodi had devised a scheme to give the paparazzi the slip. The couple would leave the hotel by the rear entrance, in a new car; a diversion would be created by the couple's chauffeurs leaving from the front of the Ritz in the Mercedes and the Range Rover that had brought them to the hotel two hours earlier. Dodi had decided that he, Henri Paul, would drive them and that there would be no back-up car. The bodyguards were to travel with the decoy convoy to make it appear more authentic.

The bodyguards were annoyed. Once again Dodi was making a plan on the hoof without consulting them at all. They were perplexed because the plan ran counter to all of their Royal Military Police training and accepted custom and practice as Fayed family security men. Their immediate thought was to contact Dave Moody at their London HQ to inform them of Dodi's plan. However, Paul's final remark made that an unnecessary and potentially risky option for them. He told them, 'The plan has been okayed by Mohamed.'

The bodyguards were in a dilemma. They knew exactly what was laid down in their guidelines: 'The OC [head] of the team, the personal bodyguard, and, dependent upon the threat assessment, up to seven other bodyguards . . . operate within the immediate area of the VIP and are directly responsible for the safety of the VIP at all times' (Close Protection Instructions, point 1615).

Now their boss wanted to accompany the most famous woman in the world out of his father's hotel by himself. There would be no security other than Henri Paul, a man with no close protection training, although he was in charge of security at the Ritz. Furthermore Paul had said that Dodi did not want a back-up car which is always deemed essential in such operations when Mohamed Fayed is involved – indeed, 'recovery' and 'alternative transport' are laid down as a necessity in point 1629 of their guidelines. This was unprecedented in both bodyguards' professional experience of close protection duties, both in the forces and working for the Fayeds.

Both men were troubled by Dodi's plan – the return to the Arsène-Houssaye apartment would normally take only five minutes, but they both knew that the paparazzi were desperate to get pictures of the couple together in Paris and would not disperse until this had been achieved. The journey to the Ritz had seen the paparazzi buzzing around the couple's Mercedes and this had led to Dodi's outburst. Now the bodyguards would have no security control of any sort if they carried out Dodi's instruction to attempt to create a decoy to fool the paparazzi.

As the bodyguards contemplated their dilemma, Dodi's head popped out of the Imperial Suite. To their disappointment, he repeated the plan exactly as Henri Paul had relayed it to them and claimed that he'd spoken to Fayed on the phone and that he had approved it.[14]

Wingfield approached Dodi and started to remonstrate with him. Both men spoke in hushed tones. Dodi obviously did not want Princess Diana to hear that he was having a disagreement with Wingfield. For his part Wingfield did not want to embarrass his boss in front of 'his missus', as Diana had become known to the guards. Wingfield furiously insisted that Dodi's plan was out of order. It meant that no bodyguard would be travelling with Dodi and the Princess in the most difficult situation they had encountered since their French adventure had begun. The chaotic scenes at the Fayed apartment when they had returned there earlier in the evening were still fresh in Wingfield's mind, particularly the aggressive behaviour of some of the photographers. Dodi refused to discuss the plan in detail with Wingfield, but he did concede that one bodyguard should be allowed to travel with himself and the Princess. He insisted that the other was to join the attempt to create a diversion at the front of the hotel as his plan envisaged.

The Ritz was still besieged by scores of photographers and reporters wanting another photo of Princess Diana and her new man. The first pictures of them kissing and embracing in the South of France had sold for millions. Pictures of the lovers at night in Paris would not attract the same price but they would certainly sell. The crowd had swelled to around a hundred people, but the atmosphere was relaxed. At one point a blonde woman leaving the Ritz received a round of applause from the onlookers. It quickly faded as they realised she was not Diana.

During this period, Henri Paul appeared at regular intervals outside the front of the Ritz to evaluate the situation and chat to the photographers. Romuald Rat was surprised by this behaviour, 'M Paul came to see us several times, it was maybe between 11 p.m. and midnight. When he left I chatted with Laszlo Veres about it and we thought it was strange. That's when I found out that he was the security number two. At the Ritz, the chauffeurs and car valets are not supposed to talk to us. His [Paul's] attitude was completely the opposite of this.

At one point, he came back to show us something; I don't know whether he was showing us the sky or the Vendôme column. He was really strange. He came out two or three times in front of the queuing

---

[14] Mohamed Fayed has subsequently denied this; see p. 244.

photographers and signalled to us: five minutes or ten minutes. He was basically taunting us.'

Pierre Honsfield, another photographer, was also surprised by Paul's behaviour: 'I saw a man who I had seen before at the Ritz but whose role I was ignorant of, come to address us. He said to us, laughing: "Well lads, in a quarter of an hour, it is coming out . . . (ça sort)". The man came out a second time saying: "In ten minutes time!". He came back a third time, tapping a small cigar on his cigar box, and repeated: "In ten minutes", still laughing. We started to think that maybe they were not going to leave by the front . . .'

At one point Dourneau and Musa faked a departure, by driving the Mercedes and Range Rover around the place Vendôme. Although many of the photographers followed them, the cars simply went around the square and stopped again outside the hotel. The crowd of onlookers began to boo. Henri Paul emerged again to taunt the paparazzi, smiling as he called out to them: '1–0!'

At 00.18 Princess Diana stood with Dodi at the rear exit of the Ritz hotel, waiting for the limousine to take them back to the Fayed apartment. Jean-François Musa, one of the directors of the small car hire company Etoile Limousine, which serves only the Ritz, had made arrangements for another Mercedes to be available.

As the couple waited for the car to whisk them away from the hotel, the security camera captured Dodi placing his hand gently at the small of Diana's back. Waiting with them was Trevor Rees-Jones and Henri Paul. Outside in the rue Cambon, several journalists had gathered, anticipating that Princess Diana and Dodi might exit from the rear of the hotel as they had done earlier in the evening. Jacques Langevin, a seasoned war photographer, was there as the Sygma agency's duty photographer for the weekend; Alain Guizard, a reporter; as well as photographers Serge Benamou and Fabrice Chassery. Chassery had been in touch with one of the directors of the Etoile Limousine company, Philippe 'Niels' Siegel, three times that day by phone to try and establish details about the couple's movements. Finally, Chassery thought, he might get a picture of Diana and Dodi together.

Trevor Rees-Jones stuck his head out of the door to look for the Mercedes Dodi had ordered, and he noticed the snappers waiting. Rees-Jones's placid exterior did not betray the misgivings he harboured about the security arrangements for the journey that he was about to undertake. Because the Welshman had been needled even more badly than Wingfield by Dodi's erratic and arrogant behaviour throughout the Mediterranean holiday, the two agreed that he should accompany the couple. According to Wingfield, their idea was that Rees-Jones, who had greater experience of dealing with Dodi, would 'have it out' with his boss to clear the air when they got back to the apartment. Wingfield feared at one stage that Rees-Jones was so wound up that he would land a punch on Dodi. He hoped that sending them back together to the apartment would give Rees-Jones the chance to restore good working relations.

At 00.19 a black Mercedes S-280 pulled up in the rue Cambon at the rear of the hotel. At the wheel was Frédéric Lucard, a student who was working at the Ritz as a part-time 'vehicle jockey'. Until June, Lucard had worked as a chauffeur at Etoile Limousine. Now his job included parking clients' cars in the underground car park beneath the hotel.

Lucard drove the Mercedes to the rear exit after being ordered to do so by Jean-François Musa just after midnight. Lucard was told that the car was to be used for a 'discreet departure'. This did not come as a surprise as celebrities often exit by the rear entrance. Lucard was, however, taken aback to learn from Musa that Henri Paul would be driving Dodi and the Princess: 'He was not a normal limousine driver. I thought that my boss, Jean-François Musa himself or Dodi's chauffeur, Philippe Dourneau, would be driving, but I just did my job and followed my orders'.[15]

As Lucard pulled up and handed the keys to Henri Paul he noticed the small knot of photographers standing on the opposite side of the street from the exit. Lucard watched as Diana and Dodi made their way to the car with Trevor Rees-Jones. Henri Paul was the first member of the party to leave the hotel. Lucard recognised Paul because he had seen him arrive at the Ritz two hours earlier and had offered to park his black and white Mini for him. Lucard recalls that, as he handed the keys of the Mercedes to Henri Paul, the Ritz security chief called out to the photographers, 'Don't try to follow us, you will never catch us.'

The Ritz security camera recorded an indistinct image of Lucard watching the Mercedes leave the Ritz with Henri Paul at the wheel. According to Lucard, Paul began his fateful journey by putting his foot down hard on the accelerator. He sped off down the rue Cambon and into history in the Alma tunnel.

---

[15] Author's interview with Frédéric Lucard, May 1998.

4. THE ACCIDENT

'Tonight's accident is a terrible tragedy. The death of the Princess of Wales fills us all with deep shock and with deep grief.'

Sir Michael Jay, 05.45, 31 August 1997

Princess Diana would have had no reason for disquiet as she slid into the back of the Mercedes S-280 outside the rear exit to the Ritz on the rue Cambon. Henri Paul led the way from the door of the Ritz to the Mercedes. Trevor Rees-Jones got into the front passenger seat next to Henri Paul. Diana ignored the handful of photographers on the opposite side of the street as she walked briskly to the car and slipped into the back seat next to Dodi. The photographers were able to take pictures of the couple in the Mercedes as the car did not have tinted windows like Philippe Dourneau's vehicle. None of the passengers put on their seatbelts.

In her two previous trips to Paris with Dodi, Princess Diana had been driven by Dourneau. However, she knew Henri Paul had been driving the back-up Range Rover during the afternoon. Paul had followed Dodi's Mercedes as they left Le Bourget, and also from the villa Windsor to the Ritz.

As the Mercedes headed for the place de la Concorde, Princess Diana would not have known that Henri Paul was not a qualified chauffeur, or that he did not possess the licence that French law requires to drive a car registered as a limousine. More seriously, Diana could not have known that Henri Paul was drunk. In addition to the two Pastis he had consumed in the bar, he had been drinking earlier in the day. No one in the car knew the state Paul was in other than himself.

As the car approached the end of the rue Cambon and Paul drove into the rue de Rivoli, the paparazzi had started to chase the car. The paparazzi hunt as a pack and, as soon as Princess Diana emerged from the back of the hotel, the photographers alerted some of those waiting in the place Vendôme at the front. Rue Cambon is a one-way street, and so the Mercedes had no option but to join the rue de Rivoli. By the time it had turned right into the place de la Concorde, paparazzi who had been waiting for the departure at the front and rear exits were in hot pursuit.

Kez Wingfield had waited with Philippe Dourneau and Jean-François Musa at the front of the Ritz as Henri Paul left from the rue Cambon. They were preparing to play their part in the Fayeds' plan to fool the waiting photographers and reporters that the couple were about to use the main entrance at the front of the hotel.

Wingfield had watched as some of the paparazzi jumped onto their motorbikes and sped off in the direction that he knew the Mercedes was headed in. He remained unhappy with his orders. As envisaged by Dodi's plan, the decoy cars should have waited for five minutes but the disgruntled bodyguard instructed them to move away only two or three minutes later. Wingfield left from the front of the Ritz in the Range Rover, driven, as earlier in the evening, by Jean-François Musa. Dourneau followed in the Mercedes he had brought Dodi and Diana to the Ritz in. It was clear to all three men that Dodi's plan to fool the paparazzi had failed. However, Wingfield knew after five years of providing close protection for the Fayeds that it was impossible to argue with a plan that had been devised by Dodi and sanctioned by Mohamed.

Just before Henri Paul stopped in the place de la Concorde at red traffic lights he made a fateful decision. He decided not to turn right into the Champs-Elysées, and take the most direct route to the apartment. It was nearly half past midnight, and the best known avenue in Paris was full of people. Paul knew that there were several sets of traffic lights on the Champs-Elysées between him and the rue Arsène-Houssaye. He also knew that the purpose of Dodi's plan was to avoid the paparazzi. As the Mercedes did not have tinted windows, the photographers would find the Princess and Dodi easy prey if he turned right into the Champs-Elysées.

Paul decided to carry straight on and turn right into the cours La-Reine which runs by the Seine. This is a familiar way of avoiding the Champs-Elysées. The cours La-Reine becomes the cours Albert-1er, and provides a long stretch of dual carriageway that would give Paul the chance to outpace the paparazzi. Paul put his foot down, jumped the lights in the place de la Concorde and turned right into the cours La-Reine. He would be able to make his way back to Dodi's apartment just by the Arc de Triomphe, by turning right just after the Alma tunnel and working his way back through the backstreets. It would be a very long way round.

In the final minutes before the accident none of the occupants of the Mercedes had any idea that the tunnel which Paul was speeding towards has one of the worst accident records in Paris. In the previous fifteen years, 34 accidents had been recorded, leaving eight people dead and eight seriously injured. Strangely, the tunnel, built in 1956, is not officially registered on the plans of Paris. The cours Albert-1er dual carriageway leading into the tunnel is deceptive. There is a hump followed by a substantial dip just before the entrance to the tunnel where the road also bends quite sharply to the left. In the Alma tunnel itself there are no safety walls or crash barriers to prevent drivers hitting the pillars that form the central reservation, which is one reason why so many have died there.

As Paul sped Princess Diana towards the Alma tunnel, Dourneau and Musa followed a similar route to the one Henri Paul had just taken towards the Champs-Elysées apartment. They found themselves in the place de l'Alma, above the tunnel where they became aware of a commotion in the area and the flashing blue lights of the emergency services. Thinking that an accident on the road might have delayed the other car, Wingfield tried to contact Trevor Rees-Jones. He knew his colleague's mobile was not working, so he sent him a message on his bleeper. He wanted to check that everyone had arrived safely at the Fayeds' apartment in the rue Arsène-Houssaye.

They had not.

Henri Paul had comfortably outdistanced the paparazzi who were following his Mercedes as he sped along the cours La-Reine. The speed limit in central Paris is 50 km/hr (31 mph). The Mercedes accelerated to well over 100 km/hr (63 mph), and no photographs were taken of the car or its occupants between the place de la Concorde and the Alma tunnel. The photographers were fairly certain that Dodi was taking Princess Diana to the rue Arsène-Houssaye apartment, indeed some had gone directly there to await them. Some of them decided there was no point in chasing Paul and proceeded at a non-competitive pace. Others tried to pursue the Mercedes in vehicles and motorbikes that could not keep up.

As Paul approached the Alma tunnel, a white Fiat Uno was in the right hand lane of the cours Albert-1er, which leads into the tunnel. The Fiat could have emerged from the slip road to the right, which feeds into the cours Albert-1er. It was travelling much more slowly than the Mercedes. Henri Paul was going at a speed of between 118 km/hr (74 mph) and 155 km/hr (97 mph). As the car encountered the Fiat, Paul tried to avoid it by oversteering to the left. Failing to avoid the Fiat completely, Paul brushed the left-hand rear of the car with the right wing of his Mercedes. The brush with the Fiat occurred just as the Mercedes went over the notorious hump before the Alma tunnel. Paul then understeered to the right as the car reached the dip at the immediate mouth of the tunnel. Having lost control of the vehicle, it crashed into the tunnel's thirteenth pillar before Paul even had the chance to brake. The car did not skid and its wheels did not lock. The

Mercedes airbags functioned normally upon impact with the pillar, but none of the passengers was restrained by a seatbelt as none had put one on. Although it was widely reported after the crash that Trevor Rees-Jones had fastened his seatbelt between the hotel and the tunnel, the investigation has proved that this was not the case.

Henri Paul and Dodi Fayed died almost instantly and Princess Diana and Trevor-Rees Jones had both been very seriously injured. The front of the Mercedes had been crushed by the impact with the pillar but the rear of the car was relatively undamaged. Smoke from the car's crushed engine engulfed the tunnel. The horn blared, echoing out of the tunnel and into the night air above the place de l'Alma.

The first person to arrive on the scene was the photographer Romuald Rat. His driver Stéphane Darmon halted immediately after the wrecked car. Rat ran back and then froze in horror.

A few minutes later the first doctor arrived on the scene. He was Dr Frédéric Mailliez, who had been travelling in the opposite direction to the Mercedes through the Alma tunnel. 'I was pretty sure that the car had just crashed because the smoke was still in the tunnel and the horn was still going on . . . I saw the severely damaged car and I saw four people inside. Two were apparently dead and two severely injured.'[1]

Having assessed the situation, Mailliez briefly returned to his car and called for help. He told the emergency services, 'There are two people severely injured. I need two ambulances.'

Trevor Rees-Jones was being attended to by an off-duty fireman who was cradling his bloodied head in his hands. Mailliez went straight to Diana who he thought was 'in the best shape' of anyone in the car. Mailliez, who later said he did not recognise the Princess, saw that blood was trickling from her nose and her mouth but, apart from that, she had no visible signs of disfigurement. Not realising the extent of her internal injuries, Mailliez later told CNN that his initial assessment of Diana was that, she 'looked pretty fine . . . I thought this woman had a chance'. Mailliez slipped an oxygen mask over her face. 'I helped her to breathe with the mask and I attempted to liberate the upper respiratory passage by bending her head back slightly. I sought to unblock the trachea and prevent the tongue from blocking the oro-pharynx. She seemed a bit more agitated, thus more reactive, once she was able to breathe better.'

The first policemen to arrive at the scene of the accident had been flagged down by the crowd that had gathered around the Alma tunnel in the immediate aftermath of the crash. Lino Gaggliardone and

---

[1] *Death of a Princess*, p. 15.

Sébastien Dorzee from the city's 8th district were on night patrol. They parked their car at the entrance to the tunnel, shouting 'accident in the Alma tunnel. Send help!' into their radio, before running to the crashed Mercedes. It was now 00.30.

The two policemen had to fight their way through a crowd of photographers who were busy shooting the wrecked Mercedes and taking pictures of the victims. Sébastien Dorzee found a dazed Princess Diana trapped in the wreckage. She was facing the back of the car, having been spun round 180 degrees by the impact. She was moving slightly and her eyes were open. She spoke a few words in English that Dorzee could not understand. Then, according to Dorzee, 'I think she said, "My God", when she saw her dead friend [Dodi]. She must have been in pain . . . the Princess turned her head towards the front of the car, saw the driver and understood better what had happened, I think. She became agitated. A few seconds later, she looked at me. Then she rested her head and she shut her eyes.'[2]

It was clear to the emergency services as soon as they arrived that Henri Paul and Dodi Fayed were dead. Both men had similar fatal injuries. According to his autopsy report, Paul had died of a ruptured aorta, combined with an instantly fatal fracture of the spinal column at neck height which severed the spinal cord. He had also suffered multiple fractures of the ribs, pelvis and legs. No attempt was made to revive him. His crushed body remained trapped in the Mercedes, while the fire crew prepared to liberate the other victims from the wreckage.

Dodi had facial injuries, his right leg had been broken in four places and his left leg in three. His back was broken, his spinal cord severed and his aorta completely ruptured, injuries which had led to his immediate death. In addition, his chest had been crushed in the accident which had led to massive internal haemorrhaging.

Diana lay in the back of the car moaning as medical workers from SAMU, the emergency service (service d'aide médicale urgente) prepared to move her into an ambulance after the first aid administered by Dr Mailliez. Dr Jean-Marc Martino, a surgical anaesthetist and resuscitation specialist, tried to help Diana, while a doctor from the fire service helped his SAMU colleagues treat Rees-Jones, who seemed to all those on the scene to be the more seriously injured of the two.

According to Martino, the Princess was still agitated and crying out, not seeming to understand his comforting words. She moved her left arm and right leg as she muttered incoherent and confused words. Her

---

[2] Pontaut and Dupuis, p. 97.

right arm was folded behind her, possibly dislocated. The firemen on the scene had already placed a neck brace on the Princess, and Martino proceeded to examine her while administering a drip and sedating her. He prepared her for transfer to hospital as she was being cut out of the wreckage. Because of the way she had been wedged in the floor well, between the back seat and front right seat, this was a difficult process. Despite all of the care taken in getting her out of the car, the Princess suffered a heart attack. She was given cardiac massage and a respiratory tube was inserted into her mouth to aid her breathing. She was then transferred into the ambulance where a more detailed examination was carried out as resuscitation attempts continued. After the heart attack Martino realised how serious Princess Diana's condition was.

Ambulance driver Michel Massebeuf described how he brought the stretcher to the car on which the Princess was given artificial respiration. 'Princess Diana was then placed in the ambulance, as was our normal procedure, so that Dr Martino could look after her under the best possible conditions.'[3]

It was now just before 01.30. It had taken nearly an hour to get the Princess out of the wreckage, and to give her vital treatment for her heart attack. Meanwhile, Trevor Rees-Jones had also been freed from the wreckage as the firemen cut off the roof of the crushed Mercedes. As Dourneau watched a motionless Trevor Rees-Jones being extracted from the Mercedes and stretchered into an ambulance, he had assumed he was also dead. An entirely separate medical team led by Dr Le Hote was taking care of the bodyguard. The emergency services decided to transfer both casualties to the Pitié-Salpêtrière hospital, a stone's throw away from the Austerlitz train station, as they judged it to have the best and most appropriate facilities.

Preceded by two police cars, and surrounded by a police motorcycle escort, the ambulance carrying Princess Diana slowly made its way to the hospital. The Paris police had closed all the roads along the route to the hospital so traffic would not impede the ambulance's journey. The SAMU rescue workers stopped transmitting details about the Princess's condition on the radio. The convoy crawled along the Seine so as not to risk destabilising the Princess's blood pressure further and thus prompt a second heart attack. This is standard procedure in both France and Britain when casualties are in as fragile a state as the Princess was.

Half an hour after leaving the Alma tunnel, the ambulance still had not arrived at the Pitié-Salpêtrière hospital. Interior Minister Jean-Pierre

---

[3] Pontaut and Dupuis, p. 108.

Chevènement and his technical advisor Sami Naïr, Philippe Massoni, the Chief of Police, and Sir Michael Jay from the British Embassy, who had all been informed of the accident, had already made their way there. Massebeuf, however, had stopped his ambulance completely just after crossing the Seine. Diana's blood pressure had dropped again, and was dangerously low. 'We had reached the Botanical Gardens when the doctor asked me to stop so that he could give treatment which required complete immobility,' recalls Massebeuf. Approximately five minutes later, the convoy resumed its course and travelled the remaining short distance to the Pitié-Salpêtrière.

At the hospital, the Princess's care was entrusted to the duty resuscitation team that night, led by Professeur Bruno Riou. Dr Martino explained the situation to him: 'The Princess's blood pressure was weak and she had been put on a ventilator.'[4]

Daniel Eyraud of the hospital's Vascular Surgery team describes the Princess's state on arrival at the hospital: 'She was unconscious and under artificial respiration. Her arterial blood pressure was very low but her heart was still beating.'

As Diana had no apparent serious external injuries, the doctors proceeded to take X-rays to establish the cause of her grave condition. Their worst fears were realised when they found that she had suffered terrible internal injuries, namely internal haemorrhaging, which was constricting her right lung and her heart. The doctors set up a drain to remove the excess blood from Diana's chest, while simultaneously preparing a blood transfusion to replace the vast quantities of blood that she was losing. A full six litres was ready, a litre more than the human body holds.

The resuscitation team's job was complicated further, however, as Diana suffered a second heart attack at 02.10. As a result Professeur Riou urgently summoned Professeur Alain Pavie, a specialist heart surgeon, to help in the efforts to save Diana's life. Diana's condition was rapidly worsening and Riou decided to operate with the help of duty surgeon Moncel Dahman.

Ten minutes later Professeur Pavie arrived and took over. It was explained to him within seconds that Dr Dahman had opened the Princess's chest on the right-hand side while external cardiac massage continued: 'The Princess's vital functions were being maintained by the resuscitation efforts. I found that the bleeding was coming from a hole in the membrane around her heart.'

---

[4] All statements from the medical team are quoted in Pontaut and Dupuis, chapter 6.

Throughout the operation, a nurse injected Diana with massive doses of adrenaline to keep her heart going. According to Pavie, '. . . she would have died there and then. Her heart vitally needed the adrenaline. We then realised that we had injected her with around 150 phials of 5 ml for 5 mg, which is an enormous amount.' Despite this, the Princess needed further surgery.

By 03.00 the original incision to Diana's chest had been extended. In a desperate attempt to save Diana's life, her heart was being massaged by hand. Her superior left pulmonary vein was also found to be torn. This was duly stitched up and the internal haemorrhaging controlled. Still the resuscitation efforts continued. Despite the massive doses of adrenaline, the doctors described how she remained dependent on the cardiac massage and no spontaneous rhythm was resumed.

In a final desperate last-ditch bid to save Diana's life the team proceeded with electric shock therapy to try to get the heart going again. After two hours there was nothing more that could be done. Professeur Pavie concluded: 'Seeing that the resuscitation attempts were ineffective, all taking part in the operation agreed to stop all treatment.'

Diana, Princess of Wales was pronounced dead in the operating theatre of the Pitié-Salpêtrière hospital at 04.00 on 31 August 1997.

The expert's report detailing the treatment given to Diana that night concludes that injuries of the type endured by the Princess are usually fatal no matter what medical treatment is tried. It also states that it is exceptional for anyone with such injuries to even reach the hospital alive.

Dr Patrick Goldstein, vice-president of the SAMU of France, said, 'Could we have done more in Diana's case? We can always do more, but we can't do the impossible. Diana had no chance of making it. The accident was too violent. The internal injuries she suffered were incompatible with life.'

First news of the crash had reported that Dodi Fayed and his driver Henri Paul were dead. Early reports held that Diana, Princess of Wales, had escaped with relatively minor injuries. There was even discussion on live TV on how Diana would cope with the death of Dodi.

Such speculation was brought to a halt at 05.45 on Sunday 31 August when the British Ambassador, Sir Michael Jay, held a press conference at the Pitié Salpêtrière hospital. Flanked by the men who had fought to save her life, Professeurs Riou and Pavie, Sir Michael announced that Diana had died at 04.00.

5. THE PAPARAZZI

'I always believed the press would kill her in the end, but not even I could imagine that they would take such a hand in her death.'

Earl Spencer, 31 August 1997

The first paparazzo to arrive after Henri Paul had crashed the Mercedes was Romuald Rat of the Gamma photo agency. He arrived on the back of a motorbike driven by the agency's Stéphane Darmon. Even though he had been pursuing the car since it left the Ritz hotel a few minutes earlier, he says he was not at first sure that it was Princess Diana's car: 'I saw that it was a Mercedes, and I thought to myself that it could be the couple. I was sure of this once I reached the car and recognised Mr Al Fayed. Then I was shocked, as it was not a nice scene to see. I backed off for a few seconds. I took two photos while I was running towards the car, and I took a third when I backed off after having seen Al Fayed in the car. All this lasted less than about ten seconds.'[1]

'After several seconds I got hold of myself and tried to aid them, simply to see if they were still alive . . . I didn't call the emergency unit because I heard someone say "I've called the fire brigade". So I didn't bother to do that myself.'[2]

Serge Arnal of the Stills agency reached the Alma tunnel in a car with Christian Martinez of Angéli immediately after Rat. Arnal says he called for help on his mobile phone as soon as he arrived. He had to move away from the crash scene to get better reception, and in panic he tried to dial 12 instead of 112, the emergency number for SAMU.

Serge Benamou was next to arrive: 'I took photos as soon as I arrived, without thinking. Then I phoned Laszlo Veres to tell him to come.'

A passing pedestrian, Belkacem B., ran into the Alma tunnel. As he entered, he thought that the emergency services were present. He had mistaken the photographers' camera flashes for the lights of the emergency services, 'But when I approached the car, I realised that it was four photographers. I tried to open the car door, and asked the photographers, particularly the fattest one [Romuald Rat] who was close to the car, what to do. Rat, who was taking precise photos of the car, told me: "Don't touch anything, it's Princess Diana! She's with Dodi!" '

---

[1] Witness statements from the scene of the crash are as given to the French investigation. Unless otherwise stated, these are recorded in Pontaut and Dupuis, chapter 5.

[2] *Death of a Princess*, p. 169.

Rat's driver, Stéphane Darmon, was also sickened as he watched the photographers work around the car, 'I sat down for a short while on the curb at the tunnel's exit. Two ladies from the area came up to me and comforted me a bit as they could see I was in shock. I had a bitter taste in my mouth because I couldn't stand the fact that the photographers were taking photos. The tunnel was alight with flashes.'

Having taken some pictures Romuald Rat decided to open the back right door of the Mercedes: 'I wanted to help them as I am qualified in first aid and resuscitation. I wanted to take Diana's pulse. When I touched her, she started moaning. Her head was leaning back slightly and she seemed to be breathing. I said to her in English: "Be cool, a doctor is coming."'

Rat says he then tried to help the stricken Trevor Rees-Jones in the front seat ahead of Diana: '. . . the bodyguard started to move around quite a lot in his seat. He was making the Princess move at the same time. I got up and went to see him. The left hand side of his face was very messed up. I touched him very gently on his cheek and head so that he could feel that I was there. I said the same thing to him as I did to the Princess.'

As Rat was helping the passengers, Christian Martinez leant into the car and started taking photos. 'I was trying to get Diana; I think I used the zoom to take her. I was at maybe 1.5 to 2 metres away.'

Rat says he tried to stop Martinez. He shouted, 'Get back! Don't take any more photos inside the car!'

Martinez later admitted, 'It's true, we didn't help the wounded. Maybe it was through a sense of modesty (*pudeur*) . . . It shows a lot of arrogance going to help the people that we were following just a few minutes earlier.'

Although Martinez' admission is revealing, the paparazzi firmly denied suggestions made later that they impeded Dr Frédéric Mailliez' attempts to treat the victims. Rat said that such a suggestion was 'ridiculous and unthinkable'.[3] Mailliez told French police that the photographers all got out of his way to allow him access to the victims in the Mercedes.

Sébastien Dorzee and Lino Gaggliardone found the photographers much less helpful than Mailliez did. Dorzee remembers a group of between ten and fifteen photographers taking photos with their cameras going off like machine guns. He claims that while he tried to help Diana, Gaggliardone tried to stop the photographers taking pictures. According

---

[3] *Death of a Princess*, p. 169.

to the police, Christian Martinez shouted at them, 'You are really pissing me off! I'm going back to Sarajevo; there the cops don't mess around with us and let us work. You've only got to go to Bosnia and you will see!'

Gaggliardone shot back with, 'We are in Paris, now!'

Martinez replied, 'I'm only doing my job'.

'So am I,' replied the disgruntled officer.

Ker, Chassery and Guizard arrived. Next came Arsov. And then Veres who had been called by Benamou. Finally, Jacques Langevin arrived by chance. He had given up the quest for pictures of Princess Diana and Dodi when they left the back of the Ritz, and he was on his way to see friends.

Members of the public who witnessed the events immediately after the crash remonstrated with the photographers. They were appalled at the photographers' behaviour and their reaction to their protests. Gaëlle L. told Martinez to stop taking photos; he bluntly told her to butt out: 'Mind your own business'. Clifford G. pushed Rat away. He recalled, 'His attitude disgusted me. On no occasion did he try to help the four victims.' Another man tried to hit Rat after exchanging insults with him.

Soon the Alma tunnel was surrounded by a police cordon that Paris police chief, Philippe Massoni had thrown around the site of the accident. No traffic could pass in either direction. As the news spread that Diana was one of those involved in the crash, hundreds of people fought for a view of the crushed Mercedes from the sides of the roads leading into and out of the tunnel. Millions of viewers and listeners around the world tuned in to learn the shocking news. A television camera situated at the end of the tunnel by the slip road that feeds into the cours Albert-1er fed live pictures which were then beamed around the world. The locked-off shot showed only the back of the Mercedes which hardly looked damaged from behind.

The world was transfixed as the sad events of the night of 31 August unravelled. Few noticed a young woman arriving in the Alma tunnel on the back of a BMW motorcycle. She was dressed in a black leather jacket and jeans. Had she not been waved through the police cordon, she could have been mistaken for one of the paparazzi herself as she dismounted. In fact, Maud Coujard, in her early thirties, was the Paris duty prosecutor on 31 August. The motorbike that brought her to the scene of the accident was driven by her husband. Coujard had been summoned to the tunnel by the police as soon as word of the accident reached them. She would oversee the French investigation into the crash.

Martine Monteil, who would lead the Criminal Brigade's investigation into the crash, also arrived in the Alma tunnel. She had become the first female head of the Criminal Brigade, popularly referred to as the 'Crim', when she was appointed in 1996. The fictional detective in the Maigret novels of Georges Simenon, held the same post. Both Monteil's father and her husband made their careers in the French police. In 1990, when she was head of the Vice Squad, she was voted 'Woman of the Year' by *Biba* magazine.

The Criminal Brigade is the branch of the judicial police that investigates criminal and terrorist cases as well as unexplained deaths. Based at the famous quai des Orfèvres, the 'Crim' has over 100 officers, and boasts an enviable record of success, cracking sixty per cent of cases assigned to it. This thoroughness has earned it the popular nickname of 'rouleau compresseur', the road roller flattening everything in its path.

Paris police chief, Philippe Massoni, had arrived in the tunnel within half an hour of the crash. The white-haired police chief moved arc lights into place to illuminate the crash scene, and to aid the removal of the victims from the tunnel by SAMU.

Once this had been done, the detectives removed Princess Diana's personal effects from the car. These included a bracelet with six rows of white pearls and a clasp shaped like a dragon, a Jaeger-Lecoultier gold watch with white stones and a gold ring, also with white stones. Her black, high-heeled Versace shoes were also found. Diana was wearing only one of her gold earrings as she was removed from the car. Several weeks later the other earring was found under the car's dashboard. Dodi's effects included three watches (made by Cartier, Breitling and Citizen) some petty cash and an Asprey gold cigar-clipper. Henri Paul had 12,560 francs on him, several credit cards and his Ritz hotel identity pass. Trevor Rees-Jones's effects included his personal address book, and the bleeper that Kez Wingfield had tried to message him on during the fatal journey. Dodi's mobile phone was not listed as having been found.

The crumpled Mercedes was photographed from every conceivable angle as the detectives began to gather evidence and preserve the scene of the crash.

Investigations into traffic accidents would normally be handled by Massoni's judicial police. On this occasion Maud Coujard, a prosecutor specialising in investigations of traffic accidents, felt justified in assigning the Criminal Brigade to the case. Coujard made her decision on the spot in the Alma tunnel having first spoken to police on the scene, as well as to several eyewitnesses to the crash. Her decision, made before

Princess Diana had died, was the first indication that the accident would be treated as a potential criminal case.

Criminal Brigade commander, Jean-Claude Mulès, had arrived to direct the operation. Mulès was a veteran of the Criminal Brigade's lengthy and ultimately successful hunts for 'Carlos' the terrorist and the *Action Directe* terrorists who caused so much havoc in France in the 1970s and 1980s. Mulès was at the heart of the unfolding tragedy on 31 August 1997. As the survivors of the crash, Trevor Rees-Jones and Princess Diana were taken to hospital, Mulès directed the police operation in the Alma tunnel. He could be briefly glimpsed in the TV pictures sent around the world that night. While the gendarmes arrested some of the paparazzi who had been chasing the Mercedes, the veteran detective ensured that every piece of evidence was collected. The tunnel was cordoned off and the scene of the crash and the crumpled Mercedes were photographed from every conceivable angle. For the next year Mulès worked silently at the head of what was to become the most investigated car crash in French history.

On 31 August Mulès helped his officers collect debris and fragments of glass from the scene; he personally collected and sealed shards of red glass in the tunnel that were later to help forensic scientists establish that the Mercedes had been in collision with a Fiat. The glass was later found to have come from the Fiat's rear brake light. Having ordered the Alma tunnel to be reopened Mulès made his way to the Pitié-Salpêtrière hospital to help Professeur Dominique Lecomte with her external examination of Princess Diana's corpse. Mulès took notes during the examination and recorded that, although Diana had undergone surgery as the doctors had tried to save her, her body showed little evidence of having been in a crash. Lecomte was informed that no autopsy would be necessary on the Princess; her body was then covered in a yellow sheet.

The two senior French officials then left for the morgue at the Institut Médico-Légal where Henri Paul's corpse had been taken. Mulès attended part of Paul's autopsy which Professeur Lecomte, who is also one of the IML directors, conducted. The autopsy started at 08.00.

Prince Charles had flown to Paris with Diana's sister, Sarah McCor-quodale, as soon as he had heard news of her death and, later that bleak morning, Commander Mulès returned to the Pitié-Salpêtrière hospital to perform his final, poignant duties. In the presence of President Jacques Chirac and the Prince, Mulès closed Princess Diana's coffin lid before her last journey to Britain began. Before he signed the documents necessary to ship the coffin to England, he signed Diana's death certificate.

Martine Monteil discussed the situation with Patrick Riou, the director of the Paris judiciary police, at the scene of the accident. Within an hour and a half of the crash, Monteil had drafted her first report, after posing initial questions of her own. She said that the Mercedes had been 'pursued and interfered with' by the photographers which had caused it to lose control. She recorded that seven of them had been arrested, and also noted that the photographers had been so busy taking pictures that they had 'ignored the basic gestures of assistance'. Photographers Serge Arnal, Nikola Arsov, Christian Martinez, Jacques Langevin, Romuald Rat and Laszlo Veres were arrested at the scene of the crash. Romuald Rat's driver Stéphane Darmon was also arrested. The pictures of the bedraggled-looking men being transported from the Alma tunnel under the harsh light of a police van were flashed around the world, and became one of the enduring images of the night.

After the BAC 75 (Brigade Anti-Criminalité) arrived, the tunnel was cleared of everyone who was not involved in trying to help the victims. Onlookers were moved on, and the photographers were pushed about 50 m back to the tunnel exit from where they carried on taking photos.

The seven paparazzi who had been arrested by the police were taken to the first division of the judiciary police in the rue de Courcelles. All of them, even those who had not been driving, were tested for any signs of alcohol in their blood: all seven tests were negative. Then they were transferred to the quai des Orfèvres by the Seine where they were questioned individually about the circumstances of the accident, and the events immediately preceding it. The policemen who had been in the tunnel, Sébastien Dorzee and Lino Gaggliardone, had given a particularly damning account of some of their activities around the Mercedes.

The world assumed that the paparazzi were guilty, and some of the French police did too. They were held in custody for two days as a debate raged throughout France and the rest of the world about journalistic ethics and the limits of press freedom. The photographers claim that they were roughly treated, and reported that they were strip-searched twice.

The photographers' cameras were confiscated and their films were developed by the police. They found that no photographs had been taken by those under arrest during their pursuit of the Mercedes from the Ritz. The first photos taken by Rat, Martinez and Arnal in the Alma tunnel had been of the wrecked Mercedes with its door shut and no one else around.

Later photos on the rolls of those arrested showed Dr Mailliez helping the Princess while she was still lying in the car. These photos show that Diana had no apparent injuries except for a trickle of blood running down her face from her forehead. Several dozen photos showed the frantic scenes in the tunnel after the fire brigade and SAMU arrived.

The first hypothesis of how the crash happened emerged during the early hours of the morning on 31 August. It held that the driver of the Mercedes could have been blinded by the flashes of the photographers' cameras, or possibly blocked by one or several of their vehicles. In a statement made on the day of the crash, French Interior Minister, Jean-Pierre Chevènement said that 'preliminary investigations show that the princess's car was being chased by journalists who were trying to take photographs'.[4]

Maud Coujard had a heated discussion with her overall boss, Gabriel Bestard, the chief Paris prosecutor, over what charges the paparazzi should face.[5] Bestard wanted the photographers to be taken before a criminal court and investigated on manslaughter charges. Coujard argued that charges of involuntary manslaughter and non-assistance under France's so-called 'Good Samaritan' law would be more appropriate. Coujard prevailed.

Both charges carry a maximum penalty of 5 years in prison, or a fine of 300–500,000 francs. Judge Hervé Stéphan's task was to determine how many of the photographers should face charges of involuntary manslaughter and failure to assist people in danger. He would be formally appointed by the prosecutor's office on Tuesday 2 September to lead the investigation into the crash. He had been summoned to the Alma tunnel on the night of the crash as he was on duty that weekend. In his forties, Stéphan has a methodical, sharp mind, and is well respected by the French legal community. Judge Marie-Christine Devidal, a colleague and friend of Stéphan, was appointed to join him on the investigation. She has a reputation for being hard hitting and feisty. Together the two judges would share the prodigious workload, and they would make a formidable team.

Some photographers were questioned but not charged, and others fled the Alma tunnel before they could be arrested. Serge Benamou got on his bike and rode off very quickly when he heard the sound of sirens. David Ker followed him, allegedly stopping to say to Darmon on the way, 'They are destroying the job. They are irresponsible. These things should not be done.' As well as Ker, Fabrice Chassery and Alain Guizard also managed to evade arrest.

---

[4] Agence France Presse, 31 August 1997.
[5] *Death of a Princess*, p. 182.

Ker recalled hearing from Chassery that Laurent Sola, the head of Laurent Sola Diffusion (LSD), who'd initially tipped them off about Diana's presence in Paris, wanted to speak to them immediately:

'During that night, Laurent Sola decided to develop the photos. We were scared that they might be leaked. He insisted, saying that we would see how they turned out and then decide what to do. There was no hurry, we could wait to hear more news about what had happened before deciding what to do. As far as we knew, at that time the Princess and Dodi were only injured.'

The photos showed the Mercedes in the Alma tunnel, its occupants, and the first help they were given a few minutes after the accident. By the time the photos had been developed, news of the accident was breaking all over the world, and the papers were scouring Paris for pictures which might have slipped through the fingers of the police.

At 03.00, Sola called in Dominique Petit as he contemplated his options. Petit specialises in scanning photos onto computers. 'For the first hour I didn't know whether or not I was going to use these photos. I sent five photos of Diana receiving the first medical attention by e-mail to my English colleague, who sent them on without my knowing to an American counterpart. The proofs sent to the USA were low definition and so could not be used by the press, but the proofs sent to England were high definition, so they could have been used.'[6]

As a result of the photos being sent to the USA, offers flooded in. Sola accepted an offer of $250,000 from the *National Enquirer* in New York. However, at 05.45 when he heard of the Princess's death he cancelled all negotiations, instructing his English colleague to do the same. By that time, up to £1M was being offered by British papers. Newspapers in other countries, including Spain, Italy and Germany were also very keen. Sola says he then destroyed all trace of the photos that LSD had put on line in order to avoid pirating.

Ker agreed that all sales should be cancelled as soon as he heard of Diana's death: 'It was out of the question for us to make money out of these events.'

Sola did, however, select sixteen photos which he thought might be publishable: two of Diana in Sardinia, eleven of the couple at Le Bourget, and in the streets of Paris, and three long-distance shots of the Mercedes and rescue teams in the tunnel. These last pictures are so unclear it is difficult to make out who the victims are.

------

[6] Witness statements concerning photographers' pictures are quoted in Pontaut and Dupuis, chapter 7.

Sola scanned these pictures into the computer, and sent them to the same people in England, and to the USA, Spain, Italy and Germany. He also offered hard copies of the photos to French outlets. Several offers were made, but none exceeded 50,000 FF as the photos were not exceptional material.

However, Sola also entrusted the negatives of 49 photos to his computer specialist, Dominique Petit. Marc Selle, a salesman for LSD, proposed selling some of the photos to the *Nouveau Detective* magazine. He was seized by police during a rendezvous with *Nouveau Detective* in a bar in the Meridien-Montparnasse hotel.

Sola began to feel the heat, knowing that he was possibly the last person in Paris to have these highly sought-after photos. He also knew that the police were on his tail. He called the Ritz to try to get in touch with the Fayed family, but he was not taken seriously by the hotel switchboard, who simply told him, 'We are making no statements to the press'.

On the night of 31 August, Sola called the British Embassy in Paris at 23.12 and spoke to Michael Price, the Head of Management. Sola explained, 'I thought I might be able to give these photos to an English diplomat who could pass them on to the Al Fayed or the Royal family, so that both families would realise that these photos had not been exploited. I wanted guarantees, that is I wanted to entrust my negatives to a recognised authority in the embassy who I could identify.'

Sola did not ask for money, only an official letter of receipt for his negatives. Price met Sola and secretly taped the conversation he had with him. Price immediately informed the police who then questioned Sola about his sales.

However, some photos did manage to slip through the rapidly tightening net. On 1 September *France-Dimanche* produced a special edition featuring four of David Ker's photos, one of which showed the Mercedes surrounded by the emergency services.

On Thursday 4 September, Ker and Chassery decided to go and see the police after advice from lawyer Jean-Louis Pelletier. They were questioned in the same fashion as the other seven photographers who had been arrested at the scene. On the same day Serge Benamou also turned himself in to the police, evidently shaken by the catastrophe.

In the tunnel, I didn't think, I took photos as soon as I arrived. But I felt bad and wanted to leave. I got on my scooter which was outside the tunnel. It was 1 a.m. and my mobile phone had run out of batteries. I called Michel Dufour [a colleague] from a public telephone on the avenue Rapp, in the VIth arrondissement. I went to the office and waited for him there. He arrived at 2 or 3 a.m. I was lying on the sofa – I needed to. I told him I had taken photos and that I wanted to throw them away. He said 'No, I'll deal with it.' So I left the photos at the office. I left at about 4 or 5 a.m. to go home but I couldn't sleep, I just stayed on my sofa. Then I went to take refuge at my parents' house . . . Two days later, Michel Dufour came to see me. He had developed both of my films. I didn't look at the photos which were in negative form anyway. I don't want to see them, I don't want to because I took those photos and now I know that those people are dead. It is a horrible memory.

Meanwhile, the SEFTI agency (Service d'Enquete sur les Fraudes et les Technologies de l'Information) went swiftly into action to check that none of the photos had made it onto the Internet. It found evidence of negotiations taking place, but not of photos being sold. Two Internet websites revealed that the asking price for images of Princess Diana in the wrecked Mercedes was over £600,000. The *News of the World* claimed a French photographer tried to sell similar pictures for £200,000.

As the news of Diana's death travelled around the world, most assumed that the photographers had caused the crash. The TV pictures of the arrested, exhausted-looking paparazzi were sent by satellite to every corner of the planet. Diana's death appeared to be an open and shut case: the most famous woman in the world, chased to her death by a horde of picture-hungry paparazzi. In the opinion of Diana's brother, Earl Spencer, the press had 'blood on its hands'.

6. 'A MODEL EMPLOYEE'

'Jesus denounces all the judgements, rumours and lies we repeat about others without verifying them, without taking into account the complexity of the facts.'
Leon Théraud, parish priest at Henri Paul's funeral,
20 September 1997

Henri Paul was not buried until three weeks after the crash. His delayed funeral took place at the Sainte-Thérèse Church in Lorient, where his family live, on 20 September 1997. Frank Klein and Claude Roulet led a contingent of more than a dozen mourners from the Ritz hotel. The media turned out in force to watch Paul's parents, Gisèle and Jean Paul, bury their son. Judge Stéphan, who knew it was possible that Paul's body may be required for further examination, had ordered the family to bury rather than cremate their son.

When Princess Diana was buried a fortnight earlier, her brother, Earl Spencer, had roused the multitude following the service outside Westminster Abbey on giant video screens to applause, with an attack on the paparazzi who were chasing her on the night she died: 'Of all the ironies about Diana, perhaps the greatest was this – a girl given the name of the ancient goddess of hunting was, in the end, the most hunted person of the modern age.'[1]

Diana's mother and Dodi's father were among the mourners who listened to the people's applause drifting into the abbey. Both parents and their families knew by then that the gaze of the world as well as the French investigation had started to shift from the paparazzi who were pursuing the Mercedes to the man who had been driving it. The devastating news that Henri Paul had been drunk when he crashed had shocked the world. He had been between three and four times over the French alcohol limit to drive a car when he died.

Mohamed Fayed did not attend Paul's funeral. His spokesman, Michael Cole, said that he would 'spit on Paul's grave' if the blood tests that had been carried out were correct, and Paul had indeed been drunk when he crashed.[2] Mohamed Fayed himself could not accept the autopsy's findings. He entered a state of chronic denial over Henri Paul's condition. Fayed was to remain in denial throughout Stéphan's

---

[1] All of Princess Diana's funeral details are taken from the Buckingham Palace website (www.royal.gov.uk/start.htm).

[2] *Guardian*, 12 September 1997. Cole later apologised for this comment – *Guardian*, 13 September 1997 – admitting it was 'inappropriate and potentially offensive'.

investigation. Sixteen months after the crash, as Judge Stéphan was preparing to hand his completed investigation to the prosecutor, Maud Coujard, in February 1999, Dodi's father was still saying that, 'Henri Paul was not drunk'.[3]

The prosecutor's office had issued a statement on the results of Paul's autopsy on 1 September 1997. Two separate tests had been conducted on blood samples extracted from Paul's corpse during his autopsy. Such autopsies are standard procedure when drivers are involved in fatal car crashes. Professeur Dominique Lecomte had begun Henri Paul's autopsy at 08.00, seven and a half hours after the crash. Lecomte found that Paul's spinal cord had been snapped, and a complete rupture of the aorta had occurred. This would have been 'instantly fatal'. Lecomte also found that Paul had suffered multiple fractures to his pelvis, legs and ribs. In her written report to the investigation, completed the day after the crash, Lecomte confirmed the emergency services' report that Paul had been dead before they arrived. In Lecomte's opinion, all the injuries to Paul had been inflicted by the crash.

The samples Lecomte took from Henri Paul's body included five phials of blood from his chest area, urine and fluid from his eyes. Two tests on these samples showed that Paul had a blood/alcohol level more than three times the legal driving limit of 0.50 grams per litre. When the blood samples were analysed by Dr Ivan Ricordel in the police lab, they showed a level of 1.87 grams per litre. The second analysis, conducted by Dr Gilbert Pépin at TOXLAB, an independent laboratory, using extracts from the same samples, indicated a level of 1.74 grams per litre. Lecomte's autopsy showed that Paul had been drinking on an empty stomach.

The Paul family shared the world's shock at these findings. The day after these results were released, the Pauls requested further tests on their son's body, unable to believe that he had been drunk when he crashed the Mercedes. Judge Stéphan took this opportunity to personally oversee a second set of samples being extracted from Paul's corpse. On Thursday 4 September, Stéphan watched the process as it took place. Ensuring that every step of the entire process was photographed, Stéphan witnessed two blood samples being taken from Paul's femoral vein, in the groin area, as well as samples of muscle and hair. The tests on these samples showed a blood/alcohol level of 1.75 grams per litre. Furthermore, a test on the eye fluid, which was taken at the autopsy, showed a level of 1.73 grams per litre. The Stéphan-

[3] *Sunday Mirror*, 10 January 1999.

supervised tests had thus confirmed the two analyses performed upon the samples extracted by Professeur Lecomte during the autopsy. Paul had been more than three times over the French drink-drive limit of 0.50 grams per litre when he died.

Tests on the Stéphan-supervised samples of 4 September also revealed traces of the antidepressant fluoxetine, the principal ingredient of Prozac, and traces of tiapride, a tranquilliser commonly used in the treatment of alcoholism. Taken with alcohol, these drugs would replicate and exaggerate the feeling of being drunk, slowing reactions as well as giving the user a feeling of wellbeing. The manufacturers of such drugs warn against combining them with alcohol, and they specifically warn against driving having taken them. The tests on the Stéphan-supervised samples provided decisive confirmation that Henri Paul was both drunk and drugged when he had driven the Mercedes into the thirteenth pillar of the Alma tunnel. It was a devastating finding both for the Paul family and for Mohamed Fayed.

Further tests showed that Paul had not only been drunk on the night he died, but that he had also been fighting alcoholism. Released on 17 September, a more sophisticated analysis by Dr Pépin at TOXLAB revealed that Paul had been in a state of 'moderate chronic alcoholism' for at least a week before his death. The test was capable of detecting Paul's condition for only a week before his death, so he could have been in this state for even longer. Tests on the urine extracted from Paul's bladder indicated that the alcohol in his body had entered the 'elimination phase'. This was further proof that his drinking in the Ritz bar could not have been the only alcohol he had consumed.

The tests on Paul's corpse raised two immediate questions: first, how did he get so drunk on the night of 30/31 August and, secondly, did anyone at the Ritz know of his alcoholism? A third, related, question sprang from attempting to answer the first two: why was Paul allowed to drive Diana in this condition? Precisely how Paul managed to consume enough alcohol to take him to between three and four times over the French drink-driving limit remains a minor, unsolved mystery.

After returning to the Ritz at approximately 22.08,[4] Paul was observed drinking in the bar Vendôme, where he sat with the bodyguards Wingfield and Rees-Jones at table No. 1. The meal started at 22.06 and

---

[4] Timings from the heavily edited Ritz security videotape which was released to the press. However, the timecodes shown by the cameras were not synchronised on 30/31 August 1997. Thus the edited videotape shows Henri Paul arriving in his Mini at 22.09 and then walking through the revolving doors of the Ritz at 22.07.

was signed to the Imperial Suite at 23.11. The bill (No. 4891) for that table was for 1,260 francs. It recorded the purchase of two Ricards. The bodyguards did not drink alcohol, because they were on duty. They were under the impression that Paul was not drinking alcohol either. When cut with water, Ricard turns a yellow colour. The bodyguards thought Paul was drinking pineapple juice and mixing it with water.

No one saw Paul drinking after he left the bar Vendôme, less than an hour before leaving on his fatal journey. The autopsy indicated that, when he died, the alcohol in Paul's blood was in its 'elimination', or passing-out, phase. Precisely when and where the alcohol passed into his system remains unclear.

Henri Paul's movements between 19.05, when he stopped working at the Ritz, and 22.08, when Ritz security cameras captured him returning at the wheel of his Mini, were never definitively established by the French investigation. During its intense period of interviewing witnesses immediately after the crash, the Criminal Brigade did, however, pick up important clues.

One of the two security guards at the Fayeds' rue Arsène-Houssaye apartment, Didier Gamblin, remembered speaking to Paul just after Dodi had stood Paul down at the Ritz a little before 19.00. 'He had finished his working day, and was going home – he told me this word for word.'[5] When Martine Monteil's detectives went to Paul's home in the rue des Petits Champs, they found no evidence that he had returned to his apartment that evening as he told Gamblin he was intending to do. When the detectives entered his home, which is just off the rue de la Paix close to the place Vendôme, they did find evidence of Paul's *penchant pour la boisson* (fondness for alcohol). In a cupboard in the hall, they found several open bottles of aperitifs: crème de cassis, Ricard, Suze, port, beer. They also found unopened bottles of red wine and champagne. Also in the entrance to the apartment was a table bar containing open bottles of Martini Bianco, vodka, Pinot, Suze and wine. In the kitchen, in another cupboard, they found open bottles of Ricard, Martini Bianco and Four Roses whisky. In the fridge they found a bottle of champagne, two beers and a bottle of Martini Bianco which was nearly empty.

Despite an intensive hunt of the bars surrounding the Ritz, Martine Monteil's team was unable to double-source or confirm a single reliable sighting of Paul between his leaving the Ritz at 19.05 and returning at approximately 22.10. Statements by several witnesses about his move-

---

[5] Pontaut and Dupuis, p. 53.

ments were contradictory. Josiane Le Tellier, owner of Champmeslé, a lesbian bar in the rue Chabanais, said she saw him just before he returned to the Ritz. She knew Paul well as he often drank in her bar. At around 22.00 he popped his head around the door and, according to Le Tellier, said, 'See you later, girls!' She said, 'We saw him get into his car, a black Mini which he usually parks in front of our bar. He waved and left very calmly. He came from the direction of his house, and was holding a little white bag.'[6]

Other sightings of Paul in another bar in the rue des Petits Champs could not be confirmed, but had the ring of probability about them. After the crash and the publication of the results of the autopsy, detectives found that proprietors of bars in Paul's neighbourhood were reluctant to be identified as owners of an establishment where Paul got drunk before he drove Princess Diana and Dodi Fayed to their deaths.

François Tendil had summoned Paul back to the Ritz just before 22.00, following Paul's instructions to alert him if the couple returned. According to Tendil, Paul picked up his mobile phone straightaway, and replied, 'I'm not far. I'll be there in a minute!'[7] When Paul arrived at the Ritz, the 'vehicle jockey' Frédéric Lucard offered to park his Mini for him. Paul told him that would not be necessary. Because he did not recognise Paul, Lucard was slightly suspicious of him. The 'jockey' asked a colleague who the bespectacled figure striding through the hotel's enormous revolving door was. He was informed that Paul was the head of the hotel's security.[8]

Once inside, Paul chatted with Ritz security guards, gave some instructions and paced the corridors before entering the bar Vendôme. He was seen repeatedly looking at his watch, adjusting his jacket and wiping his glasses. Occasionally, he approached the entrance gates to evaluate the paparazzi situation outside the building. François Tendil, who had known Paul for ten years, remembered how he behaved: 'Mr Paul was just as usual that evening. He joked around and laughed with a few people. At no point could I imagine that he was drunk. He was no more excited/nervous than usual; he went outside several times to the Vendôme "peristyle" and spoke to the journalists.'[9]

Several photographers confirmed that Paul had appeared outside the front of the Ritz in the build-up to Princess Diana's and Dodi's departure

---

[6] Pontaut and Dupuis, p. 52.
[7] Pontaut and Dupuis, p. 52.
[8] Author's interview with Frédéric Lucard.
[9] Pontaut and Dupuis, pp. 172–3.

from the hotel. Their statements contradicted Tendil's assessment of Paul's condition. Serge Benamou was to photograph the Princess and Dodi leaving from the rear of the hotel later in the evening. He was later arrested in the Alma tunnel after the crash. Benamou was familiar with Paul, and told the police that he thought that the security chief had behaved strangely: 'I saw him in front of the hotel. He was laughing, and he was annoying us a bit. He smiled constantly, he seemed merry, I couldn't understand why. This man had never behaved like this in the past. Normally he ignored us. He treated autograph seekers and photographers in the same way. I thought that he was not in his normal state and I even said to some people, around 22.30, that he must have been drinking, judging by his state.'[10]

Attempting to establish precisely what staff at the Ritz witnessed Henri Paul saying or doing became much more difficult after the results of the blood tests were published. According to Ritz insiders, all staff were summoned to a mass meeting the following day, Tuesday 2 September. They were told by Frank Klein that they would face the sack if they spoke to journalists. All communication with the investigation would emanate from his office. Staff were also ordered to report any journalists found on Ritz premises to Frank Klein's office. Once identified, journalists would be instantly expelled. Accounts by Ritz staff describing Paul's drinking were periodically leaked, anonymously, to the media throughout the investigation. On 3 September a member of the Ritz staff, with his voice distorted to disguise his identity, told Europe 1, 'Paul wasn't a chauffeur, he had no business being in that car. He was recalled to the Ritz because Dodi Fayed came back . . . He should have been off duty and he had already "tippled" a little, we all knew that . . . everyone knew that, when he wasn't at work, he "tippled".'[11]

A Ritz barman, Sébastien Trote, told Judge Stéphan's investigation that he remembered serving Paul alcohol in the bar Vendôme: 'Mr Paul ordered a Ricard from me, which I asked for at the bar. I took it over to him together with two small silver bowls of almonds and dried fruit. The Ricard measure was a normal one, and I saw him fill the thirty-three-centilitre glass three-quarters full with water.' Philippe Doucin, the Vendôme's head barman on 30 August, served the second round: 'At one point I cleared table number one. I took away the bodyguards' empty plates, and I offered them dessert and coffee, which they accepted. I also took away an almost empty glass of Ricard, which

---

[10] Pontaut and Dupuis, p. 173.

[11] Reuters news agency, 3 September 1997.

was in front of Mr Paul, and he asked me for another one. I brought over their order, some petits fours and another glass of Ricard – five centilitres – together with a carafe of water.'[12]

Other bar staff who observed Paul in the Ritz gave Stéphan conflicting accounts of his behaviour. Another barman, Alain Willaumez, claimed to have a vivid recollection of Paul: 'Mr Paul was drunk. His eyes shone, he seemed excited. When he left the bar with the two bodyguards, he bumped into Mr Lhôtellier, the head barman, and staggered to the exit.'

Strangely, Vincent Lhôtellier himself failed to recall this incident in his statement to police. The bodyguards, who had been eating at the same table as Paul in the bar Vendôme, did not recall Paul staggering out of the bar either. Indeed, they both told the French police that they did not realise that Paul had been drinking alcohol. Kez Wingfield told detectives that he and Trevor Rees-Jones had been under the impression that Paul was drinking 'pineapple juice, which he cut with water'.

Wingfield was adamant that Paul had not exhibited any signs of drunkenness before starting his final journey: 'He did not smell at all of alcohol, and he was less than a metre away from me. Besides, if he had seemed in the slightest bit drunk, then Trevor and I would have refused to let him drive the couple. It would have been inconceivable.'

When Rees-Jones had recovered sufficiently from his injuries to be interviewed by the police, he backed Wingfield's account. According to Wingfield, if either Dodi or Diana had formed the impression that Paul had been drinking, Dodi would have sacked him rather than instruct him to drive them.

Wingfield knew that Rees-Jones did not get along particularly well with Paul, so the two of them went upstairs and waited outside the Imperial Suite. They did this partly because they did not want to sit in the bar Vendôme with Paul. They also repositioned themselves outside the suite so they would be well placed to await the couple's departure. Wingfield recalled that, during this period, 'Henri Paul came to see us twice: first, to ask if everything was all right; second, to tell us that everything [the Fayeds' plan to leave the Ritz] had been arranged with Dodi. That time I noticed from his breath that Henri Paul had just smoked a cigar. He absolutely did not smell of alcohol, and his behaviour was completely normal.'

At the end of the evening, needled by having to deal with yet another of Dodi's ad hoc travel arrangements, Wingfield or Rees-Jones would have been able to prevent Paul from taking the wheel very simply. As

---

[12] Quoted in Pontaut and Dupuis, p. 54.

Dodi had ordered both men to execute an exit plan with which they claim they both disagreed, they could simply have told him that Paul had been drinking. The result would have been the instant abandonment of Paul's role in the plan, if not his dismissal.

Furthermore, Rees-Jones would have been taking an extraordinary and foolhardy risk himself, as well as on behalf of the Princess and his boss's son, had he permitted Paul to drive in the knowledge that he had been drinking. There is no evidence to suggest that this was the case. Rees-Jones did not enjoy Paul's company, and so misplaced feelings of loyalty or affection would have been unlikely to prevent him from informing Dodi that Paul had been drinking. Wingfield had never met Paul before he encountered him at Le Bourget airport. Ben Murrell remembered that, at the villa Windsor that afternoon, Paul was behaving in a slightly strange manner, more expansively than usual. Murrell thought he had probably been drinking. Wingfield had no standard by which to judge Paul.

Neither the waiters who served Paul pastis nor the two bodyguards had any notion that Paul would be required to drive the Princess later that night. All were unaware at this stage that Dodi had formulated his unconventional plan to leave the Ritz.

The man whose position Paul had assumed at the Ritz, the security chief Jean Hocquet, provides an insight into Henri Paul's dilemma when Dodi asked him to drive the Mercedes: 'Driving cars or chauffeuring people was not at all part of Mr Paul's duties. As regards the night of the 30/31 August, the following could very well have occurred: Mr Dodi asked Mr Paul to drive him. You must remember that Mr Dodi had already asked for Mr Paul to come to Le Bourget on the 30 August 1997 in the capacity of driver. Knowing Mr Paul, I think that he would have been incapable of refusing to drive Mr Dodi if he had asked him to. For my part, I did not appreciate the way Mr Dodi used to ask everything and anything from any Ritz employee, regardless of their status.'[13]

When he asked Paul to drive the Mercedes rather than the Range Rover he had driven throughout the day, Dodi was probably unaware that he did not have a permit to drive the Mercedes S-280. Defending Henri Paul after the first blood tests were released, Michael Cole stated that Paul had been 'qualified in every respect to drive the car'.[14] It was true that Paul had a clean driving licence and was, therefore, qualified to drive any model of car. However, to drive cars of any description that

[13] Pontaut and Dupuis, pp. 174–5.
[14] Harrods' press conference, 5 September 1997.

are registered as limousines in France requires a special permit, which Henri Paul did not possess.

After the Alma tunnel crash, Roland Biribin, the president of the French Association of Limousine Companies, made the position clear: 'This permit is absolutely essential in order to be able to drive hire cars. It's the same legislation as for taxis, but a little more stringent. Paul was qualified to drive a car, but not a hire car. He had a driving licence but didn't have a hire-car permit, so he should not have driven that car. I don't think that the crash could possibly have happened with a professional chauffeur.'[15]

Biribin's comments have history on their side. His members have a proud tradition: no properly qualified chauffeur has ever had a fatal crash. Dodi Fayed's regular Paris chauffeur knew better than anyone else that Paul was not a professional driver. Before Paul drove to meet Princess Diana's party from Le Bourget on the afternoon of 30 August, Dourneau had been obliged to show Paul how to use the controls of the Range Rover he was to drive to collect the party.[16]

Philippe Dourneau felt dreadful about the events that had led to Paul's taking the wheel of the Mercedes. He had driven Princess Diana on every trip she had ever made in Paris since her romance with Dodi started. Dourneau had chauffeured the couple during their secret weekend in Paris at the end of July, and had watched them walk hand in hand on the banks of the Seine, lost and anonymous among the crowds.[17] On their last day, Dourneau had driven them everywhere they had been in Paris, until their last journey. He had been waiting to take the couple back to the rue Arsène-Houssaye apartment until the Fayeds changed the plans, and he was told to become part of the 'decoy convoy' that Dodi instructed Kez Wingfield to organise.

After the crash Dourneau had been sent to Le Bourget to collect Mohamed Fayed in the early hours. The news of Princess Diana's death came through as he waited with Kez Wingfield for Fayed to land. The bodyguard had broken the news of Princess Diana's death to Fayed. On the drive into Paris, Dourneau informed him that the word from the Ritz was that Henri Paul had been drinking before setting out from the hotel.

The forensic tests on Henri Paul's corpse may have been expected to end any argument about his condition when he crashed, but they did not. Determined to find out for himself what had happened in the Alma

---

[15] Author's interview with Roland Biribin.
[16] Bower interview with Dourneau (unpublished).
[17] *Daily Mail*, 9 February 1998.

tunnel, Mohamed Fayed decided to send a team of experts to Paris as soon as the results of the autopsy were released to 'assist the French investigation'.

Led by his two security chiefs, John Macnamara and Paul Handley-Greaves, the team also included Peter Vanezis, Regius Professor of Forensic Medicine and Science at Glasgow University. A Londoner, Vanezis was a former associate of Macnamara's from the latter's days at Scotland Yard. The two got to know each other as Vanezis performed autopsies for the police in South London.[18]

The team had extremely limited success in Paris, as it became clear that the French investigation did not require or welcome their assistance. Macnamara was cold-shouldered by Martine Monteil's detectives. Professor Vanezis was refused permission to conduct a second autopsy on Paul's body. Neither Macnamara nor Vanezis had any legal standing in the eyes of the French investigation. Vanezis was permitted, however, to read Professeur Lecomte's autopsy and the results of the blood tests.

Upon their return to Britain, the news conference at Harrods was called, the day before Princess Diana's funeral. Michael Cole hosted the conference with Paul Handley-Greaves present to talk the journalists through Ritz security-camera tapes. These showed the last pictures of Princess Diana with Dodi and Henri Paul.

Inevitably, most interest was generated by the last pictures of Princess Diana. She was seen frequently in the 26-minute edit of her two-and-a-half-hour stay in the hotel. The tape showed a grim-faced Princess in a black top, a black jacket and tight white trousers entering the Ritz, followed by Kez Wingfield, Dodi and Trevor Rees-Jones. Later the party was seen waiting to leave the Ritz with Henri Paul, and then emerging from the hotel to walk the short distance to the Mercedes waiting in the rue Cambon. The pictures were released by Mohamed Fayed after consultation with the executors of Princess Diana's will.

Handley-Greaves told the press conference that he had been able to speak with all the relevant Ritz and security personnel while he was in Paris. He made clear one of the purposes of the conference: 'We're just trying to demonstrate the fact that this man did not have 1.75 millilitres of alcohol in his blood.'[19]

Handley-Greaves talked the press through an edited version of the pictures that the hotel's security cameras had taken of Henri Paul on the

---

[18] Author's interview with Professor Peter Vanezis.
[19] Harrods' press conference, 5 September 1997.

fatal night. In the pictures he appeared to be walking around normally, and chatting to colleagues in the Ritz. The video edit shown to the press appeared to show that Paul was not drunk when he was in the Ritz.

Professor Vanezis was introduced briefly at the end of the Harrod's press conference. He said that the purpose of his visit to Paris had been to carry out a second autopsy on Henri Paul on behalf of Mohamed Fayed. The professor confirmed he had not been able to do this, or test the samples that Professeur Lecomte had extracted. Vanezis had been able to study only the autopsy reports. Having seen them, however, he felt able to cast some doubt on the autopsy's findings: 'In my view, given that M. Paul died a violent death with extensive internal injuries, the possibility of contamination of the blood is a real one and must be seriously considered. Therefore under such circumstances an isolated finding as has been reported to the press, cannot be treated as reliable.'

When asked about the possibility of retesting the samples, the professor expressed doubts: 'It depends very much on how they are stored. And I am particularly worried about how the blood was obtained and stored in the first instance.[20]

Professor Vanezis spoke in good faith. However, he was unaware that, as he left Paris the previous day, Judge Stéphan was personally overseeing the taking of fresh samples from Paul's body for the second round of tests, which would confirm the findings of the first.

Dodi's father appointed an international panel of scientists in the USA, Switzerland and Britain to join Professor Vanezis in examining the official findings of the autopsy on Henri Paul. None of these experts has ever gone on the record to dispute the French investigation's findings.

As he presided over Henri Paul's burial, the Sainte-Thérèse parish priest, Leon Théraud, told the congregation: 'Jesus denounces all the judgements, rumours and lies we repeat about others without verifying them, without taking into account the complexity of the facts.'

By the time Paul was buried, two incontrovertible scientific facts stood out from the 'complexity' of which Théraud spoke. First, that Paul was drunk in charge of the car in which he died. Secondly, that the drugs he was taking would have made this condition worse. The importance of a third fact, that Paul was not qualified to drive the Mercedes, would combine with the scientific evidence to undermine many of the myths that arose about the Alma tunnel crash.

---

[20] Harrods' press conference, 5 September 1997.

7. THE FINAL HOURS, THE FIRST MYTHS

'I have one question; is there any good in all this speculation? I ask that because there is clearly a lot of harm in it. All we, her family, ask is that Diana's memory be respected, and that sensational speculation be left out of the public arena.'

Earl Spencer, 12 February 1998

The Princess Diana industry did not cease production as Henri Paul's Mercedes ploughed into the thirteenth pillar of the Alma tunnel. When she was alive the Princess's friends moaned on her behalf that 'everyone wanted a part of Diana'. In the Diana death industry everyone could take what they wanted, and production underwent a massive initial boost. Between 31 August 1997 and the outbreak of NATO's war against the Serbs in March 1999, Princess Diana's life and death became the most ploughed field in world journalism, comfortably outstripping even the attempted impeachment of President Clinton in that eighteen-month period.

At Diana's Westminster Abbey funeral her brother, Earl Spencer, implored people not to attempt to sanctify his sister, but by then the process had already started. Some excellent journalism illuminated Diana's life, times and death. She had undoubtedly become the most widely known and charismatic British royal of recent times. Her status as the mother of two heirs to the British throne ensured that historians, as well as her public constituency, mourned her brief life. Many wrote that they had been surprised at the depth of their own reaction to her passing. Poignant and insightful articles abounded about the Princess and her life, in a market that became virtually insatiable during the eighteen months it took Judge Stéphan to conclude his report into the crash. While Stéphan's comprehensive investigation progressed slowly and silently, the world's multi-tongued media rapidly and noisily left unexplored few conceivable aspects of the tragedy. Those who would sanctify Princess Diana, and those who would attribute her death to unidentified 'conspirators', proliferated.

The first 'conspiracy' website about Princess Diana's death was created while she was still alive. The Conspiracy Theory Discussion Board claims that it created a 'discussion website' two hours after the crash took place. At the peak of Internet interest, 36,000 'Diana websites' were reported to exist. Cyberspace is an atmosphere in which theories can thrive and prosper unencumbered by inconvenient facts. The confusion and initial uncertainty over how the best-known woman in the world could come to die in such mundane circumstances provided fertile ground for the conspiracy-mongers, particularly as media outriders were in pursuit of the Princess when she died. As soon as facts about the crash started to emerge, they were instantly challenged by the death industry, initially in cyberspace, but it was not long before such challenges found terrestrial expression.

When Henri Paul was proved to have been drunk when he crashed, the results of the autopsy were called into question. The debate initiated about Paul's condition when he died became a cornerstone of the death industry. 'Fears' were generated that he may have been mysteriously poisoned, or that his blood samples may have been switched in order to fool the world that he was drunk when, in reality, he had not been. Animated discussion was also to follow about whether Diana could have been saved, and whether she had received the best possible treatment after the crash. Suggestions that the Princess had been murdered by a combination of British, French and US intelligence agencies first appeared on the Internet before finding terrestrial expression in newspapers and on television. Such theories were to become standard offerings of the Diana death industry. That industry was fuelled by the reluctance of millions to believe that the best-known and most glamorous former member of the British Royal Family could possibly have died in such circumstances. Saturday-night drunks do not kill princesses in the semifictional world that the British royalty inhabits for many people around the world.

The conspiracy subdivision of the Diana death industry involves pickling two staple products inspired by the dead Princess: stories about how she died and stories about what she would have done had she lived. Unburdened by the need to produce credible evidence, conspiracy theorists had few problems concluding that Diana represented such a threat to certain vested interests that 'dark and sinister forces' had decided to eliminate her.

These theories would impute a variety of motives to bodies as diverse as British intelligence, the CIA and Mossad for assassinating the Princess and Dodi Fayed. A typical, breathless scenario would run as follows: because Diana was planning to marry Dodi (and may already have been pregnant with his child), the British government, unable to entertain the prospect of Muslim half-brothers for Princes William and Harry, ordered Diana's assassination.

Two days after the crash the head of a US organisation calling itself 'Executive Intelligence Review' (EIR) went public with the view that Princess Diana had been murdered. Her death had been the result of a 'vehicular homicide', according to EIR's president, Lyndon Larouche.

The virtual silence from the French investigation made rumours appear more credible to some. However, sober examination of the evidence about the crash, and the claims that Diana and Dodi were murdered, that Diana could have been saved, and what she was really planning for her immediate future, reveals such theorising as meaningless and, in some cases, self-serving. Had Stéphan been conducting his investigation in Britain or the USA, a news conference, or official or informal briefings, would have been held to dispel some of the more fanciful rumours. However, France's secrecy laws would not permit such attempts at enlightenment. Making exceptions to the legal system's custom and practice, let alone its laws, was never a possibility.

It was not Judge Stéphan's task to prevent the elaborate mythology about the crash taking root while he conducted his investigation. However, the mythologising process helped prolong the probe. During the course of his investigation, Stéphan exercised his power to commission several reports – known as *expertises* – by independent experts to complement and copper-bottom the investigations into the accident by Martine Monteil's 'Crim', and the Pitié-Salpêtrière medical team's reports on the victims. Some of Stéphan's *expertises* appeared to be commissioned to dispel some of the more strongly rooted rumours as he tried to demonstrate to Maud Coujard that he had conducted a thorough investigation into the most infamous car crash in French history.

The efforts made by certain branches of the media to translate into a terrestrial form the 'fears' from cyberspace about how Princess Diana died were assisted by the slow pace of Judge Stéphan's investigation. Unfortunately, the French legal system created the necessary conditions for such fantasising to incubate by creating an information void about the tragedy. The *secret de l'instruction* (secrecy of the investigation) provides for an investigation to be conducted in complete secrecy. Nobody involved in the investigation is allowed to communicate with the press or the public about any aspect of the case unless authorised to do so by the prosecutor in charge. During Judge Stéphan's investigation, there were only five brief communications with the press issued by Coujard's office. Two concerned the forensic tests carried out on Henri Paul's corpse. The third was a brief summary of progress made in the investigation just before the first anniversary of the crash, and the last two in January 1999 were concerned with the timetable for the closure of Stéphan's probe.

French secrecy laws are also designed to protect the rights of those who might be accused of crime. Similarly harsh laws – *le secret médical*

– govern details of medical treatment given to patients. Both laws have honourable intentions – they are designed to protect the victims of crime and patients. During Judge Stéphan's investigation into Princess Diana's death, however, the *secret de l'instruction* and the *secret médical* combined to produce a dangerous information void. This in turn produced a flood of distorted and skewed coverage of Diana's death. Nowhere was this more apparent than in the myths that arose from her final hours, and events that occurred on the morning of her death, 31 August 1997. Confusing mythology was woven around the 'last words' the Princess was alleged to have uttered, a description of her dead body and, most disturbingly, whether her life could have been saved.

Such speculation reached a peak nearly six months after the crash, in February 1998, as Mohamed Fayed broke his post-crash silence to give his first media interviews. The sole survivor of the crash, Trevor Rees-Jones, also gave his first media interview – to the *Mirror* – at the beginning of March 1998. The *Mirror*'s headline claimed the bodyguard had heard Diana calling out for Dodi as she lay dying in the wreckage of the Mercedes. The bodyguard's reported claim fuelled what had become a transatlantic debate over whether or not Diana could have been saved. *Death of a Princess – An Investigation*, a book written by two American journalists, Thomas Sancton and Scott MacLeod, with the cooperation of Dodi's father, had first sparked the debate. Speculation intensified in Britain that, if Diana was able to speak after the crash, then maybe she could have survived had she received better care. Headlines such as 'COULD DIANA HAVE LIVED' adorned British front pages, as debate ensued about whether the delay in getting her to hospital may have 'killed' her.

Death of a Princess was serialised over a week in *The Times*, and the BBC reported its contention that, had the accident happened in the USA, Diana could have been saved. Sancton claimed on CNN that 'if she had gotten there [to the hospital] let's say within an hour of the accident, probably they could have gone in there and repaired the tear in the pulmonary vein and saved her life.'[1]

From New Orleans to New Jersey, US medics lined up to question the French response on the night of the crash. On the East Coast, Dr David Wasserman claimed, 'Spending all that time on on-site treatment was absolutely the wrong kind of approach. If they had gotten her to the operating room sooner, she would have had a far greater chance.'[2]

---

[1] CNN, 8 February 1998.
[2] *Death of a Princess*, p. 30.

The decision to treat Diana at the scene was also condemned by American heart specialists such as Dr John Ochsner, the chairman emeritus of surgery at the Ochsner Clinic in New Orleans. He opined that Diana could have been saved, as the authors asked, 'What was going on all that time?'[3]

The first French doctor to arrive at the scene of the crash added force to such speculation, even though he did not share the Americans' view on the failure of the French medical service. Dr Frédéric Mailliez reported that Diana looked in the 'best shape' of any of the victims and that he thought she had 'a good chance'. The extended period of time the emergency services took to get Diana to the Pitié-Salpêtrière hospital was heavily criticised, in what quickly developed into a set-piece debate between two rival schools of thought over how victims requiring emergency aid should be treated. US medics, who work on the principle of transferring victims to hospital as soon as possible, locked horns with their French counterparts, whose standard procedure involves attempting to stabilise victims before moving them.

None of those invited to comment in *Death of a Princess* appeared to have been aware of the testimonies of Dr Jean-Marc Martino's SAMU team. They had informed Stéphan's investigation that Diana had her first heart attack as she was cut out of the Mercedes. They had also reported to him the enormous difficulties in keeping her alive as they drove her to the hospital. Debating which approach would more likely have 'saved' the Princess in this context certainly shifted copies of books and newspapers, but was actually an exercise in futility. However, the momentum and the profile that the debate attained in early 1998 meant that the French government felt obliged to rebut the attack on the competence of its medical service. Its Health Minister, Bernard Kouchner, stepped into the debate to confirm the official French view that the vessels to Princess Diana's heart had been so badly ruptured in the accident that she had no chance of surviving, whatever care she had received.

Ministerial intervention increased the pressure on Judge Stéphan's investigation to produce the most comprehensive account possible of the medical treatment afforded to the Princess. Stéphan was eventually to commission an *expertise* to assess the medical condition of the three who died on 31 August, as well as the care that they received. It was conducted by two professors, André Lienhart and Dominique Lecomte, who had conducted Henri Paul's autopsy.

---

[3] *Time* magazine, 16 February 1998.

The professors advised Stéphan that Diana was conscious when SAMU arrived at the scene of the accident. However, she was in such a serious 'haemodynamic state' that her pulse was impossible to take. The professors concluded that, 'The treatment afforded was in order with the current facts of medical knowledge considering the operating circumstances and the lesions observed . . . No cases of survival after such a wound to the pulmonary vein exist in world medical literature.'

The *expertise*, which was signed by the two professors in November 1998, came to the graphic conclusion that, 'The Princess's heart was knocked out of place [displaced] within her chest' by the violence of the impact, 'thus causing the pulmonary vein to be ripped', and fatal haemorrhaging. It also stated that it is exceptional for anyone with such injuries to even reach the hospital alive.

The Pitié-Salpêtrière's emergency team had cut open Diana's chest, and held her heart in their hands as they tried vainly to massage life back into the dying woman. They knew that they had given Diana everything in their professional power to save her life, and found the commentary offered by their US counterparts distasteful in the extreme. France's health professionals were, however, hamstrung by the medical secrecy laws that forbade them from revealing any details of how badly Princess Diana had been injured. This was one reason why Kouchner stepped into the debate. The Health Minister felt he had a duty to set the record straight, as those who had fought to save Diana's life were legally gagged by the *secret médical*.

One of the most dramatic moments in the week that followed the Paris tragedy occurred on the eve of Diana's funeral. Mohamed Fayed's spokesman, Michael Cole, informed the press conference, 'When he was in Paris on Sunday, Mr Al Fayed was approached by someone who I must not name, who had helped the Princess during her final hours. That person vouchsafed to Mr Al Fayed the Princess's final words and her requests, and yesterday those words were conveyed to the appropriate person at a private meeting here [at Harrods].'

Enormous speculation followed as to what the words might have been and to whom they were conveyed. At the time, Michael Cole refused to reveal the who, the what or the whom. However, during the February 1998 debate about whether or not Princess Diana could have been saved, Fayed decided to break his silence over his 'last-words' claim. By doing so he fuelled the arguments of those who claimed that if she could speak after the crash, she could have been saved.

His revelation came in an interview with the authors of *Death of a*

Princess. Fayed told them that a medical worker who had treated Diana in the Alma tunnel had told him that Diana's last words were, 'Tell my sister Sarah to look after my children'.[4]

In the week that *Death of a Princess* was published, Mohamed Fayed gave a second interview, also billed as a 'world exclusive', to the *Mirror*. In it he claimed that a nurse from the Pitié-Salpêtrière hospital had told him that Diana's last words were, 'I would like all my possessions in Dodi's apartment to be given to Sarah including my jewellery, and my personal clothes, and please tell her to take care of my boys . . .' He told the paper, 'She wanted to give a message for her kids. I was the first person there and I know what happened.'[5]

Fayed told the *Mirror* that the nurse who had told him this was 'insistent that nobody would know her identity'.

The Pitié-Salpêtrière medical community had been upset over Michael Cole's initial claim that Diana had uttered 'last words', well before Fayed decided to disclose what the words allegedly were. There had been relief that Cole had not made them known, but great consternation at the idea that one of their number could have passed on such a message despite the *secret médical*.

As soon as Trevor Rees-Jones had been discharged from the hospital's care in October 1997, a hospital spokesman, Thierry Meresse, spoke to the London *Evening Standard*. The paper's 6 October headline was unambiguous, 'FAYED'S NURSE NEVER EXISTED'. The subheading, 'Paris hospital denies employee heard dying words of Princess Diana', was equally emphatic. The report quoted Meresse on the 'last-words' claim: 'This is entirely false. To make the story more credible, the name of the nurse was given who did not really exist . . . Moreover, the Princess never regained consciousness after arriving at the hospital.'

The *Evening Standard*'s Paris-based show-business correspondent, Toby Rose, was the somewhat unlikely author of his paper's rare scoop in the journalistic battle to reveal the precise circumstances surrounding Diana's final hours. Rose had written the article after pursuing Meresse following a dull press conference to announce Trevor Rees-Jones's departure from the hospital. In news terms, it had been a nonevent. Rose had been asked to cover it for the *Standard*'s news desk on the off chance that something interesting may emerge. After the conference ended, Rose pressed Meresse for more details. To his surprise, he found the spokesman willing to express the anger that the hospital felt about

---

[4] *Death of a Princess*, p. 32.
[5] *Mirror*, 12 February 1998.

the 'last-words' claim now that Rees-Jones had left the Pitié-Salpêtrière's care.

Rose recalled, 'One of the big bugbears at the hospital was that there was all this talk that one of the hospital staff had passed on to Mr Fayed Diana's last words. This was one of the key elements in all the speculation that had followed her death. What Meresse wanted to correct was that none of the hospital staff had passed on any last words and that, as far as they were concerned, this was fantasy . . .

'None of the hospital staff had come forward and spoken to Mr Fayed to pass on these last words. Obviously to have done so would have breached their Hippocratic oaths. To go up to somebody who's foreign to the service, somebody who's not part of the hospital, is not one of the embassy staff, the Foreign Ministry staff, and say, "Well, we'd just like to tell you, by the way, that Diana said this, that and the other just before she died." The hospital obviously felt aggrieved that this rumour had gained currency, and was keen to nail it.'[6]

Meresse said that the last words were 'an invention by Mr Al Fayed . . . The Princess was unconscious on arrival, and then she had a heart attack. She was not capable of speech in her last hours. It is utterly untrue to suggest that she was.'[7]

The Spencer family had taken grave offence at Michael Cole's first mention of Diana's 'last words'. The 'appropriate person' to whom Fayed had personally relayed Diana's 'last words' was her sister, Lady Sarah McCorquodale. At a meeting at Harrods the day before Cole's press conference, Fayed had apparently told her his account. Diana's sister later described Fayed's claims as 'preposterous', dismissing the words attributed to her sister as 'unbelievable'.[8]

That the 'last-words' claim was unbelievable was subsequently supported by medical evidence gathered in the course of Judge Stéphan's investigation, which indicated that Diana was incapable of speaking any 'last words'. It was not part of Stéphan's brief to establish if Princess Diana had spoken after the crash, or what she may have said. However, the SAMU paramedics who had come to the Princess's assistance in the Alma tunnel knew that she had said nothing coherent before she arrived at the hospital.

Staff at the Salpêtrière also knew that Diana had not uttered the words attributed to her. By the time Diana arrived at the hospital, she was in

---

[6] Author's interview with Toby Rose.

[7] Daily Telegraph, 9 October 1997.

[8] Sunday Telegraph, 14 September 1997.

a nonresponsive coma. According to André Lienhart and Dominique Lecomte, 'Despite surgery and active resuscitation, cardiac activity could not be resumed.' In such a condition a patient is not capable of speaking.

The doctors' conclusion was also borne out by several eyewitness statements to Judge Stéphan. It is clear from the statements made by those who had attempted to help Diana on the night of the crash that she could not have spoken. Had she done so, some of the following witnesses would have heard what she said.

The first person to arrive at the crashed Mercedes was the photographer Romuald Rat. He said he tried to comfort Diana, but stated that she did not speak to him. The SAMU team, which removed Diana from the Mercedes and placed her in its ambulance, reported that she suffered her first heart attack during this process. In their statements to Stéphan's enquiry, they said that Diana moaned in pain, but they did not report that she said anything coherent at all.

By the time SAMU arrived in the Alma tunnel, Diana had an oxygen mask on. It had been slipped over her face by Dr Mailliez, who was the first doctor to treat her. He was widely quoted at the time: 'She might have spoken some words, but the last moments of any patient are confidential. I do not know how Fayed could know these things.'[9]

Toby Rose's story was a scoop because he was the first to report that Mohamed Fayed's story that Princess Diana uttered last words before dying was not true. It was followed up by British national newspapers the following day, and scores of other outlets around the world. Michael Cole let fly at the hospital spokesman who had undermined his 'last-words' claim, Thierry Meresse. In an uncharacteristic lapse, Cole was none too subtle in his rebuke: 'Maybe M. Meresse had one or two too many Ricard when he spoke.'[10] Meresse contemplated legal action against Cole but settled for a forthright denial: 'Evidently, I would be less than honest if I was to say that I never drank a Ricard in my life. But, in my work, I reassure the world that I never drink.'[11]

The contradictory accounts Fayed gave of Diana's 'last words' were particularly hurtful to the Spencer family. Princess Diana's mother, Frances Shand Kydd, spoke out on behalf of her grandsons, Princes William and Harry, as the controversy over her daughter's 'last words' reached its peak: 'The speculation is so upsetting. Imagine what effect it

---

[9] *Daily Telegraph*, 9 October 1997.
[10] *Evening Standard*, 7 October 1997.
[11] Author's interview with Thierry Meresse, 2003.

has on the boys.' Privately Mrs Shand Kydd had made a point of writing to the Pitié-Salpêtrière team to thank them for their efforts to save her daughter's life. She did not believe the 'last-words' claim. Sami Naïr, senior adviser to Jean-Pierre Chevènement, supported her view: 'She did not utter a single word. I remain extremely formal on this point.'[12] An immediate complaint by Fayed about the *Evening Standard* story was rejected by the Press Complaints Commission.

The 'last-words' story should have been a sharp warning to Mohamed Fayed that publicly fantasising over the intimate and heart-rending details of Diana's last moments alive was unacceptable. In the furore that engulfed Fayed and Cole as their 'last-words' story was challenged, Cole stated categorically, 'Mr Fayed will never say another word about this matter.'[13] By February 1998 Fayed had changed his mind.

Since the crash the families of those who died had been forced to endure the tragedy being reported, distorted, revealed and analysed. Many reports were complete fiction particularly those arising from Diana's dramatic but confusing final hours. An early edition of a British Sunday paper on 31 August, reported that, although Dodi Fayed had been killed in the crash, Princess Diana was not seriously hurt. The paper reported that she was receiving VIP guests in a private hospital room where she had been taken for a check up. On 24-hour news stations, TV 'royal watchers' were persuaded into studios to speculate in the early hours of the morning. The market for details of almost any description about Princess Diana after she died swiftly became insatiable, with extra sales and profits guaranteed by stories containing even the slightest reference to her.

French politicians felt obliged to come to the assistance of the Pitié-Salpêtrière hospital once again because of another claim made by Dodi's father which caused further offence. In the *Mirror* in February 1998, Mohamed Fayed gave a detailed account of his own visit to the Pitié-Salpêtrière hospital in the early hours of 31 August 1997 in which he claimed that he was given the opportunity to see Princess Diana's body. His moving description of his visit to the hospital bears careful comparison with the facts as it demonstrates why the families of the other victims of the crash, particularly Diana's relatives, had reason to feel aggrieved by his behaviour.

Unsupervised by Michael Cole, who knew nothing of the interview until it was published, Fayed claimed, 'I know what really happened at

---

[12] Author's interview with Sami Naïr.
[13] *Scotsman*, 7 October 1997.

that hospital because I was there — and was the first to arrive.' The article continued, 'Mr Al Fayed arrived ahead of the official party of British Ambassador Sir Michael Jay, French Interior Minister Jean-Pierre Chevènement and police chief, Philippe Massoni.'

This account was almost entirely fictional. There was no 'official party': the officials from the two governments made their individual ways to the hospital as quickly as possible from their homes in different parts of Paris when they were informed where Diana was being treated. All the officials named by Fayed arrived before him. According to the bodyguard Kez Wingfield, who met him when he touched down, Fayed landed at 04.55 at Le Bourget just outside Paris. At that time, the British Ambassador, Sir Michael Jay, and the French Minister of the Interior, Jean-Pierre Chevènement, were preparing to host a press conference to announce Princess Diana's death at the Pitié-Salpêtrière hospital. The press conference started at 05.45.

Fayed claimed that when he arrived at the airport Kez Wingfield 'confirmed that Dodi was dead but that Diana was alive.' This contradicts the bodyguard's account. Wingfield says he informed Fayed as soon as he got out of his helicopter that Diana was dead, and he gave a detailed description of his reaction to the news.

Sami Naïr arrived at the Pitié-Salpêtrière hospital well before Diana's ambulance at 01.10, nearly four hours before Fayed touched down at Le Bourget. Naïr kept a detailed diary of everything that happened between Diana's arrival in the ambulance at 02.00 and his own departure from the hospital long after Prince Charles had left with Diana's coffin. Naïr watched the officials referred to by Fayed arrive. He then recorded Fayed's arrival with Wingfield at 05.30[14] in the Mercedes driven by Philippe Dourneau.

Fayed's account continued, 'Diana was already in the mortuary and I had the opportunity to go and see her body, but I said no. It was just too shocking for me to go and see her. The thought of this beautiful, serene princess who I loved so much lying dead would have been too awful.'

It was true that Fayed did not see Diana's body. However, he was incorrect to say that it was taken to the hospital mortuary. The body was not taken there at any stage. Fayed continued his elaboration, claiming that he stood 'in stunned silence' on the floor where Diana had died. He did not. Diana died in the basement in the operating theatre. Her corpse was then taken in a secure lift to the first floor. According to all present,

---

[14] Author's interview with Sami Naïr.

Fayed never left the ground-floor entrance hall – indeed he did not enter the hospital itself. According to every British and French government official present, and all the medical staff who saw him, Fayed departed after a stay of less than five minutes in and around the entrance hall. Kez Wingfield's account matches those of the French officials precisely.

Few of the *Mirror's* millions of readers would have been aware of Fayed's account of the same moment in *Death of a Princess*, which was published in the same week as the *Mirror* interview.[15]

In interviews recorded at the end of 1997 for *Death of a Princess*, Fayed had given Sancton and MacLeod a different account of events. He accurately described how he had been met at the hospital by Sir Michael Jay, Minister Chevènement and the police chief, Pierre Massoni. However, Fayed then invented a visit to see the body of the Princess, building on Michael Cole's account at the Harrods' press conference: 'I saw her and I prayed. She looked beautiful, peaceful and serene.'[16]

Fayed did not request permission to see Diana's body, and he would not have been granted permission had he done so because he was not a member of her family or her household. To have seen the Princess's body, Dodi's father would have required permission from the British Ambassador. Sir Michael Jay is clear this did not happen. Jean-Pierre Chevènement's adviser, Sami Naïr recalls, 'A decision was taken that entry to the room in which Lady Di's body was laid out would be strictly prohibited. I can confirm that the Minister of the Interior himself gave the order.' Commander Mulès carried out Chevèrement's orders. He knows from his own experience of entering the hospital to assist Professeur Lecomte that the security he organised did not permit Fayed to gain access to her corpse, 'To gain access to the body I myself had to pass through many security checks and identify myself as Professeur Lecomte was waiting for me. So I very much doubt that anyone else could have gained access. You needed a passsport to penetrate the security to see Princess Diana's body!'[17]

Without Michael Cole to advise and remind him, Fayed could not remember precisely what he had told to whom in the gap between giving his differing accounts. The virtually simultaneous publication in February of Fayed's two accounts of that sad night eroded his credibility enormously.

---

[15] *Mirror*, 12 February 1998.
[16] *Death of a Princess*, p. 32.
[17] Author's interviews with Sami Naïr (1998) and Jean-Claude Mulès (2003).

On the night of Princess Diana's and Dodi Fayed's deaths, government officials from Britain and France expressed sincere condolences to Mohamed Fayed on behalf of their respective countries.[18] The officials present in Paris on the night of the tragedy had been struck by the Egyptian's dignity and bearing when he arrived at the Pitié-Salpêtrière on what must have been the worst morning of his life. Sami Naïr remembered, 'He had very great dignity, the dignity of a lord. He said, "He is dead, it is fate. It is fate. Now all I want is to collect my son. I want to take him with me." '[19]

Within weeks of the Princess's death some of the most virulent myths had taken root. Fayed's inventions about seeing the 'peaceful and serene' body of the Princess and having received her last words from an intermediary have travelled around the world many times. They will continue to be believed by millions to the distress of her family and friends. All the available evidence points to the fact that they are inventions. The more serious assertion that Princess Diana's life should have been saved by the French did not owe its existence to Fayed, but it has equally little foundation in fact.

---

[18] Author's interview with British Embassy officials and Sami Naïr.
[19] Author's interview with Sami Naïr.

8. DIANA'S FAYED FUTURE?

'Imagine the situation: Diana and Dodi get married. They have two beautiful children. They spend their time between Malibu, Paris and London. The world still beats a path to Diana's door. Their glamour, looks and radiant happiness make a striking contrast with the House of Windsor . . .'

Mohamed Fayed, *Sunday Times*, 14 June 1998

Myths and legends surrounding Princess Diana's short relationship with Dodi Fayed started to sprout in the public imagination well before her funeral. It became accepted by millions around the world that the lovers were intending to get married when Henri Paul's car hurtled into the Alma tunnel. It was reported that Dodi had bought Diana a fabulous engagement ring, which was found in the car. Dodi's butler said he was chilling champagne for the couple upon their return from the Ritz, in anticipation that the Princess would accept his master's proposal of marriage. Mohamed Fayed claimed that they were, 'on Monday', going to 'declare their engagement'.[1] According to what some papers took to calling the 'romance of the century', the couple planned to divide their time between the sumptuous Fayed family residence in Malibu and the villa Windsor, which they had visited on their last afternoon. The couple were said to be so besotted with the villa that they had met an Italian designer who had been commissioned to convert this former home of the Duke and Duchess of Windsor into a 'nest' for Diana and Dodi. Introducing a Channel 4 television programme from the villa Windsor in 1998, the presenter, Angela Rippon, informed viewers, 'What made the villa perfect for the Duke and Duchess made it perfect for Diana and Dodi.' Within months of the crash, the dead couple's thwarted plans for a future together were firmly established in the British national consciousness. Unfortunately, none of it was true.

Immediately after the crash an intense debate ensued about what Diana had been planning when she died. The speculators evolved into two irreconcilable camps: Mohamed Fayed and his employees bullishly maintained Princess Diana and Dodi were on the threshold of marriage, and were making plans for a life together; those closest to the Princess vehemently disagreed. Her family endured the furore in silence.

Mohamed Fayed claimed on British television in June 1998 that the couple told him they were engaged before they made their fateful

---

[1] *Diana – Secrets Behind the Crash*, ITV, 3 June 1998.

departure from the Ritz early on 31 August: 'She was completely full of happiness. Full of joy. At the end of the road, you know, she find someone she can feel, you know, fill her life and be happy, and fulfil all her dreams which she lost and she missed for years. She find the family she can be – you know – related to.'[2] Fayed's statement, nine months after the crash, represented a substantial development in the engagement hypothesis.

The news that Dodi had acquired a ring for Diana ensured that the speculation began even before the Princess was buried. On the day before the Princess's funeral, Michael Cole confirmed that the ring existed, but he did not comment on headlines that had proclaimed, 'DIANA DIED WEARING DODI'S RING.' Cole himself was noncommittal about its significance, as he read a script approved by Fayed: 'What that ring meant we shall probably never know. And if the planet lasts for another thousand years I am quite sure that people will continue to speculate endlessly.'[3]

The Repossi ring became critical to the ensuing debate about whether Princess Diana had accepted Dodi's proposal of marriage shortly before they died. Despite newspaper headlines, only one ring is mentioned in the documents of Judge Stéphan's enquiry as having been found in the wreckage of the Mercedes. It was a ring with white stones. It is listed among items found by the French police on Diana's body but its description does not match the one that Dodi picked up from Repossi.

The ring-in-the-wreckage story is one of three contradictory versions of how the ring was discovered. A second version emerged from Dodi's butler. René Delorm said he found it several days after the crash in the rue Arsène-Houssaye apartment. He wrote in his book, Diana and Dodi: A Love Story, that he discovered the ring, still in its box, in a wardrobe several days after Dodi died:

Realising it was time to face reality again, I shook myself out of my stupor. I decided to go through the apartment to make sure everything was in order, in case Mr [Mohamed] Al Fayed came back . . . As I glanced over the contents of the wardrobe, everything seemed normal. But suddenly, something out of place caught my eye. It was some sort of box – just a little one – perched on the closet shelf in plain sight . . . With my heart pounding, I slowly lifted the lid. There it was, the magnificent, diamond encrusted

---

[2] Diana – Secrets Behind the Crash, ITV, 3 June 1998.
[3] Harrods' press conference, 5 September 1997.

ring. Evidently he had decided to wait until they'd returned to their special dinner before he proposed to her.[4]

Delorm then gives a detailed description of how he phoned Mohamed Fayed to tell him that he had found the ring. Delorm says he was taken to the Ritz to give it to Frank Klein. Claude Roulet, who had brought the ring to Dodi in the Ritz on the evening of 30 August, after he had inspected it at Repossi's shop, is quoted as saying, 'Yes, that's the ring, that's the one'.[5]

On the first anniversary of the tragedy, Mohamed Fayed came up with a third version of how the ring was found. Fayed said that *he* had personally retrieved the ring on the day of the tragedy: 'I found that beautiful ring when I travelled to Paris to bring Dodi home for burial. It was a heart breaking moment.'[6]

The three contradictory versions lead nonetheless to one incontrovertible conclusion: the ring had not been accepted by Princess Diana. Whatever Dodi's intentions may have been, the ring itself provides no evidence that the couple were engaged at the time of their deaths. The ring had either not been presented to Diana, or she had refused to accept it.

The couple had originally set out for Chez Benoît on their last night, which would indicate that Dodi was not planning to propose over dinner. It is doubtful that Dodi would have considered a restaurant open to the public an appropriate place for such an intimate moment with the most photographed woman in the world. Because of the paparazzi's attentions, Dodi decided to go to his father's hotel while en route to Chez Benoît. What the couple said to each other in the privacy of the Imperial Suite in the Ritz will never be known. However, it is difficult to believe that Dodi had proposed to Diana that night but had forgotten to take the ring with him. There is no evidence, other than Mohamed's June 1998 account of his conversation with Princess Diana, that she had, or would have accepted Dodi's proposal.

Alberto Repossi has confirmed that Mohamed himself paid the bill for the ring that Dodi had collected on the evening of his death. Claude Roulet negotiated a 'special price' on Fayed's behalf when he collected the ring from Repossi's Place Vendôme boutique. Repossi stressed that he had never himself been aware that the ring was to be an engagement

---

[4] Delorm, p. 170.
[5] Delorm, p. 171.
[6] *Mirror*, 31 August 1998.

ring.[7] He said he did not know if the ring was intended by either party to seal a proposal of marriage. The ring he sold to Dodi was not from the 'Dis Moi Oui' ('Tell Me Yes') range itself. It was custom-made for the Princess, inspired, according to Repossi, by the ideas contained in the 'Dis Moi Oui' range. Repossi's was a testimony Mohamed Fayed chose to ignore: '. . . the jewellery [sic] himself give a statement that she came to the shop, she choose her engagement ring from the selection of engagement rings.'[8]

This is not the jeweller's recollection. According to Alberto Repossi, Diana did not choose the ring he supplied to Dodi from 'the selection of engagement rings'. The first journalists to chase the story of the ring in the week after the crash selected the ring they thought Princess Diana might have chosen. They took a picture from the 'Dis Moi Oui' catalogue to illustrate their stories. This picture was then reproduced thousands of times around the world as Princess Diana's engagement ring. As a result, according to Repossi himself, every picture that has ever been published of the 'engagement ring' is incorrect.[9] Repossi retains the original sketch he made for the ring's design, and he has destroyed the ideas for other items of jewellery that he had made in preparation for Dodi Fayed's visit.

Close friends who spoke to Diana shortly before she died are adamant she was not planning to marry Dodi. On her Greek holiday, in the middle of August, Diana had talked to Rosa Monckton about Dodi. When she told her friend that Dodi was proposing to buy her a ring, she laughingly said, ' "Rosa, that's going firmly on the fourth finger of my right hand." '[10]

Coincidentally, while Diana was in Greece with Rosa Monckton, Fayed's confidant and 'unofficial spokesman', Max Clifford, sought to deny that Dodi was engaged to Kelly Fisher. In doing so, he inadvertently gave sustenance to the arguments of those who doubted that the ring Dodi bought for Diana was an engagement ring. Clifford was quoted as saying, 'He denies categorically telling Fisher he was going to marry her. Dodi has given expensive rings to lots of people, some of them beautiful women, none of whom he had been engaged to.'[11]

---

[7] Author's interview with Alberto Repossi.
[8] Interview with Marian Finucane, Radio Telefis Eireann, January 1999.
[9] Author's interview with Alberto Repossi.
[10] Sunday Telegraph, 15 February 1998.
[11] Daily Telegraph, 18 August 1997.

Clifford gave Dodi regular advice on media relations during his romance with Diana, and, having spoken to him shortly before his death, he gave the engagement claims little credence: 'It was just a few days before the tragic death, and I was in Spain on holiday, and Dodi talked to me about a John Denver record, "Annie's Song". He identified with that particular song. "You fill up my senses" is one of the lines, and that is one of the expressions he used: "Diana really does fill up my senses, and, if we're together at Christmas, then I believe we'll be together for the rest of our lives." '[12]

Other Fayed associates joined distant members of the Fayed family and Fayed employees in supporting Mohamed's idea that the couple were planning marriage. The first claims of wedding plans after the crash had come from members of Dodi's extended family. On 3 September 1997, the British press cited Hussein Yassin, claiming that the couple were about to marry. Yassin was Dodi's step-uncle – the brother of Samira Khashoggi's second husband. He never met Diana. He told *Asharq Al-Awsat*, an Arabic paper based in London, 'Dodi said that they were deeply in love, and the relationship was serious and they have decided to get married . . . We have to announce this, we will announce it.' Yassin said he had been due to meet Dodi on the afternoon of 30 August 1997. According to this account, they apparently planned to meet after the meal that night, but Dodi rang from the Ritz to cancel.

The same story emerged from Hussein's niece, Joumana Yassin, on 4 September. She was quoted in *Al Akhbar*, a Cairo paper owned by the Egyptian government, as saying, 'They had been friends for about ten years, and this friendship transformed into love after the divorce of Diana and Prince Charles . . . Dodi was insistent about the fact that their marriage would be founded on true love.'

Subsequently, a stream of Fayed employees lined up to support the claims of the family. The president of the Ritz hotel, Frank Klein, claimed that Dodi was planning to move into the villa Windsor with the Princess after they had married. 'Dodi broke some startling news: "We want to move into the villa, Frank, because we are getting married in October or November." ' Klein replied, 'That's wonderful Dodi. Really wonderful. I'll be back in Paris on Monday and we'll talk about it.'[13]

Dodi's American publicist, Pat Kingsley, was also cited, somewhat more obliquely, in support of the Diana–Dodi link being made more permanent: 'He never mentioned marriage, but he dropped enough

---

[12] Author's taped interview with Max Clifford.
[13] *Death of a Princess*, p. 127.

strong hints . . .' Dodi had apparently told Kingsley he would be back in Los Angeles towards the end of September. 'I have some great news for you . . . I'm not going to tell you about it until I get to California, but it is really great and I think you'll be thrilled for me.'[14]

This conclusion was backed up by other Fayed family employees. Michael Cole told Sancton and MacLeod of a conversation with Dodi before the final holiday: 'He said, "Michael, there will never be another girlfriend, ever." He was so emphatic about it. And he wasn't someone who was usually emphatic.'[15] On British TV in June 1998, after he had quit his post with Fayed, Cole said, 'It was a very sincere relationship. He had great respect for her and her family. He told me that they were going to go to Hong Kong, and then across the Pacific to Malibu.' Michael Cole had just watched his former boss declare publicly on TV that Diana and Dodi were certainly about to get married when they died.

A few days before Cole's indication that the couple were planning to go to Malibu, it had been reported that Mohamed Fayed had put the Californian 'dream home' where Diana and his son were planning to live on the market for $7.5 million.[16] Kelly Fisher knew the Malibu house well but Diana did not. On the video she took of her visit to the villa Windsor with Dodi on 14 July, Kelly can be heard chatting to him about furniture and design ideas for their Malibu home. Dodi left the Malibu house for his final holiday with Princess Diana ten days before he died. It is certain that Diana herself never visited it. The description of the Malibu mansion as being Diana's 'dream home' revealed more about the marketing tactics of a Californian real-estate agent than Diana's vision of her future.

On Princess Diana's side, those who had known her well before her romance with Dodi were sceptical about the claims that she was planning a long-term future with him after such a short romance. Simone Simmons, the therapist and 'healer' who worked closely with Diana following her divorce, was a close friend during the Princess's relationship with Hasnat Khan. Because of the nature of her work with the Princess, she knew as well as anyone the way her mind worked. Simmons had not been in touch with the Princess over the summer of 1997. She had fallen out with Diana, who had similar periods of noncommunication with Sarah Ferguson, Elton John and, indeed, her own mother and brother over perceived slights. Nonetheless, Simmons felt able to say,

---

[14] *Death of a Princess*, pp. 124–5.
[15] *Death of a Princess*, p. 125.
[16] *Daily Telegraph*, 2 June 1998.

If she hadn't died at the end of August 1997, I'm convinced that the Dodi episode would be remembered only as a footnote to her life, and by the time autumn passed she would have returned, rested, to her greater purposes, while Dodi would have resolved matters with his fiancée [Kelly Fisher] in America. I don't deny that some spark ignited between them, perhaps something rather more than the impulse that had made Diana want to make Hasnat jealous. Dodi was someone she already knew slightly, he was personable, had a certain position in international society, and was wealthy enough to be able effortlessly to pamper her at a time when she needed not merely to rest, but to be spoiled: . . . If Mohamed Fayed really thought that Diana and his son were on the brink of announcing their betrothal, then he was the victim of wishful thinking.[17]

Lana Marks spoke to the Princess while she was on the *Jonikal* with Dodi during her last holiday. She formed the impression that marriage to Dodi was 'definitely not on the cards' for Diana. Lana thought she was 'happy passing the summer'[18] with Dodi but reports that she made no mention of settling down with him.

Diana's journalist friend, Richard Kay, modified his own opinion over whether or not Diana would have married Dodi. When she died Kay wrote that she would 'probably' have married Dodi. However, upon reflection, and having spoken extensively to Diana's family and close friends, he judged that she would not have done: 'The Spencer family and Diana's close friends . . . refuse to believe claims which purport to cement the relationship between Diana and Dodi to a timeless permanence. The ring, for example. Dodi did give her a ring but it was a "friendship" ring rather than an engagement ring. Diana would not have hurried into a marital commitment without first speaking to her sons – especially William – and three close friends. She discussed it with none of them.'[19]

No one has sought to question the intensity of Diana and Dodi's short relationship in the summer of 1997. At her funeral, Earl Spencer paid tribute to the happiness his sister had found that summer. However, a six-week relationship between two divorcees still in the process of disentangling themselves from serious, post-divorce relationships does not suggest marriage as an immediate outcome. In the shock of Diana's

---

[17] Simone Simmons, *Diana: The Secret Years*, pp. 166–7.
[18] Author's interview with Lana Marks, May 1999.
[19] *Daily Mail*, 11 February 1998.

death many had sought to impose a kind of romantic unity on her senseless end, speculating on a marriage which would lend an air of a classical tragedy to what was a thoroughly ordinary death in an avoidable car crash.

Aside from the fictions of her engagement to Dodi, no speculation about the hypothetical future of Princess Diana caused more offence to her friends and relatives than the notion that she was pregnant when she died. Examining the facts upon which such speculation was loosely based, however, is salutary.

A remark that Diana had made to British journalists in Saint-Tropez sparked much speculation after she died. 'You will be surprised at the next thing I do,' she said on 14 July, Bastille Day. Some have posthumously interpreted this comment to mean that she was pregnant, others that she was planning to marry Dodi in the autumn. Neither is possible. The timing of the remark meant she could not have been pregnant by Dodi, or conceivably have been thinking of taking time out in the autumn to marry him. Dodi made his fateful acquaintance with Diana only that evening. The Princess had spoken to the British press during the day. Dodi was in Paris with Kelly Fisher at the time, escorting her around the villa Windsor.

Other pregnancy rumours flowed from the thousands of photographs taken of Princess Diana in Saint-Tropez. She was extensively photographed during her Mediterranean holidays, and the trimness of her body was much admired. After her death, the Saint-Tropez pictures were re-evaluated, and great significance was attached to a slight roll of fat on her tummy. Although so slight as to be hardly noticeable, it was held by some to show a woman in the first stages of pregnancy, rather than a 36-year-old former bulimia sufferer regaining a healthy figure.

In order for a pregnancy to show it needs to have advanced at least two or three months. Such a hypothetical baby could thus not have had anything to do with Dodi Fayed. Nobody who was in the South of France when Dodi and Diana met has any evidence that the couple slept together at that point. Both friends of the Princess and seasoned Diana watchers were adamant that she would not have contemplated this while her two sons were with her. It was also the case that Dodi was still involved with Kelly Fisher at this time. Fisher claims that she was sleeping with Dodi and having sex with him while she was in the South of France on 17/18 July. This is a credible claim as the couple had been dating for nearly a year, and Kelly claims they were on the brink of getting married. Indeed, Kelly Fisher claimed in a newspaper interview after Dodi had started his romance with Diana that she had unprotected sex with him on the last occasion they slept together in July 1997.[20]

If, as seems probable, Diana's physical relationship with Dodi started during their cruise on the *Jonikal* in early August, it is certain that their initial sexual encounters did not result in her becoming pregnant. Infuriated by the pregnancy rumours, Rosa Monckton felt obliged to reveal after Princess Diana's death that her friend menstruated during their Greek holiday, which ended on 20 August.[21]

The following day, as she prepared to depart for the South of France, Princess Diana visited Dr Lily at the Man Fong Mei clinic in London. Dr Lily was treating the Princess for premenstrual tension, and she knew that Diana could not have been pregnant when she died: 'She saw me on Thursday August 21 and I can say without question that she was not pregnant then. It would have been impossible for Diana to have been pregnant at the time of the crash. It makes me so upset when people say she was pregnant. It just wasn't true.'[22]

In the exceptionally unlikely event that Princess Diana had been in the first stages of a pregnancy as a result of having unprotected sex with Dodi on her last holiday with him, Diana would not herself have known she was pregnant. Even the most crazed conspiracy theorist has yet to suggest how a government intelligence agency would have known what Princess Diana herself did not know about her own body.

The pregnancy rumours were given a new lease of life with the emergence of an apparently official document in *Interviu*, a Spanish magazine. It looked authentic, as it appeared to be on the Pitié-Salpêtrière hospital's headed paper and signed by Dr Pierre Coriat. He is the head anaesthetist at the hospital's resuscitation unit. The letter appeared to be addressed to the Interior Minister, Jean-Pierre Chevène-ment. When the document was published in December 1997, the Pitié-Salpêtrière hospital explicitly denounced it as a fake. The hospital's spokesman, Thierry Meresse, put out a statement confirming that the letter was a forgery: 'No tests were taken in this regard. The role of the doctors was to save Diana's life, nothing else.'[23]

The document was a clever forgery. It did not purport to be an outright confirmation of pregnancy, reporting instead a nine- to ten-week gestation at the time of the Princess's death. Diana had known

---

[20] *News of the World*, 17 August 1997.
[21] *Sunday Telegraph*, 15 February 1998.
[22] *Mirror*, 23 February 1998, confirmed via Professor Man Fong Mei, 16 April 1999.
[23] *Death of a Princess*, p. 43.

Dodi for only six weeks when she died, so even if the document had been real it would have confirmed that Dodi could not have been the father.

The hospital's terse statement disguised what had really happened, and why the rumours had gained momentum. Official sources admitted to me that one reason why the rumour had gained momentum in the first place was because of a mistake made in the recording of Princess Diana's treatment at the Pitié-Salpêtrière.

The Paris prosecutor Maud Coujard launched a criminal investigation into the crash shortly after she arrived on the scene in the early hours of 31 August. This meant that details of medical treatment that all the victims received would automatically be transferred to the investigating team. In this case they were sent to Martine Monteil's Criminal Brigade at the quai des Orfèvres. The police inspector responsible for recording what had been done to save Diana's life mistakenly recorded that blood samples had been taken from her. Blood samples are routinely taken from every patient on admission, and he had wrongly assumed that this had been carried out on Diana. A pro forma is created on a police computer for cases under investigation, and this anticipates blood samples being taken. In Diana's case, there was simply no time to take blood samples, as her life was slipping away so quickly.

The absence of details about a blood sample in the official file, and the absence of tests upon it, led some to jump to the conclusion that something was being hidden, and that Diana may have been pregnant. However, as no samples were taken, there was nothing to cover up, other than a bureaucratic error by a weary police inspector at the quai des Orfèvres. The cock-up theory of events as admitted by officials is far more convincing than the 'conspiracy-to-cover-up-Diana's-pregnancy' theory, which has no evidence to support it.

Diana's friends and family were appalled by the pregnancy rumours. 'An absolute disgrace,' one of them told Diana's journalist friend, Richard Kay. He was similarly dismissive of the pregnancy rumours: 'Diana was not pregnant for several reasons. Everyone around her, and close to her, knew that she was obsessive about not having a child out of wedlock, and had made certain decisions to ensure it never happened. No, the Princess of Wales was not pregnant when she died. I know that for a fact . . . to her family and friends, who could have supplied the definitive answer to the question, it was a grotesque, scurrilous accusation.'[24]

---

[24] *Daily Mail*, 11 February 1998.

A logical extension, indeed conclusion, to the pregnancy and engagement myths, which emerged soon after the crash, was the idea that the dead couple had been looking for a house together when they died. It was widely reported six months after the crash that Princess Diana and Dodi had been planning to move into the villa Windsor when they were married. There was enormous poignancy in the idea that the Princess of Wales had been planning to live in the house that the former Prince of Wales, King Edward VIII, had lived in for most of his exiled life. Edward had abdicated after choosing to marry the love of his own life, Wallis Simpson, an American. The former king became the Duke of Windsor, and Wallis became the Duchess of Windsor. Now it appeared that Princess Diana had been planning to marry Dodi, a foreigner, and like Wallis Simpson, a divorcee. The couple's visit to the villa on their last afternoon was offered as evidence of the seriousness of their intentions.

When Michael Cole briefed the world's press on 5 September at Harrods, he stated that Diana and Dodi's visit to 'his' villa lasted 35 minutes; they arrived at 15.45 and departed at 16.20. No details were given beyond the statement, 'Princess Diana and Mr Fayed arrive at the villa Windsor. Dodi gives the Princess a tour of his house and of the garden.'

However, between September 1997 and February 1998 this episode, like that of the 'engagement' ring, underwent a mysterious transformation. In 1998, Fayed decided to grant access to the villa to selected media for the first time since the crash. He told British TV of the importance of the villa to the couple: '. . . she decided that this is the place she loved. She find that this is the place for her, and a very secure place, and it's just near London – she will be near home . . . and was just the right nest for her.'[25]

A number of journalists were welcomed to the villa Windsor in February. The story now told had changed since the Harrods' press conference, and the revised tale held that Diana and Dodi had actually been at the villa for 'a couple of hours'. They had been met by an 'Italian designer' who had drawn up plans to redesign the villa for the couple when they moved in. The couple had been given an extended tour of the house and its gardens by Gregorio Martin, who has worked at the villa for most of his adult life. Formerly butler and chauffeur to the Duke and Duchess of Windsor, Martin had been retained by Fayed when he took over the lease on the villa. He gave a

---

[25] *Diana – Secrets Behind the Crash*, ITV, 3 June 1998.

moving account of Diana and Dodi's visit: 'They were a very beautiful couple. They came to visit everything. They go all around the house. In the top until the basement, the kitchen, the kennel for the dogs. Everything.'[26]

That Diana's plans for the future included moving into the villa Windsor came as a surprise to friends she had spoken to immediately before her death. She had not mentioned the idea to any of them. When she spoke to Richard Kay after she had been to the villa with Dodi on 30 August, she gave him the opposite impression during a specific discussion about her plans for the immediate future: 'Diana told me that, in the foreseeable future, she would never live permanently outside England. She could not imagine ever living again in what was effectively a royal palace. Of the Windsor house, she said, "It has a history and ghosts of its own and I have no wish to follow that." '[27]

The revised version of Diana's visit to the villa came as an even greater surprise to Ben Murrell, its security chief. He had been present for her brief visit, and he knew that Gregorio Martin had not been. In fact, Martin had not even been in France when the Princess paid her short visit with Dodi on their last afternoon. Murrell and his wife Rebecca lived at the villa Windsor, as did Martin. They knew that Martin had been on holiday in Spain on 30 August. He had been recalled to Paris only after the fatal car crash. Unfortunately, Martin himself had been involved in a car crash as he made his way back from Spain to the villa. After his interview with ITV, Murrell asked Martin why he was pretending to have been present: 'He said to me, "What can I do? Mohamed wants me to say it." '[28]

René Delorm also felt able to vouch for the couple's plans to move into the villa. He was filmed by CBS at the villa adding his authority to Martin's description of the couple's visit for millions of American TV viewers. Dan Rather's 48 hours programme was broadcast on 31 August 1998, the first anniversary of the crash. For Ben Murrell, however, the sight of René Delorm escorting the CBS camera crew around the villa was 'the last straw'. The security chief had watched in growing dismay as camera teams and reporters from around the world had been fed a version of Diana's brief trip to the villa with his boss's son that bore absolutely no relation to what had taken place. The sight of Delorm performing the same tricks for US TV prompted Murrell to quit: 'René

---

[26] *Diana – Secrets Behind the Crash*, ITV, 3 June 1998.
[27] *Daily Mail*, 11 February 1998.
[28] Author's interview with Ben Murrell.

was walking through the rooms saying how much Diana and Dodi were looking forward to moving in. I couldn't stand it any more.'[29]

Murrell quit his job in dramatic fashion. He sold his story about Princess Diana's visit to the villa Windsor to the *Sun*. The most damaging evidence he produced were pictures that had been taken from the villa's security cameras. The time code, containing the date and the time of day, was burnt into every frame on the tape. The pictures destroyed the 'two-hour-visit' claim.

One frame showed Diana and Dodi emerging from their Mercedes at 15.47:46 on 30 August 1997. A second showed them exiting the villa less than 28 minutes later at 16.15:26. A third showed the Mercedes followed by the black Range Rover with Henri Paul at the wheel leaving the villa's grounds three minutes later at 16.18:27.

Trumpeting its 'world exclusive', the *Sun*'s main headline, two days after the anniversary of the crash, on 2 September 1998, read 'FAYED'S DIANA LIES', and the subheadline ran, ' "Marriage" to son Dodi was a sickening sham.'

In the *Sun*, Murrell said, 'All I have done is to tell the truth. Mohamed Fayed knows the truth and obviously the truth hurts.'

Murrell's revelations threw serious doubts about Mohamed Fayed's various accounts of his son's relationship with Princess Diana. His claim that the couple were engaged and planning to live together in the villa Windsor simply does not stand up. Such accounts have, nevertheless, formed an important part of the growing mythology surrounding the couple. They also form an essential part of the sundry schools of conspiracy theorising about the accident. Princess Diana's intention to marry Dodi Fayed was at the heart of such speculation. Their imminent marriage brought motive to the tragedy for conspiracy theorists. 'Dark and sinister' forces determined to prevent such a union were deemed to be responsible for the 'assassination' of the couple.

In the week after the crash, parts of the Egyptian press treated as fact the notion that the couple had been murdered to prevent their imminent marriage. Those who could not appreciate this were condemned by an Egyptian quoted in the *Cairo Times* as being 'either as blind as a new born kitten, or you're an agent of the same secret service Queen Elizabeth hired to bump off her daughter-in-law!' In the week after the crash, the Egyptian magazine *Al-Mussawar* put a computer-generated image of Diana and Dodi as bride and groom on their cover.

---

[29] *Sun*, 2 September 1998.

The *Independent* newspaper's respected Middle East correspondent, Robert Fisk, despaired of the Arab response to the Paris crash. He reported in October 1997 that Colonel Gaddafi had made Britain's production of the 'murderers' of Princess Diana a new precondition before he would allow the trial of the two Libyans suspected of the Lockerbie bombing to take place. Six books were published within weeks of the crash, and two film producers had announced their intention to make films about Diana, 'which will be about as true to life as Cecil B DeMille's epics were to the Bible'. One director had lined up Omar Sharif to play Dodi, according to rumour. Throughout the region it appeared to Fisk that everyone was convinced that Diana and Dodi had been bumped off by the British establishment.

In his sardonically entitled article, 'HER MAJESTY THE TERMINATOR', Fisk cited an Arab banker who told him,

> For the British monarchy, it was totally unthinkable that the mother of the future king could be married to a Middle Eastern Muslim. The British Royal Family could not contemplate the idea of a Muslim mother for the future king. Perhaps she would even have persuaded her sons to convert to Islam, and where would Britain be with a Muslim Royal Family? The Queen must have called the British Embassy in Paris and said 'Kill them!'[30]

Although Diana's relationship with Dr Hasnat Khan had been hinted at in the British press, few in the Middle East could have known that she had been dating him for nearly two years before she met Dodi Fayed. No harm had come to either of them, and the Khans are practising Muslims. When Dr Khan returned to his home from a holiday in the first week of September 1997, he found two items concerning Diana among the mail that awaited him. One was a birthday card from Diana herself, and the other was an invitation to her funeral.

Much of the British media needed little persuading that marriage between Diana and Dodi Fayed was a probability, from the moment that their relationship became known in August 1997. This was precisely the sort of pressure that Hasnat Khan had been so keen to avoid during his much longer relationship with the Princess. Diana and Dodi's transition to a posthumous marriage in tabloid heaven was thus a smooth one. It increased the tragedy's poignancy, whether or not the two lovers were deemed to be victims of a conspiracy. However, an examination of the

---

[30] *Independent on Sunday*, 12 October 1997.

facts, including those established by Judge Stéphan's investigation, reveals that conspiracy theories about the crash fall apart as surely as do the myths about Princess Diana's pregnancy and her plans to marry Dodi and live in the villa Windsor with him.

9. RED HERRINGS AND WHITE FIATS

'The more I learn about this story, the less clear it becomes. The blood sample seems – well – suspect.'

Nicholas Owen, *Diana – Secrets Behind the Crash*,
ITV, 3 June 1998

The shocking claim that Princess Diana and Dodi Fayed could have been assassinated was first made within hours of their deaths. The head of an organisation called Executive Intelligence Review, Lyndon Larouche, expressed his 'fears' the day after the blood tests on Henri Paul were released that the couple were the victims of a 'vehicular homicide'. EIR was not alone in making this claim. The rash of websites that appeared on the Internet after the Paris crash included many that were in no doubt that the British 'establishment' had murdered the Queen's former daughter-in-law. EIR itself detected the 'almost-certain involvement of MI6 personnel, through the agency's station in Paris, in the vehicular attack in the place de l'Alma tunnel', which occurred after, they claimed, Prince Philip had been in a 'murderous rage against the Al Fayeds for months'.[1]

I interviewed Jeffrey Steinberg, a director of EIR, for a film about Princess Diana's death that I was making for Channel 4's *Dispatches*. We had decided to examine the conspiracy subdivision of the Diana death industry, and our director had decreed that I should interview him in the back of a Mercedes. As we headed down the Mall towards Buckingham Palace, Steinberg regaled me with the thought that Prince Philip could have been behind the 'murder' of his former daughter-in-law. Modestly, Steinberg conceded that he did not possess 'anything resembling smoking-gun proof that Prince Philip called the shot, and ordered British intelligence to do it'. However, 'looking at the fact that several news reports indicated that he was livid over the idea of this relationship [with Dodi Fayed] and was, in fact, livid over the fact that Diana had become a very significant thorn in the side of the House of Windsor, certainly creates a circumstance where I can't rule it out in all honesty'.[2] Appropriately, Steinberg made this claim as we drove past Buckingham Palace, past the balcony on which, as newlyweds, Prince Charles and Princess Diana had kissed in front of thousands of well-wishers in 1981.

---

[1] *EIR*, 19 December 1997.
[2] *Dispatches*, 4 June 1998.

Conveniently, the 'dark and sinister' forces the conspiracy theorists profess to believe killed Princess Diana and Dodi Fayed are in no position to deny their swathes of allegations. How, for example, would 'the MI6 station in Paris' go about proving that it did not murder the mother of two heirs to the British throne?

The understandable reticence of the British and French governments to dignify such allegations with comment combined with the virtual blanket silence that French law imposed upon its investigation into the Alma tunnel crash to produce a miasma of conspiracy theories. They are worth closer scrutiny because they have gained so much space and been given so much credibility by media throughout a world that found itself unable to accept that its best-known woman could have died as she did. Diana's death made life itself appear so fragile to millions that a dose of conspiracy theory became a recommended prescription by media 'doctors' throughout the world.

The most popular strands of conspiracy theory can be divided into three broad parts. The first involved Henri Paul being blinded by a flash in the Alma tunnel immediately before the crash. As this theory could enlist the evidence of witnesses who saw photographers with flash guns pursuing the Mercedes, it gained some credibility on a superficial level. The second theory involved a white Fiat Uno which was ascribed various roles in causing the crash, from ramming the Mercedes into the pillar to providing a deliberate obstruction at the mouth of the tunnel. A third theory claimed that Henri Paul was not drunk at all, but he had been poisoned, which is held to be why he crashed. This theory purported to explain why his autopsy revealed an unusually high level of carbon monoxide in his blood.

In all these scenarios, anonymous 'dark and sinister forces' could be drafted in to play any role required in cyberspace, where hard evidence is often considered a luxury rather than a necessity. It is worth examining these three strands in some detail, as they illuminate the demimonde of conspiracy theorising, and the motives driving some of its proponents.

The first witness to claim to have been anywhere near the Alma tunnel crash came forward only hours after it happened. François Levi had an extraordinary story to tell. In the early hours of 31 August, the middle-aged Frenchman told a *Times* reporter, Adam Sage, that he had witnessed the crash in the Alma tunnel. He said that he had seen a group of motorbikes cutting up the Mercedes. Just before the crash Levi said he had seen a bright flash of light. Levi's story appeared to Sage to chime with the few facts that were known about the crash in the days that followed it. It was known that the couple were being pursued by the paparazzi on motorbikes when the Mercedes crashed. Indeed, Mohamed Fayed's spokesman had described the bikes surrounding the car as being 'like a stage coach surrounded by Indians'.[3]

Later in the day, Levi turned up at the Ritz hotel and told Mohamed Fayed's people his flash-before-the-crash story. One of the Fayed lawyers, Bernard Dartevelle, advised Levi to hire a lawyer and pointed him in the direction of the police. Having told his story to the *Sunday Times* and Fayed's lawyer, Levi became one of the first witnesses to give a statement to the investigation on the day after the crash.

Judge Stéphan was not appointed to lead the investigation until Tuesday 2 September. He made a point of recalling Levi to hear him recount his claims in person in May 1998. Levi had claimed, 'As the motorcycle swerved, and before the car lost control, there was a flash of light. But then I was out of the tunnel and heard, but did not see, the impact. I immediately pulled my car over to the curb but my wife said, "Let's get out of here. It's a terrorist attack!" '[4]

The French police to whom Levi first detailed his account advised Stéphan to treat anything Levi had to say with extreme scepticism. They did not believe his account, and no other witnesses claimed to have seen what Levi described as a 'blinding flash' immediately before the crash. Furthermore, Levi's criminal record was known to the police. He served a prison sentence in 1989 in Rouen for theft, burglary and forging cheques. There is no reason why a convicted criminal could not have witnessed the crash in the Alma tunnel, but Levi's record was not encouraging. Police records showed that his prison visitor had described him as a '*mythomane*', a vivid French expression which means 'fantasist' or 'pathological liar'.

Because of the 'secrecy of the investigation' (see Chapter 7) which is partly designed to protect witnesses to crimes from interference or intimidation, the detectives were not in a position to publicly comment on the credibility of Levi's claims or, indeed, to bring his criminal record to the attention of journalists who were in contact with Levi. As a result, Levi became one of the media's most popular 'witnesses', as he was very keen to speak publicly about what he claimed to have seen. Levi was the only 'witness' to describe a 'flash before the crash'.

Levi was persuasive and articulate when two *Sunday Times* journalists, Kirsty Lang and John Swain, took him into the Alma tunnel in the week

---

[3] Agence France Presse, 1 September 1997.
[4] *EIR*, 21 November 1997, p. 51.

after the crash to explain what he claimed to have seen. However, Lang and Swain's scepticism about Levi grew when he was unable to produce any conclusive proof to them that he was actually in Paris on the night of the crash, let alone in the tunnel when the crash happened. The following weekend the *Sunday Times* illustrated Levi's claims about motorcyclists cutting up the Mercedes in the tunnel, and quoted his account of what he claimed to have seen, but the two journalists remained sceptical.[5]

Levi subsequently insisted upon his face being obscured for an interview he gave to the French TV station, Canal +, shortly after he had tried and failed to convince Lang and Swain that he had witnessed the crash. In the French documentary his face was pixelated. It later transpired that Levi had become notorious in the Rouen area under the name 'Levistre'. His notoriety, however, did not stem from his record as a petty criminal in the 1980s. After his release from prison he had tried to sell a baby he had had with a woman twenty years his junior to a childless German couple for 50,000 French francs. This had brought him infamy, as he appeared on French TV to justify his actions, and the case provoked outrage in France. Tweaking his name and pixelating his image prevented his claims about the Alma tunnel crash being linked to the François Levistre who was regarded by many as a lunatic.

The authors of *Death of a Princess*, apparently unaware of Levi's colourful past, strained to give him credibility. They described his account accurately as 'much maligned', but gave it some grudging credibility. Nine months later, Levi was one of the key witnesses in a British television documentary which, as its title suggested, purported to expose the 'Secrets Behind the Crash'.[6] It was broadcast on ITV and watched by 12.5 million viewers, which ITV boasted was the largest TV audience 'in a generation'. The *mythomane* had made it into the international mainstream. The programme makers illustrated his claims with a lavish reconstruction of his flash-before-the-crash claims. The tape caused gales of laughter in the Criminal Brigade's headquarters in Paris when they watched it.

The AFP news agency in Rouen also roared with laughter when it discovered that its local *mythomane* had managed to persuade British TV that he had witnessed the crash that killed Princess Diana and Dodi

---

[5] Author's interview with Kirsty Lang.
[6] *Diana – Secrets Behind the Crash*, ITV, 3 June 1998.

Fayed. Having heard Levi in person Judge Stéphan declined to invite him to the witness summit he held in Paris in June 1998.

A much more enduring mystery surrounding the crash concerns a white Fiat Uno car. Neither the Fiat nor the driver has been found, despite the most intensive hunt of its kind in French history. The Fiat has played a role in a number of fictional scenarios in causing the crash. Some theories claim it had been specially weighted down with sand or concrete bags in order to force the Mercedes off the road. The (unspecified) height of the scratches on the Mercedes was held to be proof of this. Others claimed that the Fiat could also have been powered by a turbocharged engine to enable it to outpace Paul's Mercedes S-280. This could have enabled the small car to have rammed the Mercedes into the Alma tunnel's thirteenth pillar.

Martine Monteil's detectives embarked upon their hunt in late September 1997 after small scratches found on the right-hand side of the wrecked Mercedes were found to have been made by a white Fiat Uno. No witness has ever claimed to have seen the Mercedes colliding with a white Fiat Uno. However, a phenomenal piece of forensic work on the wrecked Mercedes, as well as debris found at the scene of the crash, clinched the identification of the vehicle for Judge Stéphan.

Shards of red and white glass recovered by Jean-Claude Mulès and his team at the mouth of the Alma tunnel were the first clues that the Mercedes may have collided with another car. The white glass was from the shattered lights of the Mercedes, but the red glass intrigued analysts based at the Institut de Recherche Criminelle de la Gendarmerie Nationale (IRCGN). The IRCGN has an unparalleled reputation for identifying cars from forensic tests, and holds one of the world's most comprehensive banks of data. It studied the fragments at its Rosny-Sous-Bois headquarters just outside Paris, and provided the first clue as to the car's identity. The IRCGN concluded on 18 September 1997 that the red glass was from the rear light casing of a Fiat Uno, manufactured between May 1983 and September 1989. However, this discovery did not in itself prove that the Mercedes had been in collision with an Uno – the fractured glass could have been left in the Alma tunnel by an earlier prang.

The scratches on the Mercedes, some of which could be observed as it was towed away from the crash scene, provided more compelling evidence that a second car may have been involved. The IRCGN boffins, whose database includes samples of every sort of paint used on cars anywhere in the world, came up with the vital evidence in October 1997. Black scratches, barely visible on the front door of the Mercedes, included traces of material used to make bumpers on Fiat Unos. This analysis supported the results of the tests on the fragments of red glass, yet it still did not provide conclusive proof that an Uno was the mystery car. The deposits found were of polypropylene, which is used to make bumpers for a wide range of cars.

Analysis of the two white scratches on the right side of the Mercedes finally clinched the matter for the IRCGN experts, Patrick Touron and Thierry Cournede. The marks were found on the wing mirror and the front door, and they were 124 and 80 centimetres long, and 1 to 4 centimetres wide. The paint scratches were from a type of white paint used on several models of Fiat. The white paint was a 'solid basecoat' known as Bianco Corfu 224. That the scratches had most probably been made during the accident was confirmed by an Etoile Limousine chauffeur who had taken the Mercedes to an Esso car wash earlier in the day. He confirmed that the car had no scratches on it at that time.[7] The height of the lower of the two scratches on the Mercedes, 81.5 centimetres from the ground, was also significant, as it was compatible with the height of an Uno's bumper, but not with that of other models of Fiat. The IRCGN investigators were then able to confirm to Stéphan that the field of possible white Fiat Unos had been narrowed further by spectrographic analysis of the paint. This showed that the traces were caused by the sort of white paint used on 'phase 1' Fiat Unos.

These cars started production in May 1983, and the last one rolled off the production line in September 1989. From its Turin HQ, Fiat told the IRCGN scientists that Bianco Corfu (code 224) was used only on Fiats between May 1983 and August 1987. Thus it was a phase 1 Fiat Uno made in this period that Henri Paul had grazed seconds before crashing. The IRCGN analysis was the only firm evidence presented to Judge Stéphan of the Mercedes being in collision with another vehicle. Touron and Cournede were also able to tell Stéphan that the IRCGN analyses indicated that the Mercedes was travelling more quickly than the Fiat.

The forensic scientists and vehicle engineers Judge Stéphan commissioned to assess the IRCGN's work would eventually conclude that the Mercedes had only a minor 'brush' with a white Fiat Uno immediately before colliding with the pillar. The evidence demonstrated that the Fiat could not have rammed the Mercedes. That final conclusion was not confirmed to Stéphan until 18 November 1998. Meanwhile, the Criminal Brigade and the *gendarmes* had embarked upon their hunt for

---

[7] Pontaut and Dupuis, pp. 177–8.

the vehicle, and the mystery of the white Fiat Uno had spread across the world.

The Fiat 'mystery' was based entirely on the identification of the car by the IRCGN. As detectives made their way through dozens of witnesses who claimed to have been in or around the tunnel at the time, none claimed to have seen the Mercedes in collision with a second car. Some of those who had mentioned seeing a second car close to the time of the crash had spoken of a dark-coloured vehicle. The IRCGN's evidence ruled out many of their testimonies, unless the orange fluorescent lights in the tunnel and the darkness outside were playing tricks with witnesses' perceptions of the second car's colour.

No witnesses claimed to have seen a white Fiat in the tunnel at the time of the crash. However, two witnesses who made statements on 18 September had given accounts of seeing such a car near the scene of the crash. They were a French couple, Georges and Sabine Dauzonne, who were driving on the slip road feeding into the exit from the tunnel when the crash occurred. The couple were driving back from a dinner date with friends when, they say, they almost crashed into an 'old and shabby' white Fiat with a broken exhaust as it exited the tunnel.

Georges Dauzonne was at the wheel. 'The Fiat zigzagged as it came out of the tunnel', he said, 'swerving from the right lane into the left lane, so much so that it almost hit my car on the left hand side as we drove side by side. I thought that the driver must be drunk, and was scared that he might hit me, so I sounded my horn. The man stared into his rear-view mirror as he drove, and he slowed down so that I was able to overtake him. I had joined the road at 30km/hr so he must have been driving really slowly. He was looking into his rear-view mirror so much that I got the impression that he was going to reverse. Once I had overtaken him, I noticed that the Fiat had yellow front headlights. Its exhaust pipe backfired loudly.'

Georges thought the driver's behaviour was strange: 'The driver was really worried about something; he seemed to want to stop and was transfixed by his rear-view mirror.'

Georges told detectives that the reason he noticed so much detail about the Fiat Uno was because his mother-in-law owns a similar car. 'It also had three stripes along the side of the white doors, like my mother-in-law's car. It also probably had a blue or green line at the door handle height and all along the car. I remember its rear lights being weak like on an old car, but I don't remember a broken or faulty light.'

Georges' wife, Sabine, was able to add more detail to her husband's description of the Fiat Uno and the driver's erratic behaviour.

'We were driving very slowly ... we noticed a white Fiat Uno, identical to my mother's. The man came out of the tunnel like a zombie. He seemed drunk, he was haggard. It seems strange that a driver coming out of a tunnel should not look in front of him. The car came close to our car as it was drifting across the road. The driver was looking behind using both mirrors. He didn't see us and he almost hit the front left of our car as he swerved right. My husband then tried to overtake him, but he swerved back into the left lane as if he was trying to stop us from passing him. He was zigzagging and not looking ahead. He only looked in his left and interior rear-view mirrors. He was leaning too, to see behind him, so much so that I thought he must be waiting for someone far behind him in the tunnel. The car stopped about 30 metres from the exit of the tunnel.

'The Fiat Uno was white, with two doors, a bit worse for wear but not particularly dirty. The driver was European, Mediterranean looking. His eyes were dark, and he had short dark brown hair. Aged between 35 and 40 years. In the back of the car there was a big dog with a long snout. It might have been a German Shepherd. It had a bright red or orange bandana or muzzle.'

The Fiat that the Dauzonnes reported seeing was heading out of Paris to the West. Furthermore, Georges thought the registration number could have been 78, which is the number given to cars registered in the Yvelines district, or 92, the number for the Hauts-de-Seine area to the west of Paris.[8] Stéphan ordered an intensive search of the area, which Commander Mulès oversaw. 'We concluded the direction the Fiat was heading led to those two départements in west Paris. Considering the time [00.26], we thought that this person was going home. So we searched all the registrations to find out who had the same type, make, model and colour of car. We checked more than 5,000 cars.

'We interviewed the owners of such cars one by one, every day, for three or four months. More than fifteen or twenty police inspectors personally went to check the cars in all the towns within these départements, but we found nothing.'[9]

---

[8] Ibid.

[9] These statements are quoted in Pontaut and Dupuis, pp. 182–7. A third person to claim to have seen a white Fiat Uno near the Alma tunnel at the time of the crash was a British lawyer, Gary Hunter, who was in a hotel room with his wife several hundred yards from the crash. He claimed to have heard the crash, and then seen a Fiat heading eastward at speed (in the opposite direction from Georges and Sabine Dauzonne) towards the centre of Paris a few minutes afterwards. He said this car was being pursued by a 'white Mercedes'. The French police decided Hunter's information was of no value, and did not take a statement from him.

At times over half of Martine Monteil's 110-strong Criminal Brigade were involved in the hunt for the Fiat with help from the *gendarmes*. Every owner of a white Fiat Uno in the Hauts-de-Seine area was required to report to Monteil's detectives with their car and relevant papers. Each was required to account for their whereabouts on the night of the tragedy. Their cars were closely examined for signs of damage or recent repair to the left rear bumper or left taillight. Any cars that had been resprayed were given particularly close scrutiny and garages were pressed for details of recent repairs on white Fiat Unos. As the hunt extended towards Christmas 1997, the scores of detectives involved muttered darkly about needles and haystacks, while many commentators derided the intensity of the effort being put into solving what many saw as a simple car crash.

Martine Monteil's detectives became very excited when they thought they may have found the mysterious Fiat in the Hauts-de-Seine region in November. It seemed that a Fiat owner, Le Van Thanh, must be their man. A second-generation Vietnamese immigrant, Le Van Thanh is a plumber who owned a 1987 Fiat Uno with a registration number of 92. Detectives established that his white Fiat had been sprayed red the day after the Alma tunnel crash by Thanh's brother in a suburb of Paris. Furthermore, the Fiat had a dog grille. Sabine Dauzonne told the police that the driver she saw fleeing the Alma tunnel had a dog in the back of the car.

The Crim swooped on Le Van Thanh on 13 November 1997. He was arrested and held for six hours. However, detectives realised very soon after they captured Thanh that he was not the man seen fleeing the Alma tunnel. The shocked plumber had a cast-iron alibi. At the time of the crash he had been working as a nightwatchman in Gennevilliers. He had clocked on for his job as a security guard at 19.00 on 30 August and clocked off at 07.00 on 31 August. By coincidence, the white paint on his Fiat did match the scratches found on the Mercedes. However the forensic tests at the IRCGN later confirmed that the left rear of his car had never been involved in an accident.

A disappointed Martine Monteil said, 'Yes, it was an extraordinary co-incidence. He was arrested, interviewed and released because he was innocent.'[10]

The failure of the French investigation to locate the white Fiat Uno or its driver was frustrating to Judge Stéphan, not least because he had no reliable eyewitnesses to the crash, and the driver's testimony could

---

[10] *Sunday Times*, 25 January 1998.

potentially be invaluable. However, the untraceable Fiat did not seem to be of enormous importance to Stéphan's team. Martine Monteil's detectives started to wind down their hunt for the car from the beginning of 1998, while keeping their file on the crash open. The IRCGN's forensic analysis of the Mercedes had indicated to Judge Stéphan and Martine Monteil's detectives that the Mercedes' 'brush' with the Fiat was not the determining cause of the crash. The entirety of the damage to the vehicle was caused exclusively by the impact with the thirteenth pillar of the Alma tunnel, apart from the scraping of the front right wing with a Fiat Uno. However, the Fiat was fast assuming a mythical status in the reporting of the crash around the world.

In January 1998, for example, an anonymous source 'close to the investigation' was quoted as saying, '. . . if they [the investigation] come up with a blank, doesn't that indicate even more thoroughly that whoever it was has secreted the vehicle? That makes it even more sinister.'[11]

The failure to find the Fiat or its driver is the most noticeable single failure of the French investigation into the crash. In fairness, it should be pointed out that the presence of the Fiat was established only because of the brilliance of the IRCGN's forensic team. Although the IRCGN also demonstrated to Judge Stéphan's satisfaction that the car did not play a determining role in the crash, the driver could have provided valuable first-hand testimony, and killed much of the errant speculation. By the time the investigation had made it clear that a white Fiat was being sought, nearly three weeks after the crash, virtually anything could have happened to the car or its driver. The incentive for its driver to identify himself and thus take his place in history as having been involved in the death of Diana, Princess of Wales, and Dodi Fayed was negligible. The driver presumably knew what the IRCGN boffins were later to establish: that he was grazed by the speeding Mercedes, and that he could have done nothing to prevent this happening.

Straightforward explanations to account for the failure of the Fiat driver to present himself to the police were far less appealing to much of the world's media than theories with sinister connotations. In Britain, some of the media followed Mohamed Fayed's spokesman, Michael Cole, in referring to the white Fiat Uno as the 'grassy knoll' of the investigation – an allusion to a 'second gunman' said to have shot John F Kennedy in 1963 from a 'grassy knoll' close to his car in the Dealy Plaza in Dallas.[12]

---

[11] *Sunday Times*, 25 January 1998.

[12] Live ITV broadcast, *Wednesday Night Live*, following *Diana – Secrets Behind the Crash*, 3 June 1998.

There is no evidence that a Fiat Uno was involved in the 'assassination' of Princess Diana, but the mystery of the unidentified Fiat will probably never be solved. It is possible that the driver of the Fiat fears that he may face prosecution. He may have been a criminal making his way home after committing a crime or have been drunk at the time. Perhaps his car was not insured, or he could have been returning home to his wife from a liaison with a mistress.

Any such reason could have caused the Fiat's owner to drive the car out of France, or to the bottom of a lake. After all, the French authorities took nearly three weeks after the accident to start looking for the car. Many similar reasons, equally plausible and mundane, could have given the driver good reason not to identify himself. His failure to do so, however, gave conspiracy theorists, and those hostile to the French investigation, ample scope to attack Judge Stéphan's probe. Commander Mulès commented, 'Let us not forget, the driver of the Fiat Uno was the victim of the crash, not the one at fault. We see how the press killed Henri Paul a second time – he was already dead, but they killed him socially as well by tarnishing and bringing down his reputation. Imagine what could go through the mind of [the Fiat driver] who may have had a bit to drink, or whatever. If he went to the police, what would he become? He would become the Princess's killer!'[13]

As the Fiat remained unidentified, attention switched to the man whose autopsy showed that he was drunk when he crashed Princess Diana's and Dodi Fayed's Mercedes.

The notion that Henri Paul was *not* drunk when he died became essential to most conspiracy theories. It is self-evident that, if the results of the autopsy on Paul are accepted, none of the conspiracies even begin to work unless Paul is characterised as a kamikaze driver who tanked himself up to kill Diana and Dodi. Even this does not stand up when Dodi's late instruction to Paul to drive the Mercedes instead of his regular chauffeur, Philippe Dourneau, is taken into account. No one, including Henri Paul, knew he was to drive the Mercedes until Dodi instructed him to shortly before the party left the Ritz.

The theory that Paul was not drunk was based on the following set of assumptions. After the 'assassination' of the three victims in the car, known in conspiracy parlance as a 'vehicular homicide', the samples of a sober Paul's blood were switched by secret-service agents tasked with covering up Princess Diana's murder on behalf of their governments. In

---

[13] Author's interview with Commander Mulès, 2003.

this way, the world would believe that Diana and Dodi died as a result of a drink-drive accident, and no one would ever know that they were actually assassinated.

Such theories may have their place in the novels of Raymond Chandler, John Le Carré or Frederick Forsyth, but to suggest that such scenarios could explain the deaths of the Princess of Wales and Dodi Fayed stretches credulity beyond breaking point. Assuming that Jacques Chirac's government alone is not being accused of murdering Diana and Dodi nine hours after they touched down at Le Bourget, such scenarios require the complicity of at least two governments and two sets of secret services, plus the acquiescence of the French medical service and judiciary.

Executive Intelligence Review of Washington has proved to itself, but nobody else, that this is the case. It claimed less than three months after the crash that it was 'beyond a doubt that it was high-level officials of the French Socialist government – remnants of the Fascist Mitterand machine – who personally carried out the murder of Princess Diana, who otherwise would have survived the place de L'Alma tunnel crash'.[14]

Other conspiracy theorists cited rumours about the high level of carbon monoxide found in Henri Paul's blood as indicating that something sinister had happened, either to Henri Paul or to his blood samples.

Conspiracy theorists argued that, had Paul really had such high levels of carbon monoxide in his blood, he could not have functioned at all, let alone driven a car. Therefore, it followed that the blood samples tested were not Henri Paul's, or that he had been poisoned while in the car. By failing to recognise this, Judge Stéphan's investigation was thus a cover-up rather than a quest for the truth. France's fierce medical and legal secrecy laws combined with some flawed journalism to produce an enduring but misleading controversy over the level of carbon monoxide found in Paul's blood.

Leaks concerning the level of carbon monoxide in Henri Paul's blood when he crashed started to appear in the media at the beginning of 1998. The authors of Death of a Princess, Sancton and MacLeod, noted in February 1998 that tests on Henri Paul's corpse had shown an 'unusually high level of carbon monoxide' in his blood.[15]

There had, in fact, been two tests carried out on Henri Paul samples at TOXLAB which established the level of carbon monoxide in his blood. They were carried out by Dr Gilbert Pépin. One showed a level

---

[14] EIR, 21 November 1997.
[15] Death of a Princess, pp. 238–9.

of 12.8 per cent carboxyhaemoglobin saturation – this was the proportion of iron-carrying pigment that had combined with carbon monoxide in Paul's blood to form carboxyhaemoglobin. A nonsmoker has about 1 per cent of carbon monoxide in his/her blood, whereas smokers will routinely have a level of 8–10 per cent or more if they have recently smoked. Someone with 10–20 per cent would be likely to have headaches and suffer from lethargy. As smokers habitually have a level of 10 per cent Pépin described the 12.8 per cent result as having 'no significance' to the enquiry because it had 'no chemical incidence'.[16]

The other test showed a level of 20.7 per cent. As this result seeped out from the files of the enquiry, misleading assessments emerged. The conspiracy wing of the Diana death industry pounced on the 20.7 per cent finding, and then moved into overdrive in the middle of 1998.

The ITV documentary *Diana – Secrets Behind the Crash* – which was first shown in Britain and then sold around the world – brought the result of the 20.7 per cent test into the homes of 12.5 million British viewers who watched it on 3 June 1998. In the film, the British Carbon Monoxide Support Group and two appropriately qualified doctors, including a behavioural psychologist, were introduced to say that, if Paul had such a high level when he died, he would not have been able to function properly or able to judge distance or time. Pursuing this particular thought, Dr Alistair Hay, introduced as a Carbon Monoxide Expert, told viewers that carbon monoxide disperses at the rate of 'about half every four or five hours'. So, in other words, the level of 20.7 per cent found during Paul's autopsy could have been 40 per cent several hours earlier when he died. Had Henri Paul really had 40 per cent carbon monoxide in his system, it would have been impossible for him to function at all according to Dr Hay, let alone drive a car. A level of 20–30 per cent produces strong headaches, and a level of 30–40 per cent would cause nausea, vertigo and vomiting.[17]

Pictures from the Ritz hotel security cameras showed Paul walking around, apparently normally. The pictures not only appeared to belie the finding that Paul was drunk and drugged when he died, but also showed that he certainly did not appear to have been suffering from 40 per cent carbon-monoxide poisoning. In this way the validity of the tests on the blood sample was called into question.

The presenter of the film, ITN's royal correspondent, Nicholas Owen, suggested, 'It's impossible to overstate the significance of that blood

---

[16] Author's researcher's interview with Dr Gilbert Pépin.
[17] Author's researcher's interview with Dr Gilbert Pépin.

sample [sic]. From the very start, it's defined our views of Henri Paul and virtually all our thinking – until now. But what if it is not as reliable as we first thought? The more I learn about this story, the less clear it becomes. The blood sample seems – well – suspect . . .'

According to Owen, 'the mystery deepens further' when the autopsy's evidence that Paul was three to four times over the legal limit to drive in France is put together with the 20.7 per cent carbon-monoxide level. Dr Hay agreed that the 'mystery' described by Owen was in fact 'a bit of an enigma', presumably because he had not been fully informed of the results of both of the carbon-monoxide tests.

The reality was somewhat more prosaic. By failing to incorporate both tests, ITV had told only half the story. It had also failed to report the assessments of the French experts who had actually carried out the tests. ITV preferred instead to seek the opinions of British experts who made their assessments in good faith, but on the basis of incomplete information.

As a result of the controversy that had blown up over the leaking of the information about the higher level of carbon-monoxide – and the partial and misleading assessments that had been made public about it – Judge Stéphan commissioned Lecomte and Pépin to jointly produce a complementary *expertise*. Their task was to assess the significance, or otherwise, of the 20.7 per cent level of carbon-monoxide found in Henri Paul's cardiac blood. Ironically in the context of the fuss that ensued, it is not standard procedure for a driver's carbon-monoxide levels to be assessed at all after a car crash. However, when she conducted Paul's autopsy, Professeur Lecomte was as keen as Judge Stéphan was to be seen to be conducting a comprehensive operation. Now she had to explain the results.

This carboxyhaemoglobin *expertise* was completed on 16 October 1998. It stated that the test which showed the high carbon-monoxide level of 20.7 per cent was from a sample of Paul's blood taken from his heart and lung area. However, the test, which showed the lower level of 12.8 per cent, was on blood extracted from Paul's femoral vein in the groin area. Averaging the results of their tests (20.7 per cent and 12.8 per cent), and subtracting an allowance for an average heavy smoker's carbon-monoxide level (10 per cent), the level of carbon-monoxide in Paul's blood *not* attributable to a heavy smoker was 6.75 per cent.

That Paul was smoking on the night had been reported by the photographers who had seen him tapping cigars as he spoke to them at the front of the Ritz between 23.00 and midnight on 30 August. Furthermore, Kez Wingfield had told the French investigation that

Henri Paul was puffing at small cigars while he was with them in the bar Vendôme. Wingfield had given this as one reason why he and Trevor Rees-Jones, both nonsmokers, had moved upstairs to await the departure of Diana and Dodi.

Pépin and Lecomte's joint *expertise* found an unsensational explanation for the 20.7 per cent found in the cardiac blood: in addition to the level attributed to a smoker who was puffing cigars shortly before he died, Paul's last gulp of air, taken in the wrecked Mercedes, could have contained a sufficient quantity of carbon monoxide to permeate blood from the heart, near to the lungs. However, the carbon monoxide would not have had time to reach the femoral vein, from which the 12.8 per cent sample was extracted. Paul's heart stopped beating fractionally after impact with the thirteenth pillar. Blood would have stopped flowing through his system after he took his last breath. Thus the carbon monoxide found in Paul's cardiac blood would not have shown up in the blood taken from his veins.

Pépin and Lecomte cited the Autoliv company, which produces airbags and seatbelt 'pre-tensioners', in support of their findings about the level of carbon-monoxide. Autoliv told them 'that the quantity of carbon-monoxide produced in a car by its release on brutal impact, of two airbags and two seat belt systems, is between one and several grammes. In other words, between ten and several dozen times more than the necessary quantity of carbon-monoxide to produce a level of 20.7 per cent in the blood.' The *expertise* concluded that, 'logically, the carbon-monoxide found in M Henri Paul's blood comes from this source.'

This unremarkable result from Professeur Lecomte and Dr Pépin's perspective was contained in a one-and-a-half-page summary submitted to Stéphan at the end of 1998. It was not of any concern to Judge Stéphan. He had commissioned the Lecomte/Pépin *expertise* to ensure that he had not left this particular stone unturned.

This *expertise* was not, however, beyond reproach. Dr Murray Mackay, professor emeritus of Transport Safety and one of the world's leading crash investigators, studied it at my invitation. The Birmingham University academic has studied thousands of crashes throughout the world, and is familiar with the phenomenon of crash victims inhaling carbon monoxide. He was not satisfied with the explanation from Lecomte and Pépin. Indeed, Dr Mackay said he thought that the *expertise* was 'totally misleading', suspecting that the Autoliv quote had been used 'out of context'. Mackay checked with Mercedes, and with Autoliv in Sweden. He established that the airbags used in the type of car in which

Paul died do not contain any carbon-monoxide, and the pre-tensioners only a 'tiny amount'. Thus, Mackay did not accept the findings of the *expertise*. He argued that it would not have been possible for Paul to have inhaled a sufficient quantity of gas, as the autopsy had established that he had died instantly.

Despite disagreeing with the reasons given in the *expertise*, Dr Mackay was not troubled by the results of the original tests. His view is that both levels of carbon monoxide found by the French scientists in Henri Paul's blood were 'perfectly explainable and unremarkable'. Mackay felt that mundane factors, such as Paul's intake of tobacco shortly before his death, were the most likely causes of the 20.7 per cent reading.[18]

Millions of British TV viewers were suitably baffled when they watched *Diana – Secrets Behind the Crash*. The film informed its audience of only the higher of the two carbon-monoxide tests. The single result it used became a central 'mystery' of the crash that killed Princess Diana. In a poll conducted immediately after the film, and published on 6 June, an astonishing 95 per cent of 9,877 *Mirror* readers who called the paper's 'Diana hotline' thought 'there was a conspiracy'; 93 per cent believed that Henri Paul's blood sample 'was switched'.

Ninety-two per cent of those polled also believed in François Levistre's flash-before-the-crash theory, which had featured heavily in the film. A number of critics who saw the ITV programme ridiculed it, but the programme was clearly flowing with the tide of the public opinion it had helped to create. The poll further found that 97 per cent of respondents believed the crash was 'not just an accident'.[19]

The 93 per cent of the *Mirror* poll who thought that the blood samples had been 'switched' was significant. Rumours that ITV would argue that the samples had been switched had proved unfounded. ITV had shied away from actually saying as much in its film. However, the implication was clearly made when Nicholas Owen proclaimed the blood sample – once again, note the use of the singular – to be 'suspect' and viewers had understood this. Aware that the French investigation's results were drawn from more than one sample, Frederick Forsyth disparaged the ITV film's implication that the samples had been 'switched'. Forsyth wrote in the *Spectator*, '. . . just how many spooks are we supposed to employ to moon about Paris clutching phials of doctored blood of (amazingly) just the right blood group and the right age since the death? And why has it taken ten months for these fantasies

---

[18] Author's interview with Dr Murray Mackay.
[19] All poll figures from the *Mirror*, 6 June 1998.

to emerge? . . . it is doubtful the French will dignify the allegations with action.'

Peter Vanezis, Regius Professor of Forensic Medicine and Science at Glasgow University who had travelled to Paris immediately after the crash for Mohamed Fayed, pointed out that it was biologically impossible for Paul's blood samples to have had carbon-monoxide added to them. Carbon-monoxide has to be inhaled to enter the bloodstream – it cannot simply be injected.[20]

There is not a shred of evidence that Princess Diana, Dodi Fayed and Henri Paul were murdered. The flash-before-the-crash yarn is fantasy springing from the untrustworthy lips of a *mythomane*. The white Fiat Uno was not an instrument in Diana's 'asassination'. All the forensic evidence suggests it played a minor role, if any, in the crash. That Henri Paul was 'poisoned' has been proved not to be the case, and nobody seriously believes that MI6 swapped the samples taken from Henri Paul's blood for doctored specimens.

---

[20] Author's interview with Professor Peter Vanezis.

10. THE MYTH MAKER

'Top-secret telexes, tapes and never before seen photographs will prove that Princess Diana and Dodi were assassinated in cold blood – and British and American intelligence agencies worked together to cover up their murder. That's what Dodi's grieving father, Mohamed Al Fayed told a Washington D.C. court . . .'

US Star, 28 February 1999

Kez Wingfield broke the news that Princess Diana was dead, as Mohamed Fayed disembarked from his helicopter at Le Bourget airport at 04.55 on 31 August 1997. 'I hope the British government is happy now' were the first words his boss uttered. Fayed had been told that Dodi, Henri Paul and Trevor Rees-Jones had died in the crash before he left England. The news of Diana's death was the final, devastating blow.

Kez Wingfield had been phoned with the news as he waited for Fayed to land at Le Bourget. The bodyguard put Fayed's bitter reaction to the news of the Princess's death down to grief, an emotional spasm from a bereaved father. Wingfield also knew that the only reason he and Trevor Rees-Jones had permitted Henri Paul to drive the Mercedes was that Dodi had decreed that it should be so, and he had told them that his father had approved the plan.

What Wingfield did not realise as he accompanied the distraught father into Paris was that his boss's remark about the British government anticipated the start of what would become Fayed's campaign to influence world opinion about Princess Diana's last days and how she came to die. By the time Fayed flew back to England with Dodi's body twelve hours later, the process of converting the dead Princess into an honorary Fayed had begun. By 1999, Fayed had progressed to accusing British intelligence, under Tony Blair's new Labour government, of killing his son and the Princess.

The result of Fayed's actions, which started in the bleak early hours of 31 August, was to take the world's eyes away from his hotel, and its drunken head of security who killed his son and Diana, Princess of Wales. Fayed was initially seen as a tragic figure, the 'grieving father'. The crash had simultaneously robbed the proud Egyptian of Dodi, and of his ultimate ambition of seeing his son marry British royalty. Fayed the businessman, the international wheeler-dealer whose empire, standing and family were being challenged, responded in the way he knew best: by going onto the attack. France's *secret de l'instruction*, and *secret medical*, meant that Judge Stéphan's investigation and the emergency and hospital services were required by law to remain silent. Fayed possessed a virtual monopoly on information, and on the personnel who knew what had happened on the fatal night, and, as everything he said was given great significance in a hungry media, Fayed was clearly in a strong position to influence the way in which every detail of Diana's last day was reported. As a civil party to the French investigation, Fayed would receive regular bulletins from Judge Stéphan's file as it grew to 6,800 pages in length. Even before he left France on 31 August with Dodi's coffin, Mohamed Fayed had sent his top officials into action.

At 16.30 on the day of the crash, the president of the Ritz, Frank Klein, and his deputy, Claude Roulet, presented themselves at the headquarters of the French police at 36 quai des Orfèvres. They told Patrick Riou, the director of the Paris judiciary police, that they had reason to believe that there were 'suspicious circumstances' surrounding the crash. The results of the autopsy on Paul had not been released, but it would have been surprising if either official had not known of rumours circulating the Ritz that Paul could have been drunk before he left their hotel.

The details of the 'suspicious circumstances' alleged by the Ritz officials have never been made known by Riou or his office. Mohamed Fayed, by contrast, seemed – to the outsider – to speak about little else since the tests on Henri Paul proved that he was not only drunk but also drugged when he crashed. As he sought to defend what his spokesman described as 'the indefensible' – Henri Paul's drunkenness – Fayed's one major advantage was his monopoly on information about Princess Diana's last days, which became the biggest-running story in the world for eighteen months after her death. As a veteran of the battle for Harrods, Fayed was engaging journalists on terrain that he was much more familiar with than they were.

Fayed could provide selected employees to act as sources for soft features about Diana's time in his family's care for the British tabloids and the American press. Cooks, butlers and caretakers all had their stories of serving the Princess splashed over the tabloids, as did Trevor Rees-Jones. Providing these interviews achieved one aim for Fayed – to polish the impression of a princess in love with his son, and planning her future with his family. Later these stories, many of which were embellished so as to render them unrecognisable to their sources, became essential components in Fayed's various 'conspiracy' theories. Fayed had apparently little difficulty in restoring relations with newspaper editors whose cousins had pursued his son and the Princess into the Alma tunnel. As well as being a grieving father, Fayed was also seeking to protect his personal and business interests and he could afford to hire the best available people to help him.

The head of Fayed's French legal team, Georges Kiejman, has a heavyweight pedigree. Nicknamed the 'pit bull', he had been a justice minister in President Mitterrand's government. After the Alma tunnel crash, Kiejman's first target was the paparazzi. As soon as the prosecutor's office announced that Paul had been drunk when he died, he went on the offensive.

A statement by one of Kiejman's legal team, Bernard Dartevelle, described two photographs 'confiscated by Paris police'. The lawyer said the pictures showed that Henri Paul was blinded by a flash of light during the chase towards the Alma tunnel. Dartevelle said, 'Henri Paul was dazzled by the flash, while Trevor Rees-Jones was lowering the sun visor to protect himself from the photographers, and Princess Diana was hiding her face with her arms.

'One sees very distinctly the driver dazzled by a flash. One sees very distinctly the bodyguard at his side [Trevor Rees-Jones] who, with a brisk gesture, lowers the visor to protect himself from the flash, and one sees very distinctly Princess Diana turning to look behind the vehicle, and one sees very distinctly the yellow headlights of a motorcycle.

'The photo, taken before the first photo of the accident, shows the Mercedes taken from very close ... A driver, who is maybe a photographer, and a motorcyclist, also perhaps a photographer, are very directly implicated in this accident.'[1]

The photograph actually came from a roll of film taken by Jacques Langevin at the back of the Ritz before the Mercedes departed. In his statement to Martine Monteil's detectives, Langevin described exactly how he had taken that particular photograph as the party emerged from the Ritz. 'I took some photos of Princess Diana in the car. She sat on my side [of the car]. She put her arms up against the flashes. As we, therefore, couldn't see anything, I moved in front of the car and took a picture from straight on. The car left.'[2]

Furthermore, Langevin told the police he had not pursued the Mercedes. He chanced upon the accident in the Alma tunnel while on his way home a considerable time later. Thus the photographs cited by Dartevelle did not 'directly implicate' Jacques Langevin in the accident. After the allegation that they did directly implicate the photographer had been relayed around the world, Dartevelle acknowledged that there

---

[1] Associated Press, 10 September 1997.
[2] Quoted in Pontaut and Dupuis, pp. 67–8.

was a significant time lapse between the two photos he had been referring to.

Michael Cole later conjured one of the enduring images of the tragedy – presumably on the basis of a briefing given to him, as he was in England when the Mercedes crashed: 'It was like a stagecoach, surrounded by Indians, but instead of firing arrows they were firing these lights into the eyes of the people . . .'[3]

The evidence gathered by the police proved that this was not an accurate description of what happened immediately before the accident. In all of the rolls of film seized by the police, there were no photographs that had been taken between the place de la Concorde and the Alma tunnel – the last kilometre of the fatal journey. The only person to claim to have seen anything that would have supported Cole's description was François Levi.

This lack of photographs taken during the last phase of the chase was, in fact, a crucial piece of evidence in the paparazzi's defence. It supported the contention by some of those arrested that they could not keep up with the Mercedes after Paul had jumped the lights in the place de la Concorde, and had sped off along the cours La-Reine.

Fayed's Director of Security was John Macnamara, who had worked at Scotland Yard for 28 years, rising to the rank of Detective Superintendent in the Fraud Squad. Macnamara was in overall charge of the efforts to pile up further evidence against the paparazzi as the final preparations were made for Princess Diana's funeral. His immediate target, like Cole's, was the weekend papers. *The Times*'s Paris office received a call from Macnamara's office late in the afternoon of Friday 5 September. Journalists were told that a valuable Bulgari necklace worth £250,000 had disappeared from the wrecked Mercedes. The *Sunday Times*'s Paris correspondent, Kirsty Lang, was intrigued by the story, and immediately tried to follow it up. The clear implication was that the paparazzi who had been the first to surround the car could have been responsible for the theft. If true, the story could have made the front page of Britain's biggest-selling broadsheet Sunday newspaper the day after Diana's funeral. In the court of public opinion it would have been a sensational nail in the coffin of the paparazzi – corpse robbers as well as lunatic media outriders responsible for turning Diana into the 'most hunted woman of the modern age', as her brother Charles had described her in his memorable funeral ovation.

Scouring all the photos she could find of Diana on her last night, Lang could see no such necklace around her neck. The *secret de l'instruction*

---

[3] Agence France Presse, 1 September 1997.

made the job of confirming Macnamara's tip even more difficult, as the French police were not allowed to comment on any aspect of the case. To her own surprise, Kirsty Lang did manage to get through to a police spokesman, late on the Friday night.

'I said to the spokesman, "I know you can't say anything, but please can you just tell me: has a complaint of theft been lodged with you [as a result of the crash in the Alma tunnel]?" He said, "No, I'm sorry, I can't tell you that." "Not even that?" "No, nothing, no comment." '[4]

Faced with the prospect of running a story that she could not confirm, and unable to establish any corroborating evidence, Lang advised against running the piece. The story did, however, find its way into the *Sunday Times* on the day after Diana's funeral. The story appeared on the paper's inside pages under the headline, 'FRENCH POLICE DENY GEM THEFT FROM CRASH CAR'. It led with a denial by the French police that the theft had taken place, rather than the implication that the paparazzi were corpse robbers.

The timing of this story in the *Sunday Times* was significant. Sunday papers are at their most frantic on a normal Friday evening. On the eve of Diana's funeral, as every paper rushed to publish what it hoped would be historic editions, each was hypersensitive to any new piece of information that might provide an advantage over a competitor.

Kirsty Lang's judgement in Paris was vindicated only much later. No report of a missing necklace has ever been received by the French police. Papers that ran stories stating that jewels had been stolen from the wrecked Mercedes had been conned – early victims of Fayed's disinformation campaign against the paparazzi.

At the same time, Michael Cole and Paul Handley-Greaves were planning a press conference for the eve of Diana's funeral, just as Judge Stéphan started his slow probe into how Princess Diana came to die while she was in Fayed's care.

The Princess of Wales had died while with Fayed's son, and while being driven from his hotel by his head of security. Despite his grief, Fayed had to try something to avoid going down in history as the man whose employee drove the car which killed his son and the Princess of Wales. It is worth examining the controversial Harrods' press conference in some detail because what was said became the template for many of the Fayed myths.

It came at a peculiarly sensitive time during a week of unprecedented national mourning which was reflected around the world. Many people

---

[4] Author's interview with Kirsty Lang.

were still in shock, unable to believe how a woman in the prime of her life had met such an untimely and unforeseen end. The French blackout on any news other than Paul's drunken state meant that people had either to accept that Diana had died in the most mundane circumstances or seek other explanations. The mass ranks of the world's media crowded into Harrods to hear what Michael Cole had to say, before communicating with a world that had appeared to become almost desperate for answers.

The justification for the press conference – which Michael Cole said, 'we would have preferred to have postponed or never have called at all' – was held to be Fayed's 'personal anguish', which had been increased by the media's 'unfounded allegations' of the Mercedes' last journey. Reports on the crash in the immediate aftermath had been voluminous and expansive, some of them very inaccurate. The Mercedes was erroneously reported in the British press to have been travelling at over 100 m.p.h., and to have been an S-600 model; Stéphan's investigation was to find that the Mercedes S-280 was travelling between 74 m.p.h. and 97 m.p.h. when it entered the tunnel, and between 64 m.p.h. and 70 m.p.h. on impact with the pillar. Working on the false assumption that Mohamed Fayed had provided an armoured Mercedes for his son and the Princess of the kind he insists on travelling in himself, it was reported that the car was armoured; the Etoile Limousine Mercedes was not armoured. These inaccuracies clearly irritated Fayed; but in correcting these stories, he introduced errors of his own.

Cole then gave an account of Fayed's visit to see Diana's body and quoted the words that set another fiction in motion: 'she looked peaceful and serene'. His address also initiated the 'last-words' fiction. He read out the first of several versions of how Fayed had come to hear what they were. None of them has any evidence other than Fayed's word to support them. His remarks about the ring Mohamed bought for Diana on Dodi's behalf, subsequently heavily elaborated by Fayed himself, would start worldwide speculation that the Princess was engaged to Dodi when she died.

'What that ring meant we shall probably never know,' said Cole. Fayed's subsequent distortions would nourish the transformation of the ring into an engagement ring. The 'endless speculation' would then become an important element in further speculation that the Princess and Dodi could have been the victims of an assassination by British intelligence, because a Fayed was on the brink of marrying the mother of the two young heirs to the British throne.

Responding to heavy criticism after the press conference, Cole insisted that everything he had said had been said in good faith, and that he believed what he said to be the case.[5] The passage of time has revealed that much of what he read out, in characteristically magisterial tones, did not square with the facts that would be established by Judge Stéphan's enquiry. One of the major purposes of the press conference was to challenge the French blood tests on Henri Paul. Fayed had been particularly angered by headlines that had appeared all over the world following the publication of the blood tests, which had shown that Paul had been drunk when he died. Michael Cole drew attention to one typical British headline: 'DI'S DRIVER WAS DRUNK AS A PIG'.

'We are just trying to demonstrate the fact that this man did not have 1.75 millilitres of alcohol in his blood,' said Paul Handley-Greaves. Handley-Greaves was Fayed's head of close protection, and the last time he had been seen in public, he had been piloting Diana and Dodi as they relaxed in a small craft in Saint-Tropez. The bespectacled security chief talked the press through a heavily edited video of Diana and Dodi's two-and-a-half-hour stay in the Ritz hotel. The version presented was 26 minutes long.

Although the last pictures of Princess Diana alive caught the attention of the world, Mohamed Fayed's main purpose in releasing the tape appeared to be to attempt to allow Handley-Greaves to prove that the Ritz hotel's head of security was not drunk despite the scientific evidence to the contrary. Handley-Greaves had been in Britain at the time of the accident. However, he said he had since been to Paris and spoken to 'everybody in the [video] pictures'. He told the press, 'We are satisfied that the accounts of Henri Paul's demeanour are accurate, and those accounts are that he was sober, he didn't smell of alcohol, his gait was steady.' Handley-Greaves drew on accounts by Ritz staff such as François Tendil, and Diana's bodyguard, Kez Wingfield. The accounts of Ritz bar staff who were to tell Judge Stéphan that Paul appeared drunk were not relayed to the press conference, nor was the widely held hotel view that Paul had a *penchant pour la boisson*.

The description of Paul's activity in the Ritz immediately before he drove Princess Diana and Dodi to their deaths was highly selective. Handley-Greaves said that Paul 'popped into . . . the bar where . . . my security people [Rees-Jones and Wingfield] were having a quick meal, and that was the closest he got to the bar'. What he did not say was that the Vendôme bar bill showed that the bodyguards' meal had included two alcoholic drinks. These had both been consumed by Paul.

Further security-camera video pictures showed Kez Wingfield in conversation with Princess Diana and Dodi outside the Imperial Suite.

---

[5] *Guardian*, 13 September 1997.

This conversation was said by Handley-Greaves to be about 'the amount of paparazzi and the concern that the Princess had that something would happen . . . This is the discussion concerning the paparazzi, the motorcycles, the reckless driving that had taken place by the paparazzi . . . preceding their visit to the Ritz.'

Precisely what was actually being discussed at this stage is not known, but there was no mention by Handley-Greaves that the unorthodox plan to leave the Ritz was Dodi's. The bodyguard's dissent was not mentioned, and neither was Dodi's reluctant acceptance of even one bodyguard travelling with himself and the Princess.

It had been widely reported that the photographers had claimed that Henri Paul had taunted them as he wandered outside the front of the Ritz before departure, and some had said that he had shown signs of drunkenness. The photographers had confirmed this in their sworn statements to the police. Handley-Greaves told the press conference that this had not happened, saying that Paul had not been outside the hotel. 'The furthest he got was the revolving door . . . to check on the state of the paparazzi at the front of the hotel. He never actually left the hotel.'

According to some eyewitnesses, this was not true. Paul did leave the front of the hotel according to sworn statements by several who were present. Furthermore, some of the photographers who were at the back of the Ritz state that he cried out to them as well as he left the hotel with Princess Diana's party. However, the selection of Ritz video pictures shown at the press conference of Princess Diana leaving via the back of the hotel was designed to show that 'there were no paparazzi in the immediate area', in Handley-Greaves's words. If that statement had been accurate it would have undermined the paparazzi's claim that Paul had taunted them before he left on the fateful journey. The obvious implication was that the paparazzi charged with involuntary homicide had been lying about Henri Paul's behaviour.

Michael Cole had told the press conference, 'You will remember that it was reported as a matter of fact that Henri Paul taunted the paparazzi as he drove away saying they would never catch him or words to that effect. You will see from the evidence that there were no paparazzi in the immediate vicinity when M Paul drove away, and that he drove off in quite a normal way.'

The time lapse on the video made any assessment of the car's speed very difficult, as the departing Mercedes started to exit the screen in one frame, and had completely left by the next. So the video pictures neither supported nor contradicted Cole's description of the car departing in 'quite a normal way' or Handley-Greaves's subsequent description of it pulling away 'quite sedately'. However, the absence of paparazzi in the pictures of the doomed party leaving the Ritz did appear to support Cole's claim that they were not present, and thus they must have been lying about Henri Paul's taunts and, indeed, the speed at which the car left. The video tape was also mute, so any exchanges that had taken place could not have been heard.

Handley-Greaves described the party leaving the hotel: 'Here we see Henri Paul walking out . . . The group getting into the vehicle, Trevor Rees-Jones getting into the front right-hand side, Henri Paul jumping into the driving seat, the Princess is in the rear, right-hand side behind Trevor Rees-Jones, Mr Dodi obviously behind the driver . . .'

Handley-Greaves then pointed out a blurred individual on the screen who appeared immediately after the Mercedes had left: 'This gentleman reported at the time, and he obviously had a good view of the street, there were no paparazzi in the immediate area, although he did report seeing somebody at the very far end, about 120 metres hence talking into either a mobile phone or a hand-held radio.'

It was not clear from viewing the Ritz video who the indistinct figure was. Actually he was the 'vehicle jockey', Frédéric Lucard, who had just handed the keys of the Mercedes to Henri Paul. He was the person responsible for bringing the car from the underground car park to the rear exit of the Ritz. Lucard had not spoken to Handley-Greaves. Had he done so, Lucard would have been able to inform Handley-Greaves that photographers were standing at the rear of the Ritz as Diana left: 'There were three photographers on the side of the street waiting close to the car and they were waiting for the exit of the Princess.' He would also have told him that Paul sped off along the rue Cambon: 'He put his foot down'.[6]

Lucard also says he did not see anybody talking into a mobile phone or a hand-held radio. This phrase was to set off several lines of conspiracy 'thinking', including the notion that secret-service agents were staking out the back of the hotel with mobile communications in preparation for a 'vehicular homicide' in the Alma tunnel. Whomever Handley-Greaves did talk to, it was not the man he pointed at in the video at the press conference.

It is possible that Handley-Greaves had spoken to Philippe 'Niels' Siegel, a director of Etoile Limousine. Siegel told the police that he had brought the Mercedes S-280 to the back of the Ritz for Henri Paul. Lucard was unaware that Siegel was even in the hotel on the night of 30/31 August. In his statement, Siegel had made no mention of the

---

[6] Author's interview with Frédéric Lucard.

photographers. Siegel's testimony also misled Martine Monteil's detectives. For nearly eight months after the crash, the investigators had no reason to suppose that the man who had performed the insignificant task of bringing Diana's car to the rue Cambon for Henri Paul was anyone other than 'Niels' Siegel. Lucard's evidence would blow a large hole in accounts of the departure of the Mercedes from the hotel. Most importantly, Lucard was the first Ritz employee to support the paparazzi's claim that Paul had taunted them before he set off. The photographers standing at the back of the Ritz had told police that they heard him call out, 'You won't catch me.' Encouragingly for them, Lucard gave Stéphan's investigation the same account: 'Henri Paul said, "Don't try to follow us, you'll never catch us." '[7]

Frédéric Lucard did not make a statement to the investigation until 27 April 1998. On a drizzly spring afternoon, the 28-year-old law student, wearing a full-length raincoat, arrived to see Martine Monteil's detectives in the Palais de Justice. For reasons he did not fully understand, Lucard was giving his evidence well after nearly 100 other members of the Ritz hotel's staff. He had been expecting to be called to give evidence since the night of the tragedy. Ritz staffers, including musicians, pastry cooks, bar staff and security personnel, had given statements to Martine Monteil's Criminal Brigade. Lucard had been told by Jean-François Musa, a director of Etoile Limousine that he would be called to give evidence in due course. On the night of the tragedy it was Musa who had ordered Lucard to fetch the car for Henri Paul.

Until the summer of 1997, Lucard had been a part-time chauffeur with Etoile Limousine to earn the extra money he needed to put himself through the final stages of his law qualifications. He left Etoile in June 1997, and started working as a part-time 'vehicle jockey' for the Ritz. His qualification enabled him to drive all the chauffeur-driven cars in the Ritz car park, including the large, powerful Mercedes that the Etoile company rented to clients. Lucard did not know when he spoke to Martine Monteil that someone else, 'Niels' Siegel, a director of Etoile Limousine, had claimed to have delivered the car on the night.

While Michael Cole and Paul Handley-Greaves were talking to the press, John Macnamara was approaching the press, too, about the Bulgari necklace being stolen from the wrecked Mercedes. Targetting the paparazzi was one key objective but, once it had been proved by French scientists that Paul was drunk when he died, Fayed's central objective was to discredit these findings. The press conference is the best example

---

[7] Author's interview with Frédéric Lucard.

of how Fayed's virtual monopoly on information about Princess Diana's last day served to deflect any blame from his organisation, and towards the photographers, some of whom had been arrested and charged with 'involuntary manslaughter'. It was extremely difficult for the journalists present to challenge Fayed's head of close protection during his presentation. The Ritz had barred all journalists from its premises after the crash, and the French police had released no information about the crash other than the findings of the autopsy on Henri Paul.

The press conference was part of a process that was to continue throughout Judge Stéphan's investigation. The court of public opinion threatened to reach its judgement on the crash that killed Princess Diana long before any French court was convened to assess the guilt or otherwise of the paparazzi, and Fayed was determined to sway its verdict in his favour. The danger from Fayed's point of view was that the truth of the tragedy – the unalterable fact of Henri Paul's drunkenness and excessive speed – would determine the verdict on why the Princess of Wales died. Once Judge Stéphan reached his conclusion, it was possible that Diana's family would be able to sue Fayed, so diversionary stories about the crash became a staple Fayed tactic. The Fiat Uno story is a very good illustration of this approach. By getting people to focus upon the most widely known acknowledged failure of the French investigation, Fayed's interjections served only to distract attention from Henri Paul's drunkenness.

The evidence rules out the possibility that the Fiat could have been part of a 'vehicular homicide' scheme by MI6, or anybody else. The missing Fiat was simply 'brushed' by the speeding Mercedes as it hurled into the thirteenth pillar of the Alma tunnel. But still Fayed was determined to keep the Fiat in the public mind. In January 1998, the story of the Criminal Brigade's swoop on Le Van Thanh made a full page in the *Sunday Times* complete with pictures of the unfortunate plumber, his Fiat and his dog. The raid had, in fact, occurred in November 1997, and Le Van Thanh had almost immediately been ruled out of the investigation. The summary of progress made in Judge Stéphan's investigation was circulated to the civil parties in confidence at the end of the year, including details of Le Van Thanh. Within weeks the *Sunday Times* had splashed the details of the Criminal Brigade's raid on Le Van Thanh. An entirely innocent man who had been briefly wrongly detained had found himself featured in Britain's biggest-selling broadsheet Sunday newspaper.

The spectre of the Fiat Uno arose again in mid-February 1998, this time through a team of private detectives Fayed had hired in France.

Pierre Ottavioli, one of Martine Monteil's predecessors as the head of the Criminal Brigade, was hired by Fayed shortly after the crash. If anybody could find out what the investigation was up to, then Ottavioli would be particularly well placed to do so. His Securopen company has a team of 40 permanent staff that can be augmented when the need arises. Because Mohamed Fayed had become a civil party to the investigation, he could pass on to Ottavioli any of the information he gathered from Judge Stéphan's file: 'He is free to give me access to information he holds. He wanted to take a point of view that is different from the official one, and he needed an explanation of procedure, since he was not very familiar with how these things work out in an investigation in France.'[8]

With Kiejman and Dartevelle advising on legal aspects of the case, and Ottavioli tracking the investigation, Fayed had augmented his team with some of the best-qualified individuals in France.

Few have more respectability or credibility than Pierre Ottavioli, the 76-year-old Corsican who was appointed head of the Crim in 1974, having worked his way up through the ranks. Now slightly hard of hearing, Ottavioli has fine white hair and clear blue eyes. He speaks slowly and very deliberately as he explains how, after retiring from the Crim, he had founded Securopen, a private-investigation company. The company's offices are in the rue de Turbigo in the 2nd arrondissement of Paris. Ottavioli warned his new client that he must not be seen to be launching a 'parallel investigation'. He advised that it would be illegal, and certainly counterproductive, to chase witnesses to the accident.[9] To any enquiries about the work Macnamara in London and Ottavioli in Paris were engaged in, the reply given was that Fayed was engaged in a 'review of security'. It would be a very delicate path to tread.

In February 1998, Ottavioli made a rare public statement about his efforts to find the white Fiat Uno. He told the press that his team of private detectives believed a car belonging to a journalist, 'who was very interested in the Princess of Wales', and who had been in the South of France while Diana was on holiday there, could have been the 'mystery' Fiat Uno.[10]

Ottavioli claimed that his detectives had found the Fiat in a garage in Tours in central France, and that he had tipped off the police. By the time Ottavioli briefed the press, however, the Fiat had already been examined, and dismissed, by Stéphan's investigation. Once again the reasons were quite straightforward.

---

[8] Author's researcher's interview with Pierre Ottavioli.
[9] Author's researcher's interview with Pierre Ottavioli.
[10] CNN, 13 February 1998.

When the police came across the car that Ottavioli's sleuths had alerted them to, they found it belonged to a 52-year-old photographer, James Andanson. The story would be given currency because James Andanson was a celebrity photographer, and he had photographed Princess Diana and Dodi Fayed in Saint-Tropez in the summer of 1997. Andanson was able to show Monteil's detectives car-hire documents, an air ticket and a motorway toll receipt to prove that on the morning of Diana's death he had flown from Paris to Corsica. The car had also not been in Paris on 30/31 August. In fact, it had not been anywhere for some time and Andanson was using it as a dustbin when Monteil's detectives arrived to question him.

A letter from Georges Kiejman to Judge Stéphan asking him to take a second look at the 'suspect' Fiat had been sufficient to start the story running throughout the world. The press office handling enquiries in Paris was flooded by calls for two days demanding to know why the Fiat could not have been the one involved in the crash. News agencies based in Paris would have been expected to call, but this particular development attracted attention throughout the world, and caused the phones to run hot for two full days.

Stories that flowed from Ottavioli's interview nonetheless gave the impression that the bereaved father was trying to get to the bottom of the tragedy. One of Ottavioli's detectives was quoted as saying, 'We've double-checked our information about the car, and we've let the investigating judge know'.[11] The official French investigation was not impressed, however, as the unusual swiftness of its response to the James Andanson story indicated. 'Sources close to the investigation' let it be known on the day that Ottavioli's remarks were reported that the car had been 'formally excluded from the case'.[12]

A year later, in February 1999, Fayed was still trying to keep the Fiat Uno story alive. He took out adverts in the French press offering £1 million for information about the elusive car. His security chief, John Macnamara, put it this way: 'Mohamed Al Fayed will continue his inquiries forever, long after the authorities have given up . . .'[13]

When I was initially commissioned to investigate the death of Princess Diana in Paris by Channel 4's *Dispatches*, Michael Cole was the first person I had thought of calling. We had known each other quite well when we both worked at the BBC. I had produced and directed several

---

[11] CNN, 13 February 1998.
[12] CNN, 13 February 1998.
[13] *Star*, 28 February 1998.

films which he presented as the corporation's court correspondent. While we were making 'The Uncrowned Jewels', for BBC1, we both met Mohamed Fayed for the first time. The film was about the Duchess of Windsor's extraordinary collection of jewels, which were to be auctioned in Geneva in aid of the Institut Pasteur's research into AIDS. Michael had obtained exclusive access to the jewels from Sotheby's, the auctioneers. With Fayed's permission, we had filmed in the villa Windsor for ten days in 1987, where the Duchess had lived until she died in 1986.

Cole accepted my invitation to meet for lunch in March 1998, a month after he quit his job as Fayed's spokesman. I had spoken to him on the phone shortly after the tragedy to express my condolences, but we had not met for nearly five years. He had become a household face in the immediate aftermath of the death of the Princess of Wales. (The first film Michael and I had made together was about a tour of Japan that Prince Charles and Princess Diana had undertaken in 1986.)

For me, the most surprising aspect of our lunch was that Michael was totally genuine in his support for Mohamed Fayed. I had wrongly assumed that he would be keen to distance himself from Fayed's declaration in the *Mirror* the previous month, that the crash in Paris 'was no accident'. However, during our lunch he remained loyal to the master he had served for ten years. He described the white Fiat Uno as the 'grassy knoll' of the tragedy, and stressed that there were so many 'unanswered questions' about what had happened in Paris. When I asked him who he thought best articulated the 'conspiracy-theory' school of thought that Fayed appeared to be so keen on, he had no hesitation in pointing me in the direction of Executive Intelligence Review. He told me that, in his opinion, EIR had done the 'best investigation into the tragedy', although he warned me that EIR's articles were 'eighty per cent fact and twenty per cent fiction' and was less than complimentary about EIR's leader, Lyndon Larouche.[14]

Like the 75-year-old Mohamed Fayed, the octogenarian Larouche is a multimillionaire. Also like Fayed, Larouche perceives himself as an anti-establishment figure whom the world is against. Unlike Fayed, he has been to jail – in 1988 he was convicted for fraud.

Larouche and Fayed share similar views on those who disagree with them. On EIR's website (www.larouchepub.com), Larouche proclaims, 'Clearly, all of those who have directly contrary opinions have now been proven, conclusively, to have been clinically insane.'[15] Fayed has

---

[14] Author's interview with Michael Cole.
[15] Larouche Website, October 1998.

similarly little time for those who disagree with him: 'I am the father who lost the son, I am the father who lived the tragedy, I am the father who followed the investigation with the judge day and night with my lawyers, nobody else have the right to talk because they are ignorant about what was happening, they want to cover up things.'[16]

As a result of my lunch with Cole, my *Dispatches* researcher, Sarah Mole, contacted EIR in Washington, and arranged to record an interview with its director, Jeffrey Steinberg, when he was in London. Larouche's organisation and Steinberg are of no particular interest, but the role they play in the parallel universe around the crash is. When I met him, Steinberg said that he was interviewed six times per week on average by the US media, before launching into his spiel for the camera about the Duke of Edinburgh being behind Princess Diana's assassination (see Chapter 9).

My interview with Steinberg provided an unexpected insight into the links between Fayed and EIR. The 'independent' EIR director, and leading conspiracy theorist, had tried to give Channel 4 TV the impression that he was staying at the Dorchester presumably at his own, or EIR's, expense. However, Sarah's calls to him were taken at 55 Park Lane. This is a suite of apartments close to the Dorchester owned by Hyde Park Residences. Mohamed Fayed, and the Ritz hotel's president Frank Klein, are named in HPR's company documents as directors of the company.

Fayed attempted to recruit another controversial character to his cause in the build-up to the first anniversary of the crash, as he continued to clutch at any straw that might sustain his campaign. Richard Tomlinson, who had been jailed for attempting to write a book in which he threatened to 'exhaustively expose in every detail' his secret work for MI6, wrote to Fayed in the summer of 1998 having watched the ITV documentary *Diana – Secrets Behind the Crash*.

Fayed contacted Tomlinson having received his letter by dispatching John Macnamara to meet him in Geneva at the beginning of August 1998. The former MI6 operative then travelled from his temporary base in Geneva to meet Fayed in Saint-Tropez.

Unlike MI6, Fayed was very interested in Tomlinson. After meeting Fayed in Saint-Tropez, Tomlinson travelled from Geneva to Paris to see Judge Stéphan on the last working day before the anniversary of Diana's death. The meeting was reported to have been held at Tomlinson's own request.

---

[16] BBC Radio Leeds, 25 January 1999.

The claims Tomlinson made to Stéphan were incoherent. They did not amount to allegations of a plot by MI6 to kill Diana and Dodi. As Tomlinson had left MI6 in 1995, the credibility of any claims he made about secret-intelligence operations in 1997 would have been open to doubt. Nonetheless, he told Stéphan that he suspected that Henri Paul had been an MI6 agent, and that either Trevor Rees-Jones or Kez Wingfield worked as a contact for Britain's Secret Intelligence Service.

Tomlinson told Stéphan that he had watched the ITV film, *Diana – Secrets Behind the Crash*, and had been struck by the interview with François Levistre. Levistre had described a 'flash before the crash', and Tomlinson told Stéphan that MI6 had devised a similar 'plot' to kill the Serb leader, Slobodan Milosevic, in 1992. Self-evidently, the 'plot' had not been executed.

There is no evidence to suggest that Judge Stéphan took any of Tomlinson's claims seriously but he did write to the British ambassador in Paris, Sir Michael Jay, to inform him of Tomlinson's testimony. The British Embassy wrote to the judge at the beginning of December 1998 to inform him that there was no truth in the Milosevic story. The letter also formally refuted allegations of MI6 involvement in any aspect of the Alma tunnel car crash.

After his meeting with Stéphan, Tomlinson slipped away through a back door of the Palais de Justice before he could be questioned by reporters. Tomlinson said later that he regretted his Saint-Tropez meeting with Fayed: 'With hindsight, I don't think I should have done that, as it could have discredited what I had to say in certain people's eyes. Mr Al Fayed believes in a plot. He is a broken, sad man. I obviously don't want to judge him, but I don't agree with him'.[17]

When the news broke in Paris, I phoned Wingfield to inform him of Tomlinson's interview with the judge. When I told him that Tomlinson had alleged that either he or Trevor Rees-Jones had been accused of working for Britain's Secret Intelligence Service, the Yorkshireman burst out laughing. Then he joked, 'I always thought there was something strange about Trevor's eyes. They're too close together!' I asked him for an on the record comment, and Wingfield was emphatic: 'It's bollocks, and you can print that'.

Tomlinson's extraordinary claim about one of the bodyguards being in MI6 chimed neatly with Fayed's latest throw of the blame-deflection dice. It had become clear to those like Fayed who had access to Judge Stéphan's file that the paparazzi were unlikely to be charged with

---

[17] *Nouvel Observateur*, 17 September 1998.

'involuntary manslaughter' as there was no evidence to support the charge. It was, therefore, unlikely that they would be blamed for Princess Diana's death despite Fayed's prompts. His efforts to persuade the public and the French investigation of his various conspiracy theories were flawed as blame-deflection strategies, as the forces of darkness behind the 'assassination' could never be identified.

Fayed then felt forced to attack the two bodyguards in whose hands he had placed the safety of Princess Diana and his son. In an interview for *Time* magazine Fayed accused them of messing up on the night of the tragedy: '. . . they are the people who caused the devastation and the accident through their incompetence and unprofessional practices. They had rules, and they moved away from the rules. They let me down.'

The *Time* article was published in the USA on 23 August 1998, but was omitted from the British and European editions, presumably for libel reasons. Kez Wingfield and Trevor Rees-Jones were highly offended by Fayed's outburst, and greeted it with a mixture of outrage and resignation. However, neither man was surprised that, having tried and failed to pin the blame for the crash on the photographers, and having tried with only limited success to foist his conspiracy theories on the public, their former boss should now publicly turn on them. The behind-the-scenes tensions that led to their departure from Fayed's security machine, and to this outburst, will be analysed in Chapter 12.

Fayed's decision to turn on the men in whose hands he had placed Princess Diana's safety appeared to impress few people. Indeed, the attack marked a turning point in the public perception of Mohamed Fayed. Trevor Rees-Jones was widely perceived as the hero of the Alma tunnel crash, and criticising the man who had almost paid with his life for attempting to protect Diana and Dodi was not a good move. It was noticeable that after his August 1998 attack on the bodyguards, Fayed did not return to the subject, possibly appreciating how it only helped to lower his standing in most people's eyes.

The success of Fayed's campaign against the truth of what happened in Paris should not go unrecognised. Every minute that people spend pondering the options that Fayed has put forward for them to consider is a minute that they do not spend thinking about why a drunk driver without a chauffeur's permit was allowed to speed the Princess of Wales to her death, with a fraction of the security that the family that approved the arrangement routinely insists on for itself. He has already achieved significant success in the court of public opinion and Judge Stéphan's decision not to recommend prosecution of the Ritz represented another important achievement for Fayed. Fayed knew from the moment he learnt of Princess Diana's death from Kez Wingfield at Le Bourget that there was also a danger that he would have to bear a measure of moral and possibly legal responsibility for what had happened. He has made this outcome less likely by his PR portrayal of himself as the hero of his own investigation into the 'dark and sinister forces' that 'murdered' Princess Diana. This strategy has put a barrier between Fayed and the efforts to establish why Princess Diana died while she was in his care.

By utilising some of his vast resources, Fayed has attempted, with some success, to continue to keep his critics on the back foot. His campaign may yet succeed in ensuring that the court of public opinion, as well as the French courts, never properly examines the failings of the Fayed family, its Ritz hotel and Fayed's security machine on the night of 31 August 1997. Few books, newspapers or TV documentaries since the crash have seriously analysed the mistakes made by the Fayed security on the night that Diana died, and most do not even mention the matter. On the other hand, there is a burgeoning library of books and newspaper cuttings featuring different strains of conspiracy theory and 'assassination' plots. Future historians will pay little attention to this particular draft of history other than as a guide to the thinking of the multimillionaire who fatefully invited the Princess of Wales on holiday. Mohamed Fayed has wielded a censor's pencil and eraser over the much-altered first draft of Princess Diana's demise as he has tried adopting her as an honorary Fayed.

By the beginning of 1999 he had lost many essential members of his core team. His spokesman, Michael Cole, who had represented him for ten years, announced his 'retirement' from his post less than six months after the crash, in February 1998. He said, ruefully, that his master did not listen to him anymore.[18] When pressed on live television as to whether he believed in the conspiracy theories his former boss had become so obsessed with, Cole would say only, 'My opinion is my opinion'.[19]

The head of Fayed's personal protection, Paul Handley-Greaves, quit in April 1999. The bodyguards whom Handley-Greaves had charged with protecting the Princess and Dodi, Trevor Rees-Jones and Kez Wingfield, had also both left. The villa Windsor's security chief, Ben Murrell, had followed them, as he made public the embarrassing truth about Princess Diana's visit to the villa. The bodyguards were the three crucial key witnesses to precisely what had happened from the moment Princess Diana touched down in Paris to the moment she died.

---

[18] Author's interview with Michael Cole.
[19] ITV debate, *Wednesday Night Live*, 3 June 1998.

Part of the family: The father, the son and the Princess on the *Jonikal*.

Princess Diana talked to friends all over the world from her mobile on the *Jonikal*, including her secret lover, Dr Hasnat Khan.

Above 'Mr Wonderful' – Dr Hasnat Khan, Diana's boyfriend before Dodi.

Right Kelly Fisher wearing the sapphire ring that Dodi gave her. Dodi had dumped her for Diana.

Diana and Dodi being piloted in Saint-Tropez.

Above Diana and
Dodi enter the Ritz
separately. The
waiting paparazzi
had hoped for
valuable shots of
them together.

Right Diana
enters the Ritz
followed by Kez
Wingfield.

Above The doomed party. Henri Paul, Diana and Dodi wait for the Mercedes to arrive. Trevor Rees-Jones can be seen behind them.

Left Dodi and his 'model employee' Henri Paul (right).

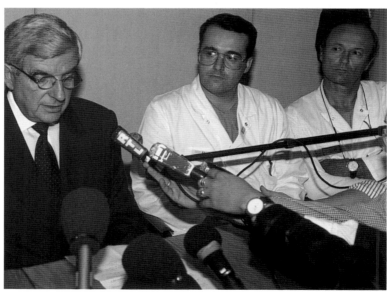

French Interior Minister Jean-Pierre Chevènement announces the death of the Princess of Wales at the Pitié-Salpêtrière hospital in the early hours of 31 August 1997. Beside him are Professeurs Riou and Pavie, the doctors who fought for over two hours to save the Princess's life.

Right Mohamed Fayed, driven by Philippe Dourneau, arrives with Kez Wingfield at the Pitié-Salpêtrière hospital on 31 August 1997.

Right Paul Handley-Greaves misidentifies a figure in the rue Cambon on the Ritz security video at the Harrods press conference of 5 September 1997. It was actually Frédéric Lucard, the 'vehicle jockey' who had just handed Henri Paul the keys to the Mercedes before he left on his final journey.

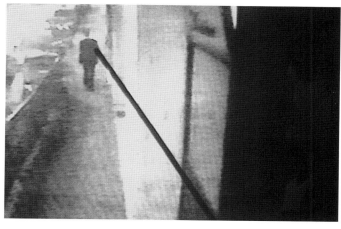

Right One of the claims made about Diana was that she was pregnant with Dodi's child when she died. However, this picture was taken on 14 July 1997, before they were a couple.

5 June 1998: Mohamed Fayed emerges from the Palais de Justice after denouncing Diana's mother, Frances Shand Kydd, as a 'snob' and a 'bad mother'. He is surrounded by his security team led by Paul Handley-Greaves (2nd on left) and Ben Murrell (bottom right). Georges Kiejman (with his hand by his chin) is Fayed's chief lawyer.

Michael Cole, Fayed's spokesman, and John Macnamara, his Director of Security, outside the Old Bailey.

Above Francois Levi/Levistre, who claimed he saw a 'flash before the crash'.

Left Former British spy Richard Tomlinson.

Right The X-ray of Trevor Rees-Jones's skull after the accident shows his numerous injuries, including both eye sockets smashed (1 and 2), both cheek bones smashed (3 and 4), his nose damaged beyond recognition (5) and the lower jaw broken in several places (6).

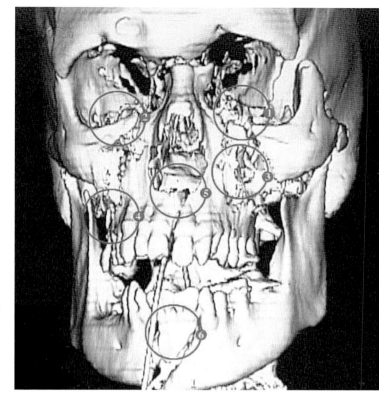

Below Back in Paris: Trevor Rees-Jones, flanked by Kez Wingfield (left) and Ben Murrell, returns to Paris on 18 December 1997 to give a statement to the French investigation.

Above Commander Mulès and Judges Hervé Stephan and Marie-Christine Devidal emerge from the Alma tunnel during their comprehensive eighteen-month investigation into the crash.

Above Coroner Michael Burgess, Martine Monteil and Commissioner John Stevens leave the Alma tunnel after their visit on 26 April 2004.

11. MOHAMED'S MEDIA

'*LIAR LIAR.*'

Sun, 17 March 1999

The death of Princess Diana was a watershed moment in many people's lives. Few will ever forget the unprecedented outpouring of public grief that accompanied her funeral, or forget where they were or who they were with when they learnt of her death. As the media prepared Diana for a secular sainthood she neither sought nor desired in life, her passing united millions in mourning a woman who was known by all, but really known by so few. The myths and legends about her life and death began to flourish even before she was buried. Editors and proprietors knew that there was little chance of circulation, viewing figures or sales diminishing as a result of running speculative stories about the crash that killed her and Dodi Fayed.

As I wrote this book, a number of people warned me that, no matter what I wrote, people would still choose to believe the fictions rather than the facts about the Paris tragedy. They believed that the myths surrounding the tragedy had formed such an impenetrable fog, that shafts of light shed by facts would fail to penetrate. Only two days after Diana's death an American conspiracy expert had warned, 'These theories will not stop just because the facts prove them wrong.'[1]

Much media coverage helped to cement myths about Diana's death and her romance with Dodi Fayed that appear almost unshakable. As has been demonstrated, the mythology about the crash, the Princess's future intentions had she lived, and the various 'conspiracy theories' have taken root. This work is perhaps best demonstrated by examining the contributions made by three different forms of media outlet: the press, a best-selling book about Diana's death and the best-watched British TV programme about the tragedy. The three have obviously not been solely responsible for nourishing the myths, but they provide examples of the seed from which the myths grew. The myths, the conspiracy theories and the counterinformation around the 1963 assassination of President JF Kennedy seeped into the world's consciousness over more than three decades. Late-twentieth-century technology helped spread the myths about Princess Diana around the world in seconds via the Internet. EIR, for example, has a highly sophisticated

---

[1] Reuters, 2 September 1997.

website which can be read in at least eight different languages. In several instances, where cyberspace led, terrestrial outlets followed.

The white Fiat against which Henri Paul's Mercedes brushed seconds before it crashed is an example of a popular myth in action. As we have seen, the role of the car in the fatal crash was proved by the French crash experts at the IRCGN to have been negligible. However, in the mythology of the accident, the significance of the vehicle has grown out of all proportion.

In October 1997, the *Independent* became the first British newspaper to raise the Fiat as 'grassy knoll' idea in the British press, followed the next week by the mass-circulation tabloid, the *People*. As no official information emerged from Judge Stéphan's investigation about the car, the scope for rumourmongering was immense. When it was reported at the start of 1998 that the Criminal Brigade was scaling down its hunt for the car, speculation intensified.

'THE MYSTERY DIANA CAR', screamed the *Mirror*'s front-page headline on 2 February over a picture of a white Citroën AX. The picture headline read, 'Paris Ritz, 12.16 a.m., August 31, 1997 . . . minutes before Diana and Dodi die.' The story started, 'EXCLUSIVE. This is the white Citroën AX car in the Princess Diana death mystery . . . it shows that the French investigators hunting the white Fiat Uno may have spent the last five months hunting for the WRONG car.'

The *Mirror* had obtained a video shot by an Australian tourist outside the Ritz on the night of 30/31 August which featured pictures of a white Citroën. The paper decided that this white car was the one that the French police should have been looking for. The reasons for this were not clear, but the story was given the full tabloid treatment for two days, including a picture of a 'Mirrorman' handing the Australian's tape to a French *gendarme* in Paris. The story collapsed on day three, when the *Mirror* noticed that the white Citroën was still outside the front of the Ritz after Princess Diana's Mercedes had left from the rear of the hotel. In fact, Kez Wingfield's decoy convoy could be seen behind the white Citroën. Given that the Wingfield convoy followed Princess Diana's Mercedes, it was unlikely that many readers would believe that the Citroën could have caused the crash, or that the French police should have been looking for it. The French police were 100 per cent certain that Princess Diana's car had not been in collision with a Citroën of any description. The 'mystery car' story served only to sow confusion about how Princess Diana and Dodi Fayed died and supplement the continuing mystery of the missing white car.

Death of a Princess ended with the thought that, unless the white Fiat is found, it will 'feed speculation about plots and cover-ups for the next hundred years. Either way the place de l'Alma will be France's Dealy Plaza' [the place in Dallas where Kennedy was shot]. Sancton and Macleod cited a British lawyer staying in a hotel about one hundred yards from the place de l'Alma, claiming that he saw a car that 'appeared to be a Fiat Uno' speeding away from the crash shortly after the accident. The authors pointed out that the route taken by the Fiat in the lawyer's account would provide a journey of 'a minute or two' to the British Embassy, which 'has a large drive-in door on the rue du Faubourg St Honoré which opens into an interior courtyard'.[2] Maps in the book illustrated the 'possible escape route of the Fiat Uno', and located the British Embassy. *Death of a Princess* was serialised over five days in *The Times* in February 1998. One of the serialised extracts posed the question raised in the final chapter, 'Was it Murder?'.

Profits from exploiting the dead Princess's memory were never threatened by the pious promises of journalistic self-restraint uttered in the immediate wake of the crash. The dead cannot be libelled, and neither can the French nation. The 'dark and sinister' forces so often held to be responsible are not capable of responding to their accusers, as they are rarely defined or named, and those that are have not bothered. For small and expansively financed cults, such as EIR, traducing Princess Diana's memory with their nonsensical theories makes commercial sense. Not many people read EIR, and stories about how the British Royal Family was behind the 'assassination' could only boost its circulation. Many British media outlets followed suit, knowing that their lifeblood profits were most unlikely to suffer as a result. In death, as in life, Princess Diana remained the most hunted woman of the modern age, with profit remaining a constant motivation of the hunters.

Mohamed Fayed was the father of many of the myths, with assorted media acting as midwives at the birth of many of them. Fayed's claim that 'IT WAS NO ACCIDENT' was emblazoned across the front page of the *Mirror* in February 1998. Beneath the *Mirror*'s dramatic headline, there were three subheadlines heralding the exclusive Fayed interview. The most striking feature of all three was that none of them were true: 'He says someone killed Diana & Dodi'; 'He reveals truth about her last words'; 'He confirms they WERE engaged.' The *Mirror* ran the interview over several days.

Death of a Princess did not go as far down Fayed's conspiracy route as he himself would have liked, finding that the evidence did not

---

[2] *Death of a Princess*, p. 245.

support the notion of the couple being murdered. However, one of its authors, Tom Sancton, confided after publication that he and Scott MacLeod had been obliged to present Fayed's views in a restrained fashion to retain their main source's credibility: 'The way we present it in the book was toned down a bit, because frankly we thought it was just a little bit over the top ... his theories about elaborate sort of space-age weapons that may have been used [to cause the crash]. He told us all that and more. I think we acted with a lot of restraint and responsibility in presenting his views.'[3]

To retain his own credibility, Fayed insisted on keeping the Americans' tapes of their interviews with him. They had to transcribe them in his presence in London. This gave Fayed and Michael Cole the capacity for 'plausible deniability'.

Television saw the chance to prosper as it alighted upon the central myth of a 'mysterious hand' playing a role in Princess Diana's death. The ITV film, *Diana – Secrets Behind the Crash*, brought such concerns into the homes of 12.5 million viewers in Britain. Fayed had been approached to help make the documentary by a television producer he had worked with in the past. Richard Belfield, a director of the independent production company, Fulcrum Productions, had made a previous programme for Channel 4 during the 'Cash for Questions' row that Fayed had precipitated in 1994. The Diana film keyed into the central Fayed-inspired myth in describing the blood tests on Henri Paul as 'suspect', without providing evidence that they were. It was, said ITV, the best-watched investigative documentary 'in a generation'. The film was given authority by its presenter, Nicholas Owen, ITN's royal correspondent, who had won respect when he fronted some of ITN's live coverage of the aftermath of Princess Diana's death on 31 August 1997.

Owen told viewers that 'a lot of people are ready to believe that there was some sort of conspiracy at work, some plot to kill Diana and Dodi by dark and sinister forces.'[4] Extraordinarily, the film's key witness feeding this particular fear was none other than the Rouen *mythomane*, François Levi, who had chosen to be described as François 'Levistre' for his appearance on ITV.

ITV illustrated Levi's flash-before-the-crash fantasy, claiming that his account was supported by 'many other witnesses', but did not specify who they were. In an experiment Levistre was shown two flashes: the

---

[3] Author's interview with Thomas Sancton.
[4] *Diana – Secrets Behind the Crash*, ITV, 3 June 1998.

first was from a camera flash gun, the second from an antipersonnel device. The *mythomane* was certain that the second flash corresponded to what he had seen. Owen reported, 'Monsieur Levistre had identified the much bigger flash [coming] from this piece of kit.'

ITN's royal correspondent then concluded part two of the film by extending Levi/Levistre's claims further than the Rouen *mythomane* had dared to himself. Brandishing a flash gun, Owen described how it could have affected Henri Paul had it been used in the Alma tunnel: 'Shine this in someone's eyes and they are stunned, blinded, disabled for several minutes. If you're driving a car when it happens, you'll almost certainly crash.

'We bought our antipersonnel flashlight in the West End of London for just over two hundred and sixty pounds. But there's another version of this piece of kit. It's not available to the public. It's infinitely more powerful, and it's used by army special forces – including the British – around the world.'

ITV's 'largest audience in a generation' were left to endure a commercial break with the uncomfortable thought that British soldiers or equipment could in some way have been involved in murdering Princess Diana. Nicholas Owen was so proud of his film's championing of Levistre's flash-before-the-crash claim that he produced his flash gun during a live debate shortly after his film finished. After the film Owen said, 'I am not for one moment saying that I believe Mohamed Al Fayed, that I believe François Levistre, that I believe any of these people.' However, thousands of viewers indicated that they had believed Levistre. In an opinion poll taken by the *Mirror* newspaper immediately after the programme, 93 per cent of respondents said that they believed that there had been a 'flash before the crash'. This was testimony to ITV's presentation of Levistre as a sober and plausible witness, rather than as the *mythomane* of Rouen who had been discounted by the French police nine months earlier.

If any of the 93 per cent of the poll respondents who believed Levistre could have known what the *People* newspaper would carry two months later they would have had a shock. The Rouen *mythomane*, still trading under the name of Levistre, persuaded the mass-circulation Sunday tabloid of an entirely different sequence of events. The *People*'s front page proclaimed, 'I CAUSED DIANA DEATH CRASH . . . Speeding driver's nightmare fears . . . His sudden appearance startled the Fiat, causing it to swerve. The Mercedes also swerved, braked and spun out of control.' Apparently relishing his unexpected appearance in the mainstream British media in the summer of 1998, the *mythomane* described how he had '. . . roared into the underpass . . . my driving may have made

Diana's car swerve and lose control.' In this version of Levi's story, the 'flash before the crash', which had beguiled millions of ITV viewers, was not mentioned. This version of Levi's story was brought to the *People* newspaper by Nick Farrell, one of the researchers on *Diana – Secrets Behind the Crash*. Judge Stéphan also ignored Levi's latest attempt to fool the world that he was the sole witness to the crash that killed Princess Diana.

There had already been embarrassment for ITV immediately after transmission when Nick Farrell wrote a trenchant article in the weekly *Spectator* magazine, dissociating himself from *Diana – Secrets Behind the Crash*. Farrell wrote, 'The programme-makers used any witness they could find whose testimony, however shaky, might support the idea of death by MI5 or paparazzi.' The researcher later conceded that his article had made him 'extremely unpopular with the people that made the programme . . . I felt like Judas.'

During filming in Paris Farrell recalled that the ITV team 'did not make much effort to talk to the French authorities . . . I suppose there wouldn't have been much point because all they would have said is that it was an accident.' As filming progressed, Farrell told me he felt that it was 'leaving reality behind and entering the realms of fiction . . . I thought we were investigating the crash with an open mind but it slowly became clear we weren't pushing the conspiracy line, i.e the Fayed line, because we believed it, but because it made good TV and would get everyone riveted to the screen.'

On reflection, Farrell was particularly critical of Levi's role in the programme. He had personally researched Levi's story but had not been convinced by him: 'It was really very difficult to pin him down on anything specific, so he was not the most credible witness. Unlike so many people who were there, [I felt] he was all too ready to speak, whereas most of them didn't want to speak.'

Farrell, a respected newspaper journalist and author who is based in Italy, saw the programme with the production team in London, and was dismayed to watch Levi's prominent role. 'I couldn't stop myself smirking even though I was surrounded by the rest of the production team who were celebrating this "major" achievement.' Farrell's worst fears were confirmed as Levi's flash-gun tale became 'one of the key events in the programme . . . I just thought, my God, this is just absurd.' As an act of what he describes as 'atonement' for his 'error' in working on the programme, Farrell wrote his *Spectator* article.[5]

---

[5] Author's interview with Nick Farrell, 2003.

Elsewhere, in media desperate for any crumbs of information about Diana's last days, other myths about her life and death also prospered unchecked. Some of the myths I examined earlier – that she could have been saved had the French emergency services done their job properly, that she conveyed her last request to a nurse before she died, and that Dodi's father saw her corpse looking 'peaceful and serene' in Paris – all took root. Tapping into a scepticism that was fuelled by a lack of official information about the Alma tunnel crash, many newspapers reflected the difficulty much of the public had in believing that Princess Diana could have died in such a mundane fashion. The myth that Diana and Dodi were about to be married is one that started within hours of their relationship being revealed in August 1997. In the tabloid imagination this heralded imminent marriage. Seventy-two hours after the news broke, on 10 August, the *Sunday Mirror* had Dodi jetting off to Los Angeles to buy an engagement ring. Media that had little problem marrying the Princess off while she was alive predictably had none whatsoever after she was dead. The myth that the couple were planning to settle in the villa Windsor was one which had been carefully nurtured by Fayed in the months after the crash. It claimed more media victims than many of the other myths that surrounded Diana's last days.

By their own account Sancton and MacLeod were escorted round the villa Windsor on 'the day that *Death of a Princess* was going to press'.[6] Their host, Gregorio Martin, was introduced as the 'major domo' of the villa. He described Princess Diana's trip to the villa to Sancton in some detail. By now the idea that an 'Italian designer' had met the couple at the villa had become a fixture in accounts of the couple's visit. Unfortunately, Gregorio Martin could not remember the name of the 'Italian designer'. Having worked closely with Fayed for months in the preparation of the book, Sancton included the designer's name without being able to check it further. The authors concluded, '. . . that they intended to marry now seems beyond question'.[7]

In 2004 further evidence confirming the provenance of this story came to light. Freelance journalist Martyn Palmer, who was preparing an article for the *Sunday Express*, was another person shown around the villa in February 1998 by Gregorio Martin in a visit supervised by

---

[6] Author's interview with Thomas Sancton.

[7] *Death of a Princess*, p. 122. Well after *Death of a Princess* was published, Sancton would admit to being 'troubled' by the 'Italian designer' story, but the unidentified person had found his way into its pages. Subsequent editions of the book omitted mention of the designer.

Michael Cole. Martin regaled Palmer with his familiar tale of Diana and Dodi's visit before Michael Cole stepped in. Palmer recorded Cole's briefing: 'The visit that they made to the villa was not a casual one. They came here straight from the airport and it was possibly one of the reasons for coming to Paris. They stayed here for two hours, the servants let them in and it was a very animated party, happy and joyful.

'They were having wonderful fun. They had just had a wonderful holiday in the Mediterranean and they were stopping in Paris on the way home and they were planning to go out to dinner that night.

'They came to the villa and spent certainly two, possibly three, hours and they walked the boundaries of the grounds, they saw the two staff buildings in the grounds and they then visited the main house from the rafters to the cellars even going as far as to inspect the central heating system and the boiler.

'They looked in the fridges which somebody who knows Diana very well says she would do a thing like that. I think the significant thing is that they met, by arrangement, a decorator – whose identity I do not know – and he went around with them.'[8]

The headline for Palmer's article was DIANA AND DODI FOUND THEIR DREAM HOME THE DAY BEFORE THEY DIED.[9] In the *Sunday Express* Gregorio Martin was described as 'chauffeur', and the 'decorator' remained anonymous.

Sunday Times journalist Andrew Alderson was told a similar story during his visit to the villa Windsor that same February 1998 weekend. In an article he co-wrote with Robert Lacey, the royal historian, they considered that Martin had provided 'the strongest pointers yet that they planned to marry [giving] greater credence to suggestions from family and friends of Dodi that the £130,000 ring that he gave Diana hours before their deaths was an engagement ring.'

Martin told the paper,

They were talking about their plans for the future. It was a beautiful day, and the princess was enjoying looking over the house . . . They looked at everything in the house: the boiler, every cupboard, the princess even opened the fridge to look inside. She had a detailed interest in everything, including the garden. The princess was asking about the rooms for the staff and security.[10]

---

[8] Michael Cole in a taped interview with Martyn Palmer February 1998.
[9] *Sunday Express*, 8 February 1998.
[10] *Sunday Times*, 8 February 1998.

The snaring of Robert Lacey was a particular coup for Fayed – his considerable reputation as a royal historian lent credibility to the story in Britain's bestselling Sunday broadsheet. When he learnt that he had been fooled, Lacey was aghast: 'I regret not going to the villa Windsor myself but, even if I had gone, there is no guarantee that I would have smelt a rat.' Lacey also regrets lending his name to an article that suggested that Diana and Dodi might have got married had they lived. He actually holds the reverse opinion: 'I can't believe that Diana would have married Dodi.'[11]

When ITV filmed at the villa Windsor, Gregorio Martin was still having problems remembering the name of the Italian designer. This was hardly surprising, as he had actually been on holiday in Spain when Diana and Dodi visited the villa on 30 August 1997. According to Ben Murrell, who greeted Nicholas Owen at the villa, 'When Martin came to speak for the camera he couldn't remember the name he had been told. I rang Mohamed in London and was put through to his office. I told them what had happened. I spoke to one of the heads of security, David Pinch, and I heard him speaking to Mohamed. I was given the name Andro Grossi, which I repeated to Martin.'

ITV's team was presumably unaware of the urgent, behind-the-scenes communication that Martin's memory lapse caused. ITV did not use the designer's name, but the film did feature Martin describing Princess Diana's visit to the villa with Dodi and the designer on her last afternoon. In broken English, the Spanish caretaker described the visit to Owen: 'Everything is ready for [them] to come here . . . He prepare the house . . . all is ready . . . If somebody comes with a designer . . . it's clear. They came to visit everything. They go all round the house . . . I think they were a very beautiful couple.'

Mohamed Fayed himself appeared next to cement the fiction that Diana and Dodi had contemplated making the villa Windsor their 'nest'.

Another curious feature of the ITV sequence with Martin was that it showed the villa Windsor full of what appeared to be the Duke and Duchess's furniture, decorations and paintings. The famous 1939 Gerald Brockhurst painting of the Duchess of Windsor was hanging in the fireplace in the main room. This was strange as the entire contents of the villa, including the painting, had been sold by Sotheby's in New York in February 1998. Brockhurst's painting of the Duchess had fetched £65,000.

ITV and its viewers were being doubly misled. Not only was Gregorio Martin absent from the villa when Diana and Dodi paid their visit, but

---

[11] Author's interview with Robert Lacey.

the fixtures and fittings had not been there either. When Alastair Miller photographed the villa for the *Sunday Times* and the *Sunday Express*, just before the auction took place in February 1998, there was no furniture in the villa at all.[12]

Nicholas Owen and Gregorio Martin were, in fact, walking around a house that had subsequently been filled entirely with replicas of some of the original furniture, decorations and paintings. The Brockhurst was a replica. Craftsmen employed by Fayed had copied many of the villa's other key items as well.

'Death, divorce, disaster – Sotheby's can take almost anything and turn it into a profitable fete . . . it has made itself the ultimate illusionist of the consumer culture,' wrote Robert Lacey at the end of his *Sunday Times* feature on the New York auction.[13] Fayed had comfortably outdone Sotheby's in creating one of the ultimate TV illusions for millions of viewers – an illusion about Princess Diana's last day alive that he hoped would live in the minds of the millions who were watching, and would bolster the myth that she was planning a future with his son. Fayed had created an illusion about her happiness, and an illusion about what she did on her last day, whom she met and what her plans might have been. The ITV sequence in the villa Windsor bore no relation to anything that Princess Diana saw or did during her visit – she had briefly toured the empty shell of the villa. According to Ben Murrell, who watched the Princess and Dodi's visit on a closed-circuit TV, the bare villa contained virtually nothing for Diana to see when she visited: 'Most of the antiques had been packed away ready to be auctioned off in New York. There was nothing much to look at, just a few animal skins that had not been packed away.' Following ITV's visit Fayed could add another significant media pelt to his collection.

'Princess Diana's life was a fairytale. Her death should not be' was the advertising copy Channel 4 used to promote my *Dispatches* film in June 1998. It was broadcast the day after ITV's programme. One of our objectives was to puncture some of the myths surrounding the Alma tunnel crash. We called the film 'The Accident' to stress to viewers that we believed that the crash that killed Diana and Dodi was not part of a 'conspiracy' to assassinate her. The central point we made in *Dispatches* was that we had found evidence that Mohamed Fayed himself had approved Dodi's plan to allow Henri Paul to drive the Princess and Dodi from his Ritz hotel on the night they died. We also showed how the

---

[12] Author's interview with Alastair Miller, May 1998.
[13] *Sunday Times*, 15 February 1998.

subsequent process of myth manufacturing about their relationship had drawn attention away from the mistakes that the Fayeds and their security machine had made in permitting Henri Paul to drive.

We filmed secretly inside the bar Vendôme where Paul drank some of the alcohol that was to prove fatal, and cited Alain Willaumez's claim that Paul had been noticeably drunk when he left the bar. We also obtained the first on-camera interview with a Ritz employee since the crash. Frédéric Lucard informed viewers that *he* had handed the keys to Henri Paul, and not Etoile Limousine's 'Niels' Siegel, who had been reported to have done this. Lucard also became the first Ritz employee to back the paparazzi's claim that Paul had sped away from the hotel, having first cried out, 'Don't try to follow us, you'll never catch us.'[14]

The day after *Dispatches* was broadcast Fayed issued a vitriolic press release claiming that the programme was a 'character assassination'. He had refused an invitation to be interviewed partly because he'd just done an interview for the ITV documentary and did not wish to give another. He indicated that he had been particularly riled by the central point that our investigation had revealed: 'The notion that Mr Al Fayed can in some way be held responsible for the tragic events last year is a travesty. The proposition is incredible and no reasonable person will believe it.'

The press release continued:

Last night's edition of *Dispatches* on Channel 4 Television was a mickey mouse production – the latest in an orchestrated media campaign against Mohamed Al Fayed. It was a grotesque caricature of an investigative programme motivated by pure malice and made no attempt to address the many serious unanswered questions about the fatal crash in Paris last August.

The programme's primary concern was not the deaths of Princess Diana and Dodi but the character assassination of Mohamed Al Fayed. There was no search for truth – just a pack of lies and distortion . . .

Today in Paris Mr Al Fayed is appearing at his own request before Judge Hervé Stéphan at a summit meeting of those who witnessed the crash. The aim is to finally establish what really happened on that night more than nine months ago. Mr Al Fayed has great confidence in the French investigation and he is doing all he can to assist it. His is a genuine search for the truth unlike last night's television programme.

---

[14] Author's interview with Frédéric Lucard.

As Fayed left the 'summit' with Stéphan he took the opportunity to launch a savage, unscripted attack on Princess Diana's mother. He left reporters at the Palais de Justice in Paris open-mouthed as he said that Frances Shand Kydd could '. . . go to hell. I don't care a damn about her.' Appearing to lose his cool completely, Fayed carried on, 'She's a snob; she thinks she is the Queen of Sheba. She walked out on her family and I don't give a damn about her.' Retaining her dignity, Diana's mother made no comment at all. It was a poignant moment that marked a turning point in the myth-making process, and the media's reporting of it, nine months after the crash.

The two bereaved parents had come face to face on 5 June 1998 at Judge Stéphan's witness summit in Paris for the first time since Diana's funeral. Judge Stéphan required the nine accused paparazzi and the motorcyclist to go through their own accounts of what happened on 31 August in the Alma tunnel. Stéphan compared and contrasted their accounts, and posed any questions he considered to be relevant. According to accounts that emerged from the summit, no real progress was made. However, the word around the Palais de Justice was that it was looking increasingly unlikely that the manslaughter charges against the paparazzi would stick. When Mohamed Fayed picked this up, possibly infuriated by the sight of the paparazzi in person, he gave vent to the private fury that had been gnawing at him since the tragedy: 'They caused the problem. They were like vultures around their bodies. It was immoral. When the car had crashed they were surrounding the vehicle taking photographs and trying to pull the bodies out of the car . . . If I were not in a court, I would hang them all.'[15]

If there was some sympathy for Fayed's attack on the photographers, there was none for his assault on Princess Diana's mother. 'REPTILE!' screamed the front page of the Sun the following day, as it led an unprecedented assault on Dodi's father, which was taken up by most other British papers. Fayed's outburst was a significant moment in the collapse of the campaign against the truth of how Princess Diana died. It was swiftly becoming clear that Judge Stéphan would not have the evidence to prosecute the paparazzi for manslaughter, as Fayed was hoping. As the prospect of the 'bastards' being charged receded, Fayed's anger was, inappropriately, directed towards the other bereaved parent present.

The Sunday after Fayed's Paris outburst against Frances Shand Kydd, the editor of the Sunday Telegraph, Dominic Lawson, had incurred

---

[15] Widely quoted in the British press, 6 June 1998.

Fayed's wrath with a powerful editorial condemnation of him entitled 'A VERY BAD MAN'. It was the seminal broadsheet condemnation of the Egyptian. It concluded that, far from being granted the British passport that he had been seeking for so long, Fayed should be deported.

Lawson's dislike of Fayed stemmed both from the myths that Fayed had manufactured about Princess Diana's last days, and his fantasies about how his son and the Princess were assassinated by the British establishment.

Fayed was, no doubt, delighted when one of the stories that the former MI6 officer, Richard Tomlinson, had been hawking around finally surfaced in *Sunday Business* in October. The paper's report that the editor of a national newspaper was in the pay of MI6 set in motion a frenzy of speculation throughout the British media.

Tomlinson had told Fayed in the summer that Britain's secret-intelligence services were making payments to the editor of a national British newspaper. Tomlinson could not identify the editor, as the individual's name appeared in code in the documents that he had seen before he left the secret service in 1995. Tomlinson told journalists he met at this time that, by a process of deduction, his best guess was that the editor could be Peter Stothard of *The Times*. It quickly became clear, however, that Fayed was certain that it was Dominic Lawson.

Lawson had impeccable credentials to be a member of Fayed's hated if amorphous 'Establishment'. The son of the former Conservative Chancellor of the Exchequer, Nigel Lawson, Dominic Lawson edited the *Sunday Telegraph*, which supported the Conservative government that Fayed had helped to destroy. To clinch matters in Fayed's mind, he was married to Rosa Monckton.

Rosa Monckton was an obvious Fayed target, and very near the top of Fayed's hate list for two reasons. She had been one of Diana's longest-standing and closest friends. Since the crash Monckton had written measured but passionate articles in the *Sunday Telegraph* that directly contradicted Fayed's agenda. In articles such as 'STOP THESE LIES ABOUT MY FRIEND, DIANA', she had calmly injected several salient facts into the debate about Diana's last days that had threatened the order within the parallel universe that Fayed and his PR team had been busy creating since the crash. She had revealed that Diana had told her in the middle of August, when they went on holiday together in Greece, that she had no plans to marry Dodi or anybody else. She had pointed out that Diana could not have been pregnant at the time of the crash, as she had menstruated during their Greek holiday less than two weeks before the crash.

Monckton was also an ideal 'Establishment' target for a second reason: she hails from a distinguished military family. Her grandfather, General Sir Walter Monckton, was a Minister in the Conservative governments of Churchill and Macmillan, and her father is Viscount Monckton of Brenchley, a retired Major-General in the British army. Rosa's brother, Christopher Monckton, served in Prime Minister Margaret Thatcher's policy unit in Downing Street in the 1980s. In the evidence-free atmosphere surrounding Planet Conspiracy, this was proof positive that the Lawson–Monckton partnership was an MI6 front determined to destroy Fayed. Fayed set about fanning the flames of the 'Lawson is a spy' story as vigorously as he could. He personally phoned the editor of one national newspaper to urge him to chase the story, even though Tomlinson himself had informed journalists he encountered that he did not actually know who the editor might be. He also admitted that he had no evidence to support any of his claims.

Punch magazine, owned by Fayed since 1996, launched an attack on Lawson. On its first cover of 1999, *Punch* featured a picture of Dominic Lawson's head on a James Bond-style body. The character was brandishing a pistol, and the headline read, 'MI6 AND THE MEDIA – BY A FORMER AGENT'. At the bottom of the cover was a note: 'Apologies to Dominic Lawson (in fancy dress). He'd shoot us if we said he was a spy.' It was hardly surprising that *Punch* failed to reveal to its readers that the most energetic circulator of the allegations was the magazine's proprietor, Mohamed Fayed.

The magazine also did not report that in the summer of 1998, Ben Murrell had quit his post at the villa Windsor. The former security chief enraged Fayed by selling his story to the *Sun*, the paper that had described him as a 'reptile'. Fayed felt that Murrell's revelations were so damaging that he ordered his lawyers to try to prevent the second episode appearing. In the High Court, Fayed's lawyers alleged that Murrell had breached his contract and his duty of confidentiality. The paper had promised that the following day Murrell would reveal 'What Fayed knew about the crash that killed Diana'.

After Mr Justice Neuberger threw out Fayed's bid to stifle Murrell and the *Sun* on the grounds of free speech, Fayed continued to pursue the newspaper, and his former Paris security chief, through the courts. Fayed's QC, Michael Bloch, acknowledged, in attempting to prevent Murrell from futher exploiting his story, that the accuracy of the *Sun*'s copy was 'not disputed'.

Richard Spearman, QC for the *Sun* and Ben Murrell, highlighted what Murrell had disclosed about Gregorio Martin's role in misinforming journalists about Princess Diana's visit to the villa Windsor. Fayed produced no evidence to challenge Murrell's assertion that Martin had been ordered by his boss to lie about Diana's visit. Indeed, there has been no response of any sort from Fayed to this important aspect of Murrell's revelations. Spearman argued that the photos Murrell had sold to the *Sun* were crucial in 'exposing serious wrongdoing' by Fayed, and 'correcting a clear deception [as part of a] sustained campaign of deception', about the last day of Diana's life.

In March 1999 Fayed's bid to stifle Murrell and the *Sun* was defeated. A picture of Fayed appeared on the front page under the headline, 'LIAR LIAR . . . PANTS ON FIRE'. The report started, 'A High Court judge yesterday ruled the *Sun* was right to brand Mohamed Fayed a liar.'[16] Judge Jacobs found that because Fayed himself had put Diana's visit to the villa Windsor into the public domain, it was 'fair dealing' for the *Sun* to publish the security-camera pictures. These showed that she had been there for only 28 minutes rather than the 'two hours' that had been claimed.

Fayed's action in the High Court cost him £25,000 in legal bills, but the damage to his campaign against the truth of what happened in Paris and in Princess Diana's last days was inestimably higher. Exactly one year after the crash Fayed had lost all three bodyguards who had been in Paris with the Princess on the day she died. The bodyguards walked away with many of the real secrets behind the crash, and a large part of Fayed's remaining credibility.

---

[16] *Sun*, 17 March 1999.

12. THE BODYGUARDS

'These guys fell down on the job. A portion of the responsibility must lie with those two bodyguards who didn't do what they were supposed to do and didn't stick by the rules.'

Laurie Mayer, Mohamed Fayed's spokesman,
48 Hours, CBS, 31 August 1998

Both of Princess Diana's bodyguards on the night she died quit their jobs with Mohamed Fayed within nine months of the Alma tunnel crash. Having made a remarkable recovery from the grievous injuries he sustained in the crash, Trevor Rees-Jones left in May 1998, and Kez Wingfield followed in June. Thus the two most important living witnesses to the fatal decisions that were made in the last hours of Princess Diana's life were now outside the Fayed camp.

Because he had not been involved in the crash, Wingfield was the more important potential witness to what had transpired before the doomed party left the Ritz. Wingfield had been the senior security officer responsible for the Princess's safety. He had been part of the personal protection team Fayed assigned to look after the Princess from the moment she arrived in the South of France with Princes William and Harry in July 1997. At that time he worked alongside Royal Protection Squad officers as the two young Princes were accompanying their mother, but when she returned alone Wingfield was in charge. He had a clear recollection of everything that had happened during the Princess's stay with the Fayeds. Most pertinently, he was with the couple throughout their final day in Paris until Dodi concocted his plan to leave the Ritz without him. In retrospect, Wingfield's hushed argument with Dodi at the door to the Imperial Suite was the moment that the Princess's fate was determined. Wingfield says that his objections to Dodi's plan to leave with no backup car, no bodyguards and a driver he had never encountered before that day, were overruled by Dodi.

Immediately after the crash, as Fayed had initially come under pressure to explain why Dodi's unorthodox plan to leave the Ritz had been executed, his employees, including the bodyguards, presented a united front. 'You've got to do the interview. We've got to get our side of the story across,' Paul Handley-Greaves told Kez Wingfield.

The bodyguard was in Ireland speaking to his boss on his mobile phone in the second week of September 1997. He had been given a break after the Paris crash and had gone to Ireland to try to buy some horses, where Handley-Greaves sent him an urgent message on his bleeper. When Wingfield responded he was told that Fayed required him to do an interview for the US TV channel, ABC. Reluctant to agree, the bodyguard was certain he had told the French police all that he knew. Qualified to provide personal security, he felt his career could be damaged by appearing on international TV. Handley-Greaves pleaded with Wingfield, saying that the programme would be broadcast only in the USA. He said it would argue that Henri Paul had not been drinking, and that there must, therefore, have been something wrong with the blood tests that showed he was drunk.

Wingfield recounts that Handley-Greaves told him, 'This will be the only interview you will have to do. Can you find it in your heart to do it? It's very important to the boss that you do.'

Feeling that he had little real choice, Wingfield left Ireland immediately to be in London in time for the filming. He took the night ferry to Holyhead, and at the port he was met by one of Fayed's cars, and driven through what remained of the night to his London HQ at 60 Park Lane.

The ABC interview took place with Cynthia McFadden later that morning; John Macnamara sat in. Wingfield repeated to McFadden some of the things that he had told the French police. He said that the paparazzi had been 'instrumental' in causing the accident, and that the crash could have been avoided. Wingfield said he twice stopped the filming to ask for guidance from Macnamara. He knew he was treading a very delicate line, and hoped he would not be asked directly about the chaos that the Fayeds' security arrangements for Princess Diana had been reduced to on the night.

As soon as the ABC interview was over, Macnamara introduced Wingfield to Chester Stern of the *Mail on Sunday*, who was preparing a major article on the crash for that weekend's paper.

The *Mail on Sunday* interview took half an hour, after which Wingfield says that he was surprised to be told, 'You're on *Panorama*!' Wingfield didn't want to do any more interviews, and certainly not for British TV, but when John Macnamara stressed to Wingfield that it would be 'in the boss's interests' to do it, he agreed. Although Wingfield felt shattered after his overnight return from Ireland, he was now back on duty, and in Fayed's Park Lane HQ. To a question about Dodi's plan to leave the Ritz which he endorsed on *Panorama*, Wingfield later said, 'What else could I do? I couldn't describe it as the best plan in the world because three people died . . . So I described it as a "good plan".'

By the time *Panorama* was broadcast, Trevor Rees-Jones was expected to survive. The ten-hour operation carried out on Thursday 4 September at the Pitié-Salpêtrière hospital had been successful, and Rees-Jones was expected to be able to speak. What Rees-Jones said, and what he remembered, could be crucial to Judge Stéphan's investigation and to Mohamed Fayed. If he repeated the retort of Dodi's about his father approving the plan, Mohamed Fayed could be implicated in the reckless decision to allow an unqualified driver to chauffeur the Princess of Wales. Trevor Rees-Jones himself might also take action against Fayed as the owner of the Ritz hotel, whose head of security had placed his life in such serious danger.

'For a few days it was touch and go as to whether Trevor would survive,' Murrell told the *Sun*. 'When it became clear that Trevor was going to live, Kez and I were taken to one side by the head of security, Paul Handley-Greaves, and told very clearly that we had to get into Trevor's room and speak to him before the police. These instructions came from Mohamed Fayed. We were told to tell Trevor he would be looked after, and he shouldn't say anything to the police about the accident. It was stressed to us how important it was for us to speak to him first.

'Because Trevor was so ill, the staff only allowed immediate family into his room. When this was relayed back to Mohamed we were told he went mad, and said we must get in to see Trevor. We had to tell Trevor not to speak with the police. That was the most important thing for Fayed. His people had to speak with him first.'

The two bodyguards were ideal choices for this delicate task. As well as having been Rees-Jones's partner on the night, Wingfield was his friend, and was concerned about his recovery. Because Murrell was based in Paris, living at the villa Windsor, he would permanently be on hand, and able to visit Trevor in hospital as soon as he was off the danger list, and as soon as his doctors allowed a visit. Two police officers from the XIIIème division of the Paris police were permanently stationed outside his door. Both bodyguards had an obvious pretext to enter the hospital as friends and colleagues of Trevor's, but their visit had to wait until the French doctors deemed Rees-Jones fit to receive them. Wingfield and Murrell's task was made easier because, although Rees-Jones was under 24-hour police guard, Mohamed Fayed had insisted on providing his own security for his employee. According to hospital spokesman Thierry Meresse, this had caused immediate tension at the hospital: 'He placed two of his own guards to watch over Trevor Rees-Jones, as well as the French police. To access the patient, the bodyguards made you pass through a sort of screen. They were very suspicious of everyone who came in and out. They always asked questions about who was there and why they were there. At the start, they quickly learned who the nurses were, who was looking after him, and the doctors. But if one didn't have a white smock one was immediately logged [by the guards]. I had to become a "go-between" between Trevor's room and the outside world.

'We had the impression that we were no longer in charge of the situation. There were so many Fayed bodyguards around Trevor that it was very difficult to get to see the patient. Staff took very badly, for example, the fact that a sort of barrier had been put in the way of getting to their patient. Great tension with the Fayed security developed very quickly.'[1]

Rees-Jones's first visitor was from the official investigation. Judge Stéphan interviewed the stricken bodyguard on 19 September. By the time Wingfield eventually succeeded in speaking to Rees-Jones, he ignored the instructions he'd been given. 'I was just happy to see my mate was still alive, and was getting better.'

Rees-Jones could not speak to his friend, but he could communicate with Wingfield by writing messages in chalk on a board with his right hand. His head was terribly swollen, he was covered in bandages and linked to drips. His left arm was heavily plastered. 'That was some overtime!' was Trevor's first scribbled comment to Kez.

Wingfield was relieved to see Rees-Jones again nearly three weeks after the two had last seen each other in the Ritz hotel just after midnight on 31 August. With the deaths of Princess Diana, Dodi Fayed and Henri Paul, the two had become the only living witnesses to the catastrophic events in the Ritz that night. Wingfield had been led to believe that Rees-Jones had died in the crash too, until he arrived at the Pitié-Salpêtrière hospital with Fayed. One of the hospital staff approached Wingfield and told him, 'Your friend is still alive.'

On returning to Britain, Kez Wingfield felt he wanted to move on from the tragedy, and regain the anonymity of his life before the crash in Paris. He was transferred from close-protection duties to minding Fayed's estates in Scotland. Although some interpreted this move as a demotion, Wingfield himself was relaxed about it. Essentially a private man, he found in his new role some peace and quiet, and a welcome return to obscurity. He was pleased to be inaccessible to journalists who might want to speak to him. After the tragedy he had started a

---

[1] Author's interview with Thierry Meresse, 2003.

relationship with Debbie Gribble, the chief stewardess on the *Jonikal*, and he was pleased to have the space in which their romance could prosper.

Several months later, however, Fayed required Wingfield to help him further. He was busy arranging interviewees for the proposed ITV programme, *Diana – Secrets Behind the Crash*. He agreed to let the programme producer, Richard Belfield, film in and around his properties in Paris – the rue Arsène-Houssaye apartment he had let Dodi use, the Ritz and the villa Windsor. Reliable staff such as the villa Windsor's Gregorio Martin were lined up as well. As Fayed saw it, Diana's bodyguards would provide essential witness in a film in which he would give his first TV interview about the crash.

Fayed started to instruct his staff as to what was required. Kez Wingfield was introduced to Belfield in somewhat disconcerting circumstances after he had been summoned to Harrods by John Macnamara. The Director of Security said he wanted the bodyguard to meet a reporter. Wingfield was led to understand that the 'reporter' was from the *Mirror*. In fact, it was Richard Belfield from Fulcrum TV. The two men both hail from Yorkshire, and they chatted amiably for a few minutes. However, when the producer suggested to the bodyguard that he should be interviewed for the ITV programme, Wingfield froze. He had fervently hoped that his September TV interviews with ABC and the BBC would have been his last. 'I just didn't want to be involved,' Wingfield recalled, 'and I tried to tell Belfield this without being rude to him.' Wingfield had reluctantly become the main performer in the BBC's *Panorama* programme immediately after the crash, and he had no desire to repeat that performance. 'I had basically said all I had to say, and I had nothing to add.'

According to Wingfield, as Belfield was trying to persuade him to change his mind about appearing in the ITV documentary, the door flew open and Mohamed Fayed himself appeared. 'I see you have met the bastard who f****d up in Paris!' he cried as he entered.[2] Trevor was the one who got f****d up in Paris, Wingfield thought.

Believing that he had made it clear that he did not wish to appear in the ITV film, Wingfield was startled to receive a call from Tam Coyle – manager of Fayed's Balnagown estate in Renfrewshire – on 17 May. Coyle told Wingfield that an ITV crew was coming to Scotland to shoot an interview with him. 'No way!' exclaimed Wingfield. 'I've already told them I won't do it.'

---

[2] Kez Wingfield in a statement to an industrial tribunal, 16 December 1998.

Wingfield had channelled his refusal to do the ITV interview through one of his superiors at Balnagown Castle, and also directly to Paul Handley-Greaves in London. Although relatively isolated on the Balnagown estate, Wingfield had become aware that the ITV programme had become a 'huge matter' to Fayed, who viewed it as being extremely important. He says he had agreed with Paul Handley-Greaves to have another 'brief chat' with Belfield, but he had stressed that he had nothing to add to what he had said in their previous meeting: 'Belfield was welcome to waste his time coming to Scotland to have another chat.'[3] When Wingfield found out it was supposed to be an on-camera TV interview, he refused to do it.

Fayed summoned him to another meeting. Wingfield drove from Fayed's Inveroykel estate where he was lodging, to Fayed's Scottish seat at Balnagown Castle on 25 May. He made the journey with a sense of foreboding – he knew how keen Fayed was for him to appear in the ITV film, and he was equally sure of his own determination not to participate.

The meeting was held in a tent pitched outside the castle. Fayed has tents erected outside his properties throughout the world from which he conducts his business. He apparently thinks they are more difficult to bug than buildings. The tent makes a curious sight outside the castle that Fayed restored and, somewhat incongruously, painted pink.

Wingfield knew his meeting would be an unusual one as soon as he walked in: 'When I entered the tent Fayed asked me to sit down. I knew it must be for a reason, because that was the first time the boss had ever invited me to be seated in his presence.'

Trevor Rees-Jones had left Fayed the previous week, on 19 May, having served his notice. Wingfield knew he would now be under even greater pressure to comply with his boss's wishes about the ITV interview. He was determined not to.

Wingfield's colleagues in Fayed's security team were able to observe on the surveillance cameras what Wingfield described afterwards as a 'blazing row'. Fayed became extremely angry when Wingfield told him he did not want to appear in the ITV programme. He started shouting at Wingfield.

'You and Trevor are to blame for the deaths of Diana and Dodi!' he told him. Referring to Trevor Rees-Jones, Fayed screamed, 'That bastard has my curse. He's supposed to be loyal but he's let me down.'

Wingfield was stunned – 'gobsmacked' was his own description.[4] In the course of the tirade, Wingfield says he had to endure some

---

[3] Kez Wingfield in a statement to an industrial tribunal, 16 December 1998.
[4] Kez Wingfield in a statement to an industrial tribunal, 16 December 1998.

incomprehensible and obscene comments about sexual deviancy and Fayed's penis.[5] After ranting for several minutes, Fayed suddenly changed tack: 'Are you loyal to me? Are you one hundred per cent loyal?' he screamed at his bodyguard. 'If you are, you will agree to do interview'. According to Wingfield, Fayed then tried to persuade him of the somewhat unlikely proposition that he would obtain ITV's questions from Belfield 'beforehand, and sort it out', so there would be no surprises in front of the camera.

Wingfield recalled, 'I told the boss that I was loyal, but I wouldn't go on TV again to repeat things he knew were not really true, such as the description I gave of Dodi's plan. It was the best plan he ever had, and it were crap,' the plain-speaking Yorkshireman recalled. 'I basically told the boss to stuff it, but in rather more polite terms, as I knew my job was on the line. I told him he was paying for his evidence of conspiracy theories, and that it wouldn't mean anything to anybody. If you pay people enough they'll say anything.

'Fayed told me that he was giving an interview for the film himself because he knew the film would support his conspiracy theories. He believes Dodi and Diana were killed by British intelligence, Mossad or the CIA.'

Wingfield had been deeply unhappy with the round of interviews he had been forced to do in the wake of the accident. Now, however, Fayed wanted a repeat of Wingfield's *Panorama* performance for millions of ITV viewers. 'He basically gave me a choice – appear in the programme or lose my job.'

Mohamed Fayed's ultimatum forced Wingfield into a major decision. Despite the trauma of the crash, he had enjoyed his security work for Fayed, and he had hoped a long career would lie ahead. He was planning a move into a house in the small village of Burstwick just outside Hull that very weekend, and to do so had taken on a large mortgage commitment. After he had moved, and after a weekend of soul-searching, Wingfield decided he had no option but to resign. He felt that the trust, which is so essential in close-protection work, had been destroyed between himself and Fayed. Wingfield instructed his lawyers to fax his letter of resignation to Fayed on 2 June, the day before the ITV film was broadcast.

I learnt of Wingfield's dramatic resignation the following day from a source who had helped me throughout my *Dispatches* investigation. I was phoned en route to Nottingham to take part in ITV's live debate about the film *Diana – Secrets Behind the Crash* in the Central TV studios

---

[5] Kez Wingfield in a statement to an industrial tribunal, 16 December 1998.

in Nottingham. Our routine request to interview Wingfield had been rejected by Fayed's office weeks beforehand, but my source phoned to say that Wingfield had quit and would speak.

We arranged to meet for breakfast at a railway station at 07.30. Wingfield had resigned less than 48 hours before our breakfast, and he had no intention of saying anything for my *Dispatches* film that was to be broadcast that evening. He told me he was committed to Judge Stéphan's investigation and would speak to him as soon as he could. (Indeed, the following month Wingfield returned to speak to the investigators to volunteer information about which he'd not been asked during his first interview.) However, he was prepared to brief me in detail about the crucial hour before Diana and Dodi left the Ritz, and also the holidays that preceded it. He had been guarding the Princess every day she was in the Fayed family's care. Wingfield was very keen that the facts should come out from beneath the cloud of misinformation that had grown particularly dense during the week in which we were speaking. He revealed that the reason he had left Fayed was that he had been pressured to appear in the ITV film that had been shown the night before we met. His comments about *Diana – Secrets Behind the Crash* conveyed his relief at having managed to avoid being in it. He felt that nothing he had ever seen on television or in print came close to reflecting what had actually happened, and why Princess Diana and Dodi had died.

Interestingly, Wingfield later said that he had spoken to Trevor Rees-Jones after the ITV programme and he, too, was furious that he was not in a position to respond. After the trauma of his virtually miraculous recovery, Rees-Jones did not find the ITV programme helpful or accurate according to Wingfield.

Within hours of the crash, Mohamed Fayed had flown Rees-Jones's mother, Gill, and his stepfather, Ernie, to Paris from their home in Oswestry with Trevor's estranged wife, Sue. The family was escorted through the massed ranks of the media by British Embassy officials. As they arrived at the Gaston Cordier wing of the Pitié-Salpêtrière hospital to see Trevor, Princess Diana's coffin was leaving. They stood in disbelief as the coffin was carried out in complete silence. The gendarmes bowed their heads as Prince Charles and Diana's two sisters, Sarah and Jane, walked red-eyed from the hospital.

Although the bodyguard's family had been told in Britain that he was still alive, they were worried that he could have died before they arrived in Paris. Naturally, they were massively relieved to find that he had survived. The Rees-Jones family was informed that Trevor did not have any life-threatening injuries. However, because Trevor's head had gone through the front window of the Mercedes, he had broken many bones in his face. The doctors told his family that they had performed an emergency tracheotomy, and his brain had swollen to enormous proportions.

The bodyguard's family was able to see him only briefly on 31 August. According to Sue Rees-Jones, the relief that the family felt at finding that Trevor was still alive was tempered by the appalling injuries he had suffered. The bodyguard was in a coma induced by the doctors. When he came round from it, at first only a fluid emerged from his mouth as he tried to react to soothing words from his family. Rees-Jones's face was held in place by wire after complicated operations to rebuild it. According to Sue Rees-Jones, when the bodyguard's parents broke the news that Princess Diana and Dodi Fayed had been killed in the crash, her husband's mouth dropped open at the shock, requiring the delicate wiring to be rebuilt. Doctors Alain Deboise and Odile Diamant Berger assessed the extent of his injuries. On a scale of one to seven, the two doctors agreed that the injuries were so severe that they rated them as 'not less than six'. They said that he would take at least a year to recover, and that they could not rule out possible secondary complications, the need for more surgery or depression in reaction to the injuries.

Distressed to hear about the bodyguard's plight, Prince Charles found time to write a personal note of support to Sue Rees-Jones:

> I can understand so well the anguish you must have felt for your husband in the immediate aftermath of last week's tragic accident. I just wanted you to know that you are in my thoughts and those of my children, and that we pray so hard for your husband's recovery from his injuries.[6]

Trevor's parents were to keep a daily vigil by his bedside as he emerged from his comatosed state. Gill recorded her son's recovery in a daily diary as the doctors conducted the complicated but ultimately successful operations to rebuild his face. Dodi's 'wholistic healer', The Reverend Myriah Daniels – who had dreamt during the last night on the *Jonikal* that the party would have an aeroplane crash on the following day – was also allowed to visit.

---

[6] Information about the Rees-Jones family's visit to Paris, including this note from Prince Charles, is from the *News of the World*, 15 March 1998. *The Bodyguard's Story*, Trevor Rees-Jones (Little Brown, 2000) confirms and amplifies this episode.

While they were in Paris, the Rees-Jones family stayed in the Fayed apartment on the rue Arsène-Houssaye, Trevor's destination on the night of the crash. Dodi's chauffeur, Philippe Dourneau, drove them to the Pitié-Salpêtrière hospital every day.

The bodyguard's first non-family visitor was from the official investigation. Judge Stéphan was received by Professeur Jean-Jacques Rouby, who was present throughout the interrogation to monitor his patient's condition. Gill and Ernie Rees-Jones were also there to help decipher Trevor's mumbled answers for the official translator, who interpreted both the judge's questions and Trevor's responses. Once the interview was over, a tape of it was transcribed by hand outside Rees-Jones's ward, and then presented to him to sign when it was finished.

The stricken guard confirmed Wingfield's assertion that it was Dodi who had devised the fated plan, and Dodi who had chosen Henri Paul to drive. Hazy memories about vehicles that the bodyguard recalled seeing from the first moments of the departure from the Ritz did not help Stéphan very much. Despite the bodyguard's best efforts, he told Stéphan little that he did not already know.[7]

A tape of the interview was obtained by the *Guardian* newspaper shortly after it took place, and thus its contents were to become widely disseminated. The paper's headline on 22 September, 'I RECALL GETTING IN THE CAR AND NOTHING ELSE', and the parts of the interview printed made it clear that the bodyguard's memory of the fatal journey was still impaired.

On 2 October, the day before he was discharged from the Pitié-Salpêtrière, Rees-Jones was interviewed again, this time by two of Martine Monteil's detectives, the Criminal Brigade's commissioner, Vianney Dyevre, and Commander Joseph Orea.

The bodyguard's memory seemed to be returning in the second interview. Kiejman and his legal team were able to read the interview shortly after the Crim's officers had submitted it to Judge Stéphan, when it was placed on the investigation's official file.

From photographs he was shown by the detectives, Rees-Jones identified two photographers who had been hounding the party during the day, Romuald Rat and Laszlo Veres. He also recognised Serge Benamou, who had been standing at the back of the Ritz hotel as he had left with Princess Diana and Dodi for their departure. Rees-Jones also began to recall details of what had happened in the Ritz. He

---

[7] Transcript of the official interview with Trevor Rees-Jones, *Death of a Princess*, pp. 203–5.

corroborated Wingfield's story about Henri Paul drinking a 'yellow liquid' in the bar Vendôme, and confirmed his colleague's impression that the hotel's head of security had appeared to be 'fine' and not drunk before departure. He also gave details of Dodi's plan to leave the Ritz by the back door. He described how Dodi had devised the decoy plan, which involved Henri Paul driving the third Mercedes.

In the margin of the transcript of Trevor Rees-Jones's interview with the Criminal Brigade is a reminder that the detectives' mission was to interview him in connection with the potential case against the photographers. The detectives were not engaged in an investigation into the Ritz hotel, or into the role Fayed himself played, at the time of Rees-Jones's interview.

One particular comment Rees-Jones made was intriguing: 'In answer to your question, to my knowledge Dodi did not receive any threats at the Ritz, or anywhere else, during the holiday. If such had been the case, I think he would have told me.'

The question Rees-Jones was responding to was possibly prompted by Mohamed Fayed's claim about the 'suspicious circumstances' surrounding the crash. The president of the Ritz, Frank Klein, and his assistant, Claude Roulet, had made this claim on the day of the crash, to the police chief, Patrick Riou, when they went to see him at the quai des Orfèvres.

The bodyguard was also starting to remember more details about Dodi's improvised plan to leave the Ritz. He repeated to the detectives his and Wingfield's joint recollection that it was Dodi's idea, and remembered that he had, indeed, objected to only one car being used, but was overruled by Dodi.

On 3 October, the day after Rees-Jones's interview with Martine Monteil's officers, he was released from hospital into the care of British Embassy officials. The hospital authorities had refused Fayed's formal request to remove Rees-Jones by helicopter from the Pitié-Salpêtrière's helicopter pad, and described a 'litany of clashes'.[8]

A British Embassy car eventually drove Rees-Jones from the hospital, where he had spent 34 days since the crash, to a heliport on the southwestern edge of Paris at Issy-les-Moulineaux. Handley-Greaves met him there, and escorted him to one of Mohamed Fayed's helicopters, which was to fly him back to Fayed's home in Oxted.

While the world was speculating first as to whether Rees-Jones would survive, and then whether he would remember anything about the

---

[8] *Evening Standard*, 6 October 1997. Confirmed by author's interview with Thiery Meresse, 2003.

crash, Fayed immediately offered to pay for French legal advice, as well as meeting his medical bills. He was keen that the bodyguard be represented by the legal firm, Klein Goddard, who were representing Henri Paul's family. However, the Rees-Jones family took a different view. Their family lawyer, David Crawford, travelled to Paris shortly after the accident. The Oswestry solicitor swiftly decided that his client's interests would be better represented by someone other than Klein Goddard, a firm that had represented the Fayed family in France for over 20 years. A friend recommended Christian Curtil, a 30-year-old lawyer, with his office on the Avenue Friedland, close to the Arc de Triomphe. Curtil is renowned for his eloquence. In 1997, he came second in the Paris bar's highly regarded debating contest, the 'conférence du stage'.

One of the first moves Curtil made was to register Trevor Rees-Jones as a civil plaintiff on 16 October 1997, after he returned to Britain to continue his recovery. Curtil thus gained the same access to Judge Stéphan's investigation as the lawyers representing the Spencer, Paul and Fayed families.

Ten weeks after his release from hospital, Trevor Rees-Jones returned to Paris to see Judge Stéphan just before Christmas. The pace of the bodyguard's recovery had been remarkable. Kez Wingfield accompanied him to Paris, and the two spent the night at the villa Windsor with Ben Murrell and his wife. The evening of 17 December was the first time the three men had been together since the day they had supervised Princess Diana's brief trip around the villa Windsor with Dodi on the last afternoon of their lives. Kez and Ben decided to take Trevor to a café off the Champs-Elysées for a meal and some drinks.

Later that night, Murrell and Wingfield glimpsed the trauma that Rees-Jones was enduring. After they returned to the villa they stayed up drinking until the early hours, as Ben Murrell recalled: 'Trevor got very upset and burst into tears as he said he was to blame for everything. It was heartbreaking to see him cry because he was so racked with guilt. We knew he hadn't done anything wrong, but the death of Diana and Dodi was getting to him. Fortunately, I think Kez and I managed to cheer him up.'

Part of the enormous pressure on Rees-Jones came from the intense, worldwide speculation surrounding what he could remember about the most infamous crash in history. Rees-Jones was aware, as he made his way back to Britain, that it was not an exaggeration to say that the whole world was fascinated to hear or read an interview with the sole survivor of the crash that killed Princess Diana. There had been leaks of his interviews to the French and British media from the files of Stéphan's investigation, but no one had ever heard or seen him tell his own story.

At the beginning of 1998 Rees-Jones returned to light duties at Harrods and, as he was still employed by Fayed, it was very difficult for the bodyguard to refuse to be interviewed for the same ITV documentary that Kez later refused to appear in. First, however, Trevor Rees-Jones was offered to the *Mirror*. The paper's editor, Piers Morgan, had splashed Mohamed Fayed's first interview since the crash over several pages and several editions in the middle of February 1998. His claim that the crash '. . . WAS NO ACCIDENT' had made waves around the world. Rees-Jones was given the same treatment.

'I SURVIVED', screamed the *Mirror*'s front-page headline on the last day of February. 'EXCLUSIVE – Diana's bodyguard Trevor Rees-Jones tells his own story.' Trailing what would follow over the next few days as 'the year's most astonishing interview', Piers Morgan was pictured sitting down talking to the man every journalist in the world would have liked to interview. His tape recorder was seen lying on the table. The headline of 28 February, announcing that the *Mirror* had secured the interview, sparked a fierce battle over that weekend between the paper and its main rivals. The *Sun* offered the Welshman a small fortune to offer his recollections to them instead. The public was fascinated to read what the sole survivor of Diana's death crash had to say, and learn of what he could remember.

Rees-Jones's interview was a moving account of how he had learnt about the deaths of his three companions in the crash from his mother once he had awoken from the coma. The bodyguard's feeling of guilt at having survived the crash was movingly conveyed, and he described watching a video recording of Diana's funeral with tears running down his cheeks. Rees-Jones's personal testimony, however, disappointed those who were looking for new revelations of any significance about the tragedy. The bodyguard had already spoken to the French investigation twice, and details of his testimony had been extensively leaked.

Like Kez Wingfield with *Panorama*, Rees-Jones felt he had been tricked into talking to the *Mirror*. On both occasions, the trickery had not been perpetrated by the journalists from the BBC or the *Mirror*, but by the bodyguard's boss. Rees-Jones had responded to a summons from Fayed to present himself at his office, and had been surprised to find himself being introduced to Piers Morgan. Once there, and with Fayed himself present at the beginning and at the end of the interview, Rees-Jones had little option but to cooperate with his boss's wishes.

It was agreed that Rees-Jones would receive no fee for the interview and that 'any proceeds accrued by Mirror Group Newspapers from selling the interview to other media will be donated to the Diana, Princess of Wales Memorial Fund and the Dodi Fayed International Charitable Foundation in equal shares.'[9]

Although Rees-Jones was quoted as saying 'I'm starting to remember more and more,' his interview did not contain information that would have been new to the judge.

The headline on the second day of the *Mirror* interviews read, 'I HEARD DIANA CALL OUT FOR DODI AFTER THE CRASH'. Rees-Jones later denied saying this. The theme of Diana's death being anyone's fault but the Fayeds' was consistent. The interview with the bodyguard was also used to support the Fayed-inspired illusion of Diana's 'last words'. Apparently without checking with French medical or police sources who had attended the stricken Princess, the *Mirror* reported that Trevor's memory of Diana calling out Dodi's name 'supports the claim made by Dodi's father, Harrods tycoon Mohamed Al Fayed, that Diana was able to speak after the crash. That it is possible she was able to utter the last words that Mr Al Fayed says were passed on to him by a nurse at the hospital.'[10]

Christian Curtil recognised that the Fayed-supervised *Mirror* interview was not how Judge Stéphan had envisaged his investigation proceeding. Rees-Jones was the only first-hand witness to the crash, and Curtil knew that Stéphan was keen to hear directly from the bodyguard about any new memories that may have returned to him.

On 5 March, Curtil requested that Rees-Jones's next interview with Judge Stéphan be brought forward to the following day. Curtil was aware that Fayed was to see Stéphan on 12 March, and was keen that his client should speak to the judge first. The trip Rees-Jones made to Paris on 6 March for his interview proved to be a watershed. It brought to a head tensions between his lawyers and the British government on the one hand, and Mohamed Fayed on the other. Fayed instructed Ben Murrell, once again, to mind the Welshman in Paris and instructed him not to let Rees-Jones out of his sight. Murrell recalled:

'Fayed sent a car [to the villa Windsor] and so did the British Embassy. We were told that under no circumstances should Trevor go in the embassy car. Fayed was convinced they were part of MI5 and wanted neither us nor Trevor to have anything to do with them. There were lots of telephone calls between Al Fayed in London, and Paris. I

---

[9] *Daily Telegraph*, 2 March 1998.
[10] *Mirror*, 1 March 1998.

heard him shouting down the phone that Trevor wasn't allowed to go with the embassy people. It was a complete farce. We were trying to persuade Trevor to come with us, and the embassy officials were insisting he went with them.'

Rees-Jones reacted badly to the friction between the two camps. He appeared to be the inadvertent cause of the escalating dispute. Fayed was becoming progressively more convinced of his own theory that the British 'Establishment' had assassinated Dodi and Princess Diana, and Rees-Jones wanted nothing to do with it.

Murrell recalled, 'Trevor just flipped and went wild. He said he was sick of everyone trying to tell him what to do. He eventually went with the embassy people. Al Fayed went crazy. He was shouting that Rees-Jones was part of MI5 and in on the conspiracy. I laughed but I felt sorry for Trevor. He resigned as a bodyguard not long afterwards.'

The trouble between Fayed and Rees-Jones started before the bodyguard had even left Britain. David Crawford had originally planned to drive Rees-Jones to France, but Fayed refused to release his employee, and insisted on flying him to Paris by helicopter. Concerned that he would have no chance to speak to his client before his interview with Judge Stéphan, Christian Curtil informed Fayed's lawyers that unless the bodyguard was present in his avenue Friedland office by 10.00 sharp on 6 March he would inform the French police that his client had been kidnapped.[11] Following the dispute at the villa Windsor over which car he was to travel in, Rees-Jones arrived to see Curtil in the British Embassy's minibus. Outside Curtil's office, the British Embassy and Fayed security teams sized each other up in the avenue Friedland as they waited in their vehicles. The Fayed car then shadowed the Embassy's minibus carrying Curtil, Rees-Jones and the British Embassy officials on the way to the Palais de Justice. At their meeting, the bodyguard explained to Judge Stéphan why the *Mirror* interview had taken place, and how, as an employee, he had had very little choice in the matter.

On 19 April, seven weeks after his *Mirror* interview was published, and six weeks after the bust-up between Fayed and the British Embassy in Paris, the bodyguard handed in his notice. In public Fayed and Rees-Jones exchanged complimentary remarks in the press. Through his Oswestry lawyers, Rees-Jones said, 'I wish to thank my employers and Mr Mohamed Al Fayed personally for the help and support they have given me through this difficult time.' He said he was leaving with regret because he wished to 'move on' with his life.

---

[11] Christian Curtil in a fax to the author, 18 May 1998.

In the bodyguard's *Mirror* interview, Fayed had been portrayed in the pastoral, protective light he had tried so hard to cultivate. It had been reported elsewhere that Fayed had offered Rees-Jones a job for life at Harrods.[12] He had started 'light duties' at the store, but one factor in his decision to leave was his dislike of being gawked at by shoppers as a form of tourist attraction – the 'freak of Harrods'.

Fayed's public statement was framed equally politely: 'I understand that Trevor must do everything possible to make a full recovery, and ultimately to put the tragic events of last August behind him.' His anger surfaced publicly nine months after Rees-Jones quit. When he was asked in a radio interview why he had let Rees-Jones leave, Fayed exploded, 'No! No! No! He resigned! Imagine, after I saved his life! Done everything, and the minute the guy started to talk and to recover, the guy turned against me. Him and other two bodyguards, was, are always working with Dodi and the Princess because they know exactly that those, one specialist Trevor Rees-Jones knows exactly what happened, and if he's, because basically it's better that he can go and, you know, is dead by now, if he's not dead what they can do, they have to turn him again against me, right, this is what I believe. How can a guy I saved his life, looked after him for five years, just leave me and go and now sue the Ritz and sue me? You see that this is fair? It's not, it's not normal.'[13]

Self-evidently Fayed would not now find it possible to force the departed bodyguard to appear in the ITV film, or undergo the series of media interviews he had envisaged for him. Nearly eight months after the tragedy, Fayed was bitterly cursing Rees-Jones's lawyers. Fayed ranted in his offices, 'It's those fuggin' lawyers that have persuaded him to leave.'

In the hope that he could leave behind the exploitation of the horrific experience he had lived through, Trevor Rees-Jones returned to live in his family's home town of Oswestry. He took a part-time job in a local sports shop.

Less than a month after leaving Fayed, Rees-Jones's rift with his former employer became formal. Christian Curtil wrote to Judge Stéphan on 12 June saying that his client 'had never accepted the same point of view as the Ritz'. Curtil requested that the investigation should be broadened to examine the role of the Ritz in the crash, and also that of Etoile Limousine. Curtil wanted Stéphan to investigate on behalf of

---

[12] *Daily Telegraph*, 12 April 1998.
[13] Radio Telefis Eireann, January 1999.

his client whether the two companies had 'put his life in danger', by allowing an unqualified drunk to cause the accident in which he was a passenger. Curtil's request opened the possibility that senior members of the Ritz, such as Frank Klein and Claude Roulet, and the two directors of Etoile Limousine, 'Niels' Siegel and Jean-François Musa, would be placed under examination for their role in the tragedy.

Fayed was furious at Curtil's move on behalf of Rees-Jones. Just before the first anniversary of Diana's death, Mohamed Fayed could contain his frustration no longer and he launched his attack on the bodyguards in *Time* magazine in the USA.

Both bodyguards were hurt but not surprised by the *Time* outburst, in which he had attacked their 'incompetence and unprofessional practices'. Fayed had said very similar things about Trevor Rees-Jones to Wingfield in private during their row over the ITV film during that spring, which had caused the Yorkshireman to quit. The bodyguards knew that they had argued that Diana and Dodi should have had more protection in Paris, not less, and now their boss, who had denied their request, was blaming them for the death of the Princess and his son.

Fayed's new spokesman, Laurie Mayer, launched an acid attack on the bodyguards: 'These guys fell down on the job. A portion of the responsibility must lie with those two bodyguards who didn't do what they were supposed to do and didn't stick by the rules . . . Why wasn't there a backup car? Why did they leave by the back door of the Ritz?'[14]

Anyone with the slightest knowledge of the events of that evening could answer those questions in one sentence – because on every detail the bodyguards were overruled, and had their professional objections crushed by Dodi Fayed hatching a reckless plan. There was no mention by Mayer that Diana and Dodi had taken exactly the same route out of the hotel earlier the same evening; no mention that Dodi had instructed Henri Paul to drive and ordered the bodyguards not to organise a backup car; and of course no mention that Trevor Rees-Jones had been allowed to travel with Diana and Dodi only after Kez Wingfield had argued with Dodi's plan to take no guards at all.

Mayer also issued a blank denial of Fayed's involvement in Dodi's getaway plan: 'I've talked to Mr Al Fayed about this many times, and it's simply not true.'

The Welshman was widely perceived as the hero of the crash that killed Princess Diana and he had fought hard to maintain his privacy since his resignation in May. His lawyers had a 'filing cabinet full' of

---

[14] CBS, *48 hours*, 31 August 1998. Laurie Mayer replaced Michael Cole in May 1998.

requests from media all over the world to interview their client, the man
he British tabloids invariably referred to as 'Di hero'. Several such offers
could have made the sole survivor of the crash that killed Princess Diana
a millionaire. All had been turned down, or put in the pending tray, as
have offers to publish books involving the bodyguard. He also instructed
his lawyers not to assist any journalistic enterprises that might upset
Fayed. Rees-Jones was determined to keep his pledge of fidelity to Judge
Stéphan's official probe.

He was understandably dismayed by Fayed's outburst and, through
intermediaries, ensured that a personal letter he wrote to Princes
William and Harry was received. Rees-Jones made it clear to Diana's
sons that he had done everything he could to protect their mother, and
that he had been devastated by the outcome. He assured them that the
allegations that Fayed was now making against himself and Wingfield
were as unjustified as they were hurtful.

At the beginning of August 1998, Rees-Jones had released a video
statement, the first and the only time the bodyguard had spoken
voluntarily in public since the crash. The purpose of the video was to
request privacy as the first anniversary of the crash approached, and to
ask the media to respect the memory of the three people who died.

'I ask you all to respect our privacy at this time and allow us all to
deal with the anniversary in our own way,' he said. 'I have at the
forefront of my mind the fact that three people were killed in the
accident last August. On this the first occasion I have spoken publicly,
I wish to extend my sympathy to the families and friends of those killed
. . . I wish to make it clear that I have told Judge Stéphan all I remember
concerning the accident.'

His lawyers made it clear that the prepared statement – which
Rees-Jones made to Associated Press TV for distribution throughout the
world – was not an 'interview'. On hearing of Fayed's attack on the
bodyguards, however, his British lawyer, David Crawford, issued a
much more combative statement: 'Trevor and Kez did all that anyone
could have done on the night, given the circumstances and the
instructions they received. They were Dodi's bodyguards. Until now no
one has disputed the fact that they were following Dodi's instructions.'

Crawford's statement also made the telling point that, when Fayed
had been interviewed by Judge Stéphan in March 1998, he had not
uttered a critical word about either man. At that time both men were
still working for Fayed.

In reality Trevor Rees-Jones had become Fayed's most dangerous
potential enemy, and Wingfield had become the Welshman's most

valuable potential ally. Rees-Jones was not only the sole surviving victim of the crash, he was also a crucial witness to the decisions made. Rees-Jones's lawyers had infuriated Fayed further by trying to persuade Judge Stéphan to investigate the Ritz hotel and Etoile Limousine. As the one living victim of the crash, Trevor Rees-Jones could become a key witness in establishing the truth about the events on the night, as well as having the right to sue the hotel for massive compensation.

Fayed's August 1998 attack on the bodyguards in the USA came as the position of the Ritz hotel appeared to deteriorate in the eyes of the French investigators. When it was made, Judge Stéphan's office was indicating that he would respond positively to Curtil's request to investigate how Henri Paul came to be placed in charge of the fated Mercedes. It had been widely reported that the president of the Ritz hotel, Frank Klein, his number two, Claude Roulet, and Etoile Limousine's director, 'Niels' Siegel, would be recalled for further interviews by Judge Stéphan.[15] The interviews took place on 25 and 26 August 1998. Their purpose was to establish whether they could shed any further light upon how Paul came to be at the wheel, and to compare their statements with those of Frédéric Lucard and Jean-François Musa. Fayed's onslaught was intended as a warning shot across the bows of the bodyguards and their lawyers, designed to let them know that they could expect a stern response if they proceeded with their respective actions against him.

What Fayed was not expecting as he attacked Wingfield and Rees-Jones was the blow from Ben Murrell, whose revelations about the brevity of Princess Diana's visit to the villa Windsor seriously damaged the credibility of Fayed's attempts to rewrite the history of Diana's relationship with Dodi. It also made it even more important to him that he should damage the credibility of the two men whom he had charged with ensuring Diana's safety in Paris on 30/31 August 1997.

Because Wingfield was not involved in the accident, and retains a clear memory of everything that occurred immediately before it, he is arguably the single most important witness to the events of the night. It became clear during the industrial tribunal into Wingfield's resignation, that Fayed was determined not only to defeat Wingfield, but also to destroy his credibility. If he achieved this, Fayed would undermine Wingfield's potential to assist Trevor Rees-Jones in future cases that the bodyguard might bring against him in France or in Britain. Before the

---

[15] Reuters, 18 August 1998.

tribunal started Fayed's lawyers made an unsuccessful attempt to exclude the press, arguing that the tribunal would involve the disclosure of 'confidential information' about his security operation. It also became apparent that Fayed would not contest Wingfield's claim in person. At this time the Egyptian had never given evidence under oath in a British witness box.

Wingfield's action was taken against Hyde Park Residences, the Fayed company that employed him. Company documents list Fayed and the Paris Ritz president Frank Klein as directors. Both sides agreed that the key to the tribunal's outcome was the conversation between Fayed and Wingfield about the ITV documentary, which took place at Balnagown Castle on 25 May, the week before the bodyguard resigned.

The bodyguard recounted his clash with Fayed in Scotland. Wingfield told the tribunal that Fayed had told him, 'Do it for me tomorrow, or you will be looking for another job.' Wingfield said he left because he felt he was being 'railroaded' into taking part in Belfield's film.

No significant detail of Wingfield's sworn statement to the tribunal had changed since the first time I met him on 4 June, two days after he had resigned, although he fleshed out some important details. Fayed's barrister, Matthew Reeve, cross-examined Wingfield at length in the afternoon. Reeve said that he would produce four or five witnesses to challenge Wingfield's statement the following day.

One of Fayed's witnesses was due to have been the producer of ITV's *Diana – Secrets Behind the Crash*. Richard Belfield had a different recollection of his meeting with Wingfield in London which set in motion the events leading to the bodyguard's departure. He says that Fayed was not present during any part of the meeting, and that their meeting did not occur in Fayed's office at Harrods. Belfield says that Wingfield agreed to record an interview for his documentary.[16]

The following morning, Fayed's team arrived looking as if they had been up all night. Fayed's lawyer announced the 'proceedings have been compromised [settled] to the satisfaction of both parties'. Fayed had reached an out-of-court settlement with Wingfield overnight by which he 'withdrew' his action. The outcome prevented any further embarrassment to Fayed in the tribunal, and removed the need for any witnesses to appear to challenge Wingfield's account of events. The details remain confidential to the parties. In an agreed statement, both parties accepted that their recollections 'differed over the circumstances leading to Mr Wingfield's resignation.'

---

[16] Richard Belfield in a letter to the author, 14 January 1999.

Once Stéphan had presented his report to Maude Coujard in September 1999, the bodyguards felt free to present their side of the story publicly. Kez Wingfield helped Trevor Rees-Jones to compile *The Bodyguard's Story*, a 300-page account subtitled *Diana, the Crash and the Sole Survivor*.[17] The two appeared on British and American TV to publicise the book, which became a bestseller. Readers were left in no doubt that neither of Diana's bodyguards give any credence to the 'conspiracy' theories of the accident that almost cost Rees-Jones his life; he describes them as 'rubbish'. The bodyguards categorically refute Fayed's allegation that they were responsible for the crash. They make it clear that, were it not for the Fayeds' instruction to permit Henri Paul to drive the Mercedes, they would not have allowed him to take the wheel or Princess Diana to leave the hotel with such scant security. At the end of the book Rees-Jones stresses how sad he is that Diana's sons will always associate his name with their mother's death. He writes of William and Harry, whom he recalls with affection from their July 1997 holiday with the Fayeds, 'If I met them, I'd say, "I'm bloody sorry. There's nothing more I could have done."'[18]

---

[17] *The Bodyguard's Story*, Trevor Rees-Jones, Little, Brown, 2000.
[18] Ibid, p. 317.

13. THE VERDICT

'There wasn't a conspiracy to murder Princess Diana, but there has most certainly been a conspiracy to cover up why she died.'

Kez Wingfield

Every month thousands of people visit the golden flame on the bridge over the Alma tunnel where Princess Diana's Mercedes crashed. Until they read the inscription many believe it stands in memory of the victims of the crash. The statue is, in fact, a detail from the American Statue of Liberty, unveiled in 1987, to commemorate the centenary of the *International Herald Tribune*, and the excellence of its journalism.

That this flame remains the place that thousands of people visit every month to remember the Princess wraps a hideous irony around their pilgrimage. The standard of journalistic excellence that the flame is said to symbolise has rarely been witnessed in the battle for her memory, or to establish precisely how she died. The bridge over the Alma tunnel is now itself a vivid indicator that much of this battle has seen a victory for form over substance, for PR over journalism, for propaganda over facts. The bridge's pale-grey concrete is covered in graffiti, wilting flowers and fading magazine pictures of the lovers who perished in the tunnel. Among messages in many languages are those that claim that Diana and Dodi were killed by MI5 or MI6, and that the crash was 'no accident'. The graffiti indicates that Mohamed Fayed's views have taken deep root in the public imagination throughout the world.

I do not believe that his campaign can withstand the force of the findings outlined in this book. By drawing on evidence from Judge Stéphan's investigation, and contributions from eyewitnesses to the events in Paris during the weekend when Princess Diana lost her life, I hope I have enabled a clearer picture to emerge.

Many people remain understandably confused about what really happened in Paris on 31 August 1997, and many feel there was something that didn't quite fit or was a 'bit odd' about the crash. Many are baffled about the precise role of the Fiat Uno. Many of these confusions occur because of the uneven reporting of the tragedy, and some because of disinformation emanating from Fayed. Ironically, none of the many members of Fayed's staff, past and present, to whom I have spoken believes the conspiracy-theorising of their boss.

Judge Stéphan's task was simply to assess whether the paparazzi should be prosecuted. In the course of his eighteen-month investigation, however, he has not found a shred of evidence to suggest that Diana, Princess of Wales, had died in anything other than a car crash, caused by a drunk driving a car for which he had no permit. The white Fiat Uno is the only missing link in the comprehensive French enquiry. The most detailed possible forensic tests at the IRCGN on the Mercedes S-280 had proved that the two cars had done no more than brush each other in the Alma tunnel immediately before the crash. The Fiat was not the cause of the crash. The widely reported 'flash-before-the-crash' theory was no more than the ravings of François Levistre, instantly rejected by French detectives, but seized on by sections of the international media after the crash. The notion that Henri Paul's blood samples may have been corrupted – a notion that owed itself to the high level of carbon monoxide found in one sample – was promoted by the selective misrepresentation of parts of the evidence submitted to Stéphan from Henri Paul's autopsy. As these myths crumbled, some conspiracy theorists dived deeper into their dark reserves of imagination to suggest that the entire judicial and medical systems were complicit in the 'cover-up' of the truth about the death of the Princess of Wales.

That the coverage of Princess Diana's death has incorporated so many of the fantasies about it is a mark of Fayed's success.

Contrary to the versions seen in the press, Fayed was not the first to arrive at the Pitié-Salpêtrière hospital, he did not see Princess Diana's body looking 'peaceful and serene', and he was not in receipt of her 'last words'.

Diana's very closest friends who spoke to her in her last days are adamant and united in their view that she had no intention of marrying Dodi Fayed. Princess Diana was not pregnant by Dodi or anybody else when she died. The only person to suggest that the ring that Mohamed bought for Dodi to give to her was anything other than a gesture of friendship is Fayed himself. There is no independent evidence to suggest that the Princess was engaged, or was planning to become engaged to Dodi. Diana said she had passed a 'blissful' summer with Dodi, but there is no evidence to demonstrate that she intended to set up home with him or that she was planning to share her life with him. The myth that she was planning to live in the villa Windsor has been disproved by Ben Murrell, who has provided incontrovertible evidence to contradict the claims that an 'Italian designer' had accompanied the couple on a two-hour visit in which they planned their future together.

The truth is that Princess Diana died because of Dodi's decision to put a drunk, drugged and unqualified driver in charge of a car which was driven dangerously and which subsequently crashed at high speed. Dodi told Kez Wingfield and Trevor Rees-Jones that his father had authorised the plan. There has been virtually no media focus on this central factor in the death of the Princess.

Fayed now seeks to expand his own views in cyberspace where he can rant against the 'animals' who disagree with him and his decreasingly credible conspiracy theories. Fayed launched his own website (www.alfayed.com) in 1998 with the 'story of Diana and Dodi', as told by Mohamed himself. The site's introductory page features pictures of some of Fayed's earthly baubles (the Ritz, the villa Windsor, his Balnagown castle) as well as pictures of Diana and Dodi. Bizarrely, one earthly possession Fayed has not been able to obtain, a British passport, floats between the picture of Diana and the villa Windsor. Princess Diana appears to be smiling at the passport.

On his Internet site Fayed moaned, 'Why is the establishment so cruel?' in an interview entitled 'I am not paranoid'. The Internet has been an important factor in the transition of Diana's death into a 'conspiracy', as it gave many conspiracy theories their first expression, and then amplified and accelerated their trajectories in the USA and in Fayed's Egyptian homeland. They have infected the first draft of the history of how Princess Diana died. An American observer of conspiracy theories remarked prophetically two days after the crash, as cyberspace vultures gathered to pick over the Alma tunnel crash, 'These theories will not stop because the facts prove them wrong.'[1]

Obtaining the facts was, of course, the principal objective of Judge Hervé Stéphan's investigation. It may have been slow in coming to its conclusions, but it could not be accused of breaching Michael Cole's entreaty, made at the Harrods' press conference, that there should be 'no rush to judgement' over who should bear responsibility for the crash. However, those expecting a report of the type Kenneth Starr produced into President Clinton's philandering will be disappointed. Only Stéphan's recommendation to the prosecutor, Maud Coujard, as to who should be prosecuted will be made public.

Judge Stéphan handed his dossier to Coujard on 19 February 1999. The 536-day investigation had produced a 6,800-page document standing over four feet high. It covered every conceivable aspect of the crash, and included over 200 statements from witnesses, including the sole survivor, Trevor Rees-Jones. Nearly one hundred of the statements were from Ritz hotel staff. Scores of photographs taken on the night of

---

[1] Reuters, 2 September 1997.

30/31 August outside the Ritz and around the crash were also included. All the medical teams that tried to save Diana, and the police who were at the scene made statements. The expert reports and those from the IRCGN were among the most significant documents.

A report delivered to Stéphan on 1 November 1998 by two crash specialists, Michel Nibodeau-Frindel and Bernard Amouroux, represented the investigation's definitive assessment of what happened in the Alma tunnel at 00.26 on 31 August 1997. The two specialists had been commissioned by Judge Stéphan to establish precisely this, taking into account the findings of the other *expertises*.

Research into the wrecked Mercedes at the IRCGN had already indicated that the car itself was in perfect working order when it crashed. The IRCGN investigators had also established that the Mercedes had only brushed a white Fiat Uno before crashing (see Chapters 4 and 7). Nibodeau-Frindel and Amouroux concurred with the IRCGN's finding: the Fiat Uno did not cause the crash.

In one sentence Nibodeau laid to rest the conspiracy theory that held that the Fiat had been used to ram the Mercedes into the pillar as part of an assassination: 'The Mercedes was more likely to have gone off course as a result of trying to avoid hitting the Fiat, rather than being knocked off course by it.'

The Nibodeau-Frindel/Amouroux report also killed other rumours – that the Mercedes' brakes could have been faulty, and that the long skid marks seen in the Alma tunnel after the crash were an indication of where the car had skidded before crashing. Nibodeau-Frindel and Amouroux found that both these rumours were not supported by evidence. The skid marks had not been made by the Mercedes, but had been made earlier by another vehicle before the accident occurred. Furthermore, Henri Paul had not used the brakes before crashing headlong into the pillar travelling at a speed of between 118 and 155 kilometres an hour. Diana and Dodi Fayed died because Paul was drunk, and he had tried to negotiate the entrance to the Alma tunnel, where the road dips and curves noticeably to the left, at too great a speed.

One of the greatest misjudgements Diana made about Dodi Fayed was that she felt he would be able to 'take the heat' of the media attention they were under. She might have been tempted into this misjudgement at least partially because of the contrast between the media-loving Fayeds and Hasnat Khan, who had refused ever to go public during her much longer and more substantial relationship with him. Diana was not prepared, however, for Dodi's panicking on the fatal night. Unless

Trevor Rees-Jones unexpectedly recovers his memory, no one will ever know what was said in the Mercedes between the Ritz and the Alma tunnel. It is known that Dodi lost his temper with the paparazzi, though, and with his bodyguards on the way to the Ritz earlier in the evening. It is known that while he was in the Ritz he dreamt up the unorthodox fatal plan to leave the hotel. No one has ever suggested that, as the two lovers hurtled towards their deaths, Henri Paul was defying Dodi's instructions by speeding. Kelly Fisher was chauffeured around frequently by Dodi's drivers during her relationship with him. From her experience, she formed the view that 'Whoever was at the wheel, Dodi was driving the car.'[2]

Unfortunately, Henri Paul was at the wheel. The Mercedes was a heavy car, difficult for Paul to control, particularly as he was unfamiliar with the car and was not qualified to drive it. Nibodeau-Frindel's report emphasised to Judge Stéphan the fact that Henri Paul did not know how to drive the powerful Mercedes S-280: 'It must be remembered that the driver was not qualified to drive this car. Excessive speed and the curve into the tunnel made the car uncontrollable.'

At the request of judges Stéphan and Devidal, the Mercedes had been returned to the Alma tunnel at 20.30 on 29 September by Martine Monteil and a Criminal Brigade delegation. IRCGN crash experts headed by Michel Nibodeau-Frindel placed the car in the position where it hit the thirteenth pillar and also the position in which it was found. Ten crash experts, criminologists and geometricians scurried around the tunnel for ninety minutes using lasers to try and work out the trajectory the Mercedes could have taken and exactly what had happened.

In their report, Nibodeau-Frindel and Amouroux concluded that the evidence indicated that Henri Paul had mistakenly put the Mercedes into neutral immediately before crashing, in an unsuccessful attempt to use its gears to slow down: 'Witnesses reported enormous engine noise before the crash. We believe the sudden revving up of the engine was due to the gear level being pushed into neutral because Paul was unfamiliar with the gearbox. Instead of acting as a brake, the motor was free-wheeling.'[3]

Furthermore, Nibodeau-Frindel and Amouroux concluded that Paul's brain, which had been shown to have been under the influence of drink and prescribed drugs, had been overloaded with information. This condition was familiar to the experienced crash investigators: 'When this

[2] Author's interview with Kelly Fisher, May 1998.
[3] Daily Mail, 19 November 1998. Confirmed in CBS interview with Nibodeau-Frindel, 2004.

phenomenon appears, we notice that the driver does the opposite of what he should do, and an accident is inevitable.'

The week before Judge Stéphan's June 1998 witness summit, or *grande confrontation*, reconstructions of the accident took place at a race track just outside Paris at Montlhery, in Essonne. The circuit had been rented on Stéphan's instructions, and police from both the IRCGN and the Criminal Brigade supervised two days of tests with Nibodeau-Frindel and Amouroux in attendance. A Mercedes S-280 was used as well as three motorcycles corresponding to those that the paparazzi had used to chase Henri Paul's car. Two people sat on the bike that had been first to arrive at the crash, to simulate Romuald Rat and his driver Stéphane Darmon. The Montlhery tests showed that the bikes that the paparazzi had been driving were more than capable of overtaking the Mercedes. However, the tests also showed that, had the bikes been travelling at the same speed as the forensic tests had shown the Mercedes to have been doing, their drivers would have lost control of their machines due to the curving dip at the mouth of the Alma tunnel.[4]

Having compared the performances of the paparazzi's vehicles with the Mercedes in the tests at Montlhery, Nibodeau-Frindel and Amouroux also concluded in their report of November 1998 that one or more motorcycles could possibly have prevented the Mercedes from leaving the Cours Albert 1er via a slip road, well before the Alma tunnel. This road would have been a more direct route to the Fayed apartment on the rue Arsène-Houssaye. To have done this, the paparazzi would either have had to block the slip road or have been illegally overtaking the Mercedes on the right-hand side of the road. This would explain why Henri Paul took the route via the Alma tunnel, which is not the most direct, or the quickest, to the Fayed apartment. However, there is no evidence or eyewitness statement to support this hypothesis. The paparazzi all claim that they were left a considerable distance behind the Mercedes by the time it crashed. In the absence of any reliable evidence to the contrary, their accounts cannot be authoritatively challenged. However, it would be wise to remain sceptical about the paparazzi's versions of their individual roles in the chase which led to the crash.

According to Kez Wingfield, Dodi said his scheme had been approved by Mohamed Fayed. The bodyguard cited this as the reason why he and Trevor Rees-Jones were not in a position to challenge the plan. When Judge Stéphan was commissioned to carry out his investigation, the paparazzi were the only subjects he was authorised to probe. Were it

---

[4] *Paris Match*, 4–11 June 1998.

not for Trevor Rees-Jones starting legal proceedings against the Ritz and Etoile Limousine, the arrangements the Fayeds made for Diana would never have become an issue, yet it is at the heart of why she died.

That Princess Diana could expect to be pursued and harassed by photographers while leaving one of the most famous hotels in Paris with her new boyfriend – who happened to be the owner's son – was nothing if not predictable. Paparazzi pursue famous quarry in the capital cities of most countries in the world every week of the year, but rarely are fatalities or even injuries reported. As Princess Diana sped into Paris on 31 August 1997, she expressed concern as her Mercedes was being pursued by the paparazzi. Her concern was not for her own safety, but for the safety of the photographers who were pursuing her.[5]

Had there been full RMP-style protection in Paris that night, Henri Paul would have got nowhere near the wheel of the Mercedes because, as some members of the Ritz staff have pointed out since the crash, 'he had no business being in that car'.[6] There has never been any suggestion that either Dodi or Mohamed had any notion that Paul had been drinking when he returned to the Ritz. Neither bodyguard believed he had been drinking when they encountered him in the Ritz. Neither felt the need to be alert to this because they had two reliable, qualified drivers outside the hotel awaiting the departure of the couple in the two cars they had been using all day. The bodyguards did not expect the Fayeds to ask Paul to drive.

Fayed himself confirmed in February 1998 that he had spoken to Dodi as he prepared to leave the Ritz. Characteristically Fayed gave two different versions of the conversation, both of which became public in the same week.

In *Death of a Princess* it was reported that Fayed claimed to have asked Dodi, 'Why don't you just stay in the hotel?' When Dodi declined that suggestion, Fayed claims he said, 'Just be careful. Don't step on it. There's no hurry. Wait until the atmosphere is perfect, get in your car and go away. Don't hide; it is unnecessary.'[7]

In his *Mirror* interview published in the same week, Fayed gave his version of events on the fatal night:

I last spoke to Dodi 15 minutes before the accident. I said to him, 'Now look, don't do any tricks when you leave the hotel. Be nice to

---

[5] Bower interview with Dourneau, September 1997.
[6] Reuters, 3 September 1997.
[7] *Death of a Princess*, p. 138.

the photographers . . . Go out of the front door and say hello. Talk to the paparazzi, they are only doing their job.' I said, 'You have nothing to hide, relax and enjoy it.' I said 'Dodi, just help them make a living'. They did the complete opposite to what I said, but what can you do? That's destiny.[8]

Fayed's contradictory accounts of his last conversation with Dodi further damaged his credibility in February 1998, the month Michael Cole retired. A year later he had declined still further in public esteem by recycling myths about the tragedy that had been widely discredited. The following remarks were made by Fayed in 1999, more than sixteen months after the crash, at a time when, in common with the other families affected by the crash, he had been advised of Judge Stéphan's findings:

Of the events of 31 August 1997
'I just get straight away my clothes on and get a helicopter, take me straight away to Paris perhaps about two thirty in the morning. And it was just a shocking state with my arrival . . . I go straight away first to the hospital, to see Diana . . .

'I saw Dodi . . . and I saw Diana too.'[9]

Of the couple's relationship
'Dodi knows Diana for a long time . . . and always Diana consider me as a second father to her.'[10]

'When she ask me if she can join me in my summer holiday in my summer house in Saint-Tropez I say fine, you most welcome. She say can I bring my kids? I say of course, you most welcome.'[11]

'As a matter of fact she invited herself. My son was going and coming from time to time and they met, they have a chat and I have no idea how it was developed.[12]

'Definitely [they were] going to get married and their engagement was gonna be declared on Monday, the night before they . . . been killed because they know, she told her friends, she told her kids . . .

' . . . And they bought the engagement ring, she choose the engagement ring already. The jewellery [sic] himself give a statement that she came to the shop, she choose her engagement ring.

---

[8] *Mirror*, 12 February 1998.
[9] Radio Telefis Eireann, January 1999.
[10] Radio Telefis Eireann, January 1999.
[11] Radio Telefis Eireann, January 1999.
[12] *Vanessa*, BBC1, 25 January 1999.

'Dodi ask me if he can take over the Windsor House in Paris, which I have restored, and bring the glory of the Windsor love story to reality. And I say fine, it's no problem. She loved the house, and she enjoyed being there. And he say if I'm gonna get married can I have the house? I say fine, it's yours. She went and visited the house the same afternoon she was killed just a few hours later.[13]

'Diana had asked me personally if she could live in the villa Windsor. She called me from the villa with Dodi and I said: The house is yours, it's an historic part of the Royal Family, but it's yours, no problem.'[14]

'It's just the natural two people, normal people, ordinary people fall in love, wanna get married . . . and for reasons of the establishment, the upper class and the aristocracy they will not accept that, that a blood Egyptian come from Egypt, his son fall in love with Diana and will gonna marry Diana . . .'[15]

On Diana's mother, Frances Shand Kydd
'She is pathetic and stupid . . . I have no respect for her.'[16]

On the accident
'I am certain that my son and the Princess been murdered by the MI6. Look the *Sunday Telegraph* editor, Dominic Lawson – he attack me in 130 articles one after the other given to him by MI6 and he is MI6 member.

'I am the father who lost the son; I am the father who lived the tragedy; I am the father who followed the investigation with the judge day and night with my lawyers. Nobody else have the right to talk because they are ignorant about what was happening – they want to cover up things.'[17]

'MI6 were behind the accident. I lost my son in this crash and I know what really happened. Henri Paul was not drunk. All this is being done by the people who were behind the accident.'[18]

There were echoes in these statements of Fayed's behaviour in the long war for Harrods and the House of Fraser in the 1980s. After lengthy investigation, the British government's DTI inspectors condemned the

---

[13] Radio Telefis Eireann, January 1999.
[14] Interview on TF1, 17 June 1998.
[15] Radio Telefis Eireann, January 1999.
[16] *Sun*, 7 June 1998.
[17] BBC Radio Leeds, 25 January 1999.
[18] *Sunday Mirror*, 10 January 1999.

Alice in Wonderland world which he had created: 'The lies of Mohamed Fayed and his success in gagging the Press created . . . a new fact: that lies were the truth and the truth was a lie'.[19] After the Paris tragedy, the facts about the unqualified Henri Paul's drunkenness became a 'lie' to Fayed, and Diana's 'assassination' by MI6 became one of his 'truths'.

The stakes in the battle for the truth about how Diana, Princess of Wales came to die while in the care of the Fayed family, were immeasurably higher than a dispute about the ownership of a chain of upmarket shops. Ever since Fayed touched down at Le Bourget an hour after Princess Diana was declared dead, he has continued to loudly portray himself as the hero of his own investigation into the 'dark and sinister forces' that 'murdered' Princess Diana, as well as the victim of an 'establishment' plot which claimed the life of his son as well as Diana. Fayed thus put his critics on the defensive. Although key employees of Fayed have chosen to quit rather than participate in this, others believe that he will continue 'long after the French investigation is over'.

The only comfort to be gleaned from tracking Fayed's media appearances is that he has devalued his own currency, and his outbursts are receiving progressively less coverage. The families and friends of all the other victims of the accident in the Alma tunnel have declined to respond to Fayed's provocation, preferring to maintain a dignified silence.

The links between some of those who remained part of Fayed's campaign to misinform the world about Princess Diana's last days were dramatically revealed in May 1999. When a list of MI6 agents was posted on the Internet, the exiled former MI6 spy, Richard Tomlinson, was widely thought to have been responsible. Even though he had previously threatened to carry out just such an action, Tomlinson denied that he had done it. The list was actually posted on the Internet by Lyndon Larouche's Executive Intelligence Review organisation. It caused outrage and resentment at MI6 as the list compromised the lives of some of the agents named, and caused great potential damage to the credibility and careers of others. The appearance of the list also revealed to a wider world the links between Tomlinson and Fayed. The Fayed/Tomlinson encounter in the South of France in the summer of 1998, and the role of EIR in devising and supporting some of Fayed's more outlandish conspiracy theories about Princess Diana's death, were widely reported thoughout the British media in May 1999 as a result. In

---

[19] DTI report into Fayed's takeover of Harrods.

one newspaper, pictures of Fayed, Tomlinson and Larouche were joined by arrows around the headline, THE CIRCLE OF FANTASY.[20]

The timing of the publication of the list of MI6 officers also appeared to be significant to Fayed-watchers. The previous week, Fayed had learnt that his application for a British passport had been turned down. The angry Egyptian had sworn revenge, and it appeared to some that the revelation of the names of British agents from the organisation he had been blaming for the deaths of his son and Princess Diana, might have been more than a coincidence. British security services launched an investigation into the links between Fayed, Tomlinson and EIR immediately after the publication of the names.

The revelation of the names also came a week before Fayed's final legal submissions to Judge Stéphan's investigation into the Alma tunnel crash which, predictably, targeted British and American intelligence. In the French Court of appeal on 21 May 1999, Georges Kiejman paid tribute to Stéphan's 'thorough and serious enquiry' but argued that he should have interviewed British diplomats who had been in Paris around the time of the crash. Kiejman suggested that they could have been involved in a surveillance operation of Princess Diana and Dodi in the days before the crash, and argued that an American official from the National Security Agency (NSA) should also be interviewed, as he could confirm the surveillance operation. Stéphan had declined Fayed's request to do this. He had also resisted Fayed's demand for a more detailed examination of the records of the arrested paparazzi's telephonic communications on the night Princess Diana died. Henri Paul's family's lawyer, Paul Brizay argued that the high level of carbon monoxide found in Henri Paul's blood could have been capable of falsifying the blood/alcohol level found in his corpse.

The appeal court's contemplation of the Fayed and Paul family challenges delayed the completion of the French investigation by several weeks. On 2 July 1999, the court rejected all the challenges, leaving the way clear for prosecutor Coujard and the two judges to assess whether any of the photographers should face charges.

When Kez Wingfield learnt that Princess Diana was to visit his boss's family in the summer of 1997, he commented, with prophetic irony, 'This'll end in tears'. After it did, Trevor Rees-Jones and Ben Murrell took the only option available to them. All three bodyguards – Kez Wingfield, Trevor Rees-Jones and Ben Murrell – became involved in legal conflict with Fayed; all the disputes related to aspects of Princess Diana's last

[20] *Sunday Telegraph*, 16 May 1997.

day in the Fayeds' care. All three bodyguards were professional British soldiers before they joined Fayed. Fayed refers to them as 'donkeys', but the three were loyal, committed members of his staff who had spent their professional lives obeying orders. They had watched in dismay as the myth maker wove his fantasies. No one, apart from Dodi, was physically closer to Diana during her last summer than Kez Wingfield. Having provided close protection for Mohamed Fayed for five years, Wingfield provided the same for Princess Diana until he was required by Dodi Fayed to stand aside moments before she started her fatal journey. After leaving Fayed's employ, Wingfield remarked, 'There wasn't a conspiracy to murder Princess Diana, but there has most certainly been a conspiracy to cover up why she died'.

14. THE JUDGES' REPORT

'. . . the accident . . . was caused by the fact that the driver of the car was inebriated and under the influence of drugs incompatible with alcohol, a state that did not allow him to maintain control of his vehicle which was travelling at a high speed on a tricky section of the road, and, in addition had to avoid a car travelling in the same direction but at a slower speed.'

Judges Hervé Stéphan and Marie-Christine Devidal,
official communiqué, Paris, 3 September 1999

After the most intensive investigation into a single car crash in French history, judges Hervé Stéphan and Marie-Christine Devidal released a short statement about their findings in Paris on 3 September 1999. That they decided not to prosecute any of the photographers who were pursuing Henri Paul's Mercedes, and that they included not a word about the myriad conspiracy theories, will come as no surprise to readers of this book.

Stéphan's vast dossier was sent first to prosecutor Maud Coujard for her consideration at the beginning of July 1999. On 17 August, she recommended that none of the photographers should be charged on either of the counts they faced. The judges agreed. Their central conclusion was that 'the loss of control of the vehicle by the driver in the Alma tunnel constitutes the main cause of the accident.'[1] The Mercedes was going so fast because Paul was drunk (see Chapter 6): 'The speed adopted by the driver can also clearly be attributed to the presence of alcohol in his blood, the effect of which was increased by the medicines, and thereby characterise the psychological effect of a driver who was totally uninhibited at the wheel of a powerful car and sure of having [out]distanced the photographers.

'Consequently, it was not shown that at the moment when the driver lost control of his vehicle, he found himself having to drive at speed, rendering the accident inevitable.

'One can only state that there is no clear underlying link between the speed of the vehicle and the presence of photographers following the vehicle.'

The judges found that the criminal liability of the photographers under investigation could only 'be considered in terms of indirect cause, since the direct cause of the accident has thus been established'; in the

---

[1] Unless otherwise stated, all quotes are from the summary of the official French investigation which is reprinted in full in the Appendix.

words of the official communiqué, 'the accident was not the result of a deliberate act.'[2] They concluded that it was not possible to sustain the view that the pursuit of the Mercedes constituted a 'hounding of the couple by the photographers'.

After Maud Coujard's recommendations that no one should be prosecuted had been sent to judges Stéphan and Devidal on 17 August, they had been extensively leaked, before the judges' decision was made public. The publication of Coujard's summary of the investigation's findings did, however, place new information into the public domain about the crucial moments in the Ritz hotel which determined Princess Diana's fate on 30/31 August. This critical period has already been examined in detail in Chapter 3.

The investigation found that, of the barmen who observed Paul in the bar Vendôme, only Alain Willaumez 'noted that Henri Paul was drunk'. However, the night manager of the Ritz, Thierry Rocher, told the investigation that he, too, was aware that Paul had been drinking. Rocher stated that he had been responsible for relaying to Paul Dodi's plan to leave the Ritz. He told Paul that Dodi had decided that he should replace the Fayeds' official driver, Philippe Dorneau, for the departure from the Ritz. Rocher told the investigation that Paul had replied that 'he was going to finish his "Ricard" with the English [the bodyguards]'.

The summary of the investigation also revealed that the director of Etoile Limousine, Jean-François Musa, had claimed that he had 'expressed reticence when he heard that Henri Paul would drive the car, notably because he did not have an ad hoc licence.' The report did not establish to whom these misgivings might have been expressed, or what form they might have taken. It simply stated that, 'no witness confirms this point'. Musa took no action to prevent the unqualified Paul driving.

That the scheme to leave the Ritz was Dodi's, was accorded crucial significance by the investigation. The report stressed that once Etoile Limousine had been asked by Dodi to provide a car for Henri Paul to drive, Jean-François Musa, who used to drive for the Ritz himself, felt he had no option but to comply: 'He justified this by reason of the fact that he could not refuse what was asked of him. Examining the nature of the commercial links which united the Ritz ... to the Etoile Limousine company, one can see the total dependence of the Etoile Limousine company on the Ritz, its only client ...'

The report also highlights the bodyguards' insistence that Dodi had made their jobs very difficult by keeping them in the dark about his

---

[2] Official communiqué of the Paris prosecutor's office, 3 September 1999.

plans with the Princess (see Chapter 3). It quoted Trevor Rees-Jones as saying, 'Dodi took an active part in security arrangements, he was the boss and in addition we did not know the programme in advance, only he knew the programme.'

Leaks to newspapers immediately before the report was published claimed that Dodi would be accused of 'over-reacting' to the presence of the photographers outside the Ritz. The published summary did not mention this 'over-reaction', but it remained the underlying theme of the part of the report which analysed the departure from the Ritz in detail. Frédéric Lucard's claim (see page 52) to have heard Paul taunting the photographers at the rear of the Ritz was given weight by the judges. The report also laid to rest the claims that there were no photographers at the rear of the Ritz when the Mercedes departed, claims that were made at the Harrods' press conference on the eve of Diana's funeral: 'Serge Benamou, Jacques Langevin, Fabrice Chassery and Alain Guizard went to the Rue Cambon and watched both the arrival of the Mercedes S280 and the departure of the couple.'

The role of the untraced Fiat Uno in the crash (see Chapter 9) was publicly clarified by the report. The nature of the collision between the Mercedes and the Fiat was described as a 'simple scrape, which had not led to a significant reduction in speed by the Mercedes'.

Having confirmed that the paparazzi did not cause the crash, the investigation also found that there were no grounds to prosecute them over the second charge: 'it does not appear that the constituent elements of the crime of not assisting a person in danger were identified.'

In fact, the investigation had established that half of those facing both charges did not arrive in the Alma tunnel until after the police, the emergency services and, therefore, the first medic, Dr Mailliez; 'there are no facts which establish the presence of David Oderkerken [referred to elsewhere in this book as David Ker], Jacques Langevin, Fabrice Chassery, Nikola Arsov and Lazlo Veres at the scene during the period of time preceding the arrival of the police and the emergency services'. Thus the investigation concluded that, 'one cannot claim that they failed to offer assistance at the scene'.

In the absence of any evidence to contradict his statement, Jacques Langevin's testimony (see page 63) was accepted by the investigation, as was that of Laszlo Veres. Veres did not join the pursuit of the Mercedes after it left the Ritz as he was one of several photographers at the front of the Ritz hotel apparently fooled by Kez Wingfield's decoy. Veres was recorded by the Ritz security camera at the front of the Ritz in the Place Vendôme at 00.26:49. The accident occurred in the Alma tunnel at

00.26:00. Veres had been waiting for Princess Diana to emerge with Dodi Fayed, after falling for Henri Paul's attempt to fool everyone that Princess Diana would leave from the front entrance.

Once Veres learnt that Princess Diana had left from the rue Cambon exit, he told the investigation that he started to head home. While en route, he received a call from Serge Benamou who informed him that Princess Diana had been involved in a car crash. Veres headed for the Alma tunnel expecting to find that the Princess had been involved in a minor scrape. By the time he arrived, the police had already formed a cordon. He used his press card to pass through the cordon, and then he took about a dozen photographs of the emergency services in action. As he was leaving the scene, a plain clothes policeman stopped him. He was arrested and taken to the quai des Orfèvres for questioning with the other paparazzi.

Having failed to find sufficient evidence to recommend prosecution of the photographers on either charge, the report did not ignore the criticism of the photographers by several who witnessed their behaviour in the aftermath of the crash. The heated exchanges between Romuald Rat, Christian Martinez (see pages 62–3) and the first police officers to arrive, had led to speculation that the two photographers might be charged. However, Coujard confined herself to remarking, 'The critical view which could be brought to bear on the manner in which the various people under examination have, during the course of the night in question, exerted their professional activity can only be recorded within the circumstances of the moral appreciation or the code of ethics hich govern the profession of journalist or photo-journalist.'

Earl Spencer, who had roused many with his attacks on the photographers immediately after his sister's death, issued a short statement when Stéphan's findings were published. 'I respect the French court's decision. They have put a lot of time and effort into the whole matter. I respect the whole decision. I believe that legally they have reached the right conclusion.' Diana's mother, Frances Shand Kydd, also accepted the report 'without reservation', and hoped that her daughter would now be 'allowed to rest in peace'.[3]

On behalf of Trevor Rees-Jones, Christian Curtil welcomed Stéphan's 'excellent decision' to acquit the photographers. 'We have always stressed that the photographers were not responsible for the accident', said Curtil. 'The prosecutor's office and the judge have underlined the responsibility of the Ritz and the Etoile Limousine company in the circumstances of the accident'.

---

[3] Spencer family quotes from *Express*, 4 September 1999.

Curtil raised the stakes in the week of the report's publication by publicly confirming for the first time that Rees-Jones had warned the Fayeds against the unorthodox plan to leave the Ritz. In an interview I held with him for *Channel 4 News*, Curtil confirmed that Rees-Jones supported Kez Wingfield's assertion that Dodi claimed Mohamed Fayed had himself approved the plan to leave the Ritz: 'He did warn the passengers as well as Dodi Fayed and Mohamed Fayed as to the plan. It did not reflect normal security . . . the security plan was not sufficient.'[4]

Through his spokesman, Fayed furiously rejected Rees-Jones's claim, saying that he was surprised that it had taken the bodyguard two years to remember this potentially damaging allegation. In reality, the bodyguard had not just remembered his warning to the Fayeds, but he had only authorised his lawyer to make it public when it became clear that Stéphan's summary of his investigation omitted this information.

Fayed had been preparing for the judge's predictable rejection of his conspiracy theorising in the weeks before the report was released by devising ever more far-fetched versions. Fayed gave interviews in the USA and Europe in August 1999, suggesting that Diana's former father-in-law, Prince Philip, the Duke of Edinburgh, had been behind the murder of Diana and Dodi. According to Fayed, the Duke organised their 'assassinations' as he did not want to see Diana bearing a Muslim child following marriage to Dodi. He told the American *Talk* magazine, 'Prince Philip is the one responsible for giving the order. He is very racist. He is of German blood, and I am sure he is a Nazi sympathiser. Also, Robert Fellowes [the Queen's private secretary and Diana's brother-in-law] was key. He is the Rasputin of the British monarchy.'[5]

Evidence-free conspiracy theorising does not get much more desperate than this. Fayed's *Talk* outburst made little noticeable impact in the USA or in France, where he repeated his claims in *VSD* magazine. In Britain, he was invited on to the BBC's *Today* programme to repeat his 'assassination' claims. The Corporation judiciously edited out his claims about Prince Philip's role, but he was permitted to ascribe the 'murder' to British intelligence.

The following extracts give a flavour of the interview, in which he also dismissed Stéphan's painstaking investigation:

Henri Paul was on the payroll of MI6 for three years as an informer. They killed him. They had to kill him, of course. He was only doing

---

[4] *Channel 4 News*, 31 August 1999.
[5] *Talk* magazine, September 1999.

about 40 or 50 miles an hour. It is all disinformation . . . The guy had not been drinking. It was not his blood. It had been changed.

I am father and I know my son had been murdered and I am not going to let them get away with it. My son's life has been taken away because they wanted to murder Diana because she wanted to be free . . . I will never stop until I find the truth.[6]

The *Today* interview marked the low point of Fayed's campaign against his enemies in what he perceives as the British Establishment, and the high watermark of his conspiracy theory campaigning. He appeared on the BBC's most influential radio current affairs programme but his interview further damaged his credibility. His sole justification appeared to be, 'I am the father who lost his son.' Because he simply recycled stale conspiracy theories, elements of which were first aired on ITV's widely discredited programme, *Diana – Secrets Behind the Crash*, few news stories flowed from Fayed's interview. Those that did, contained criticism of the BBC for interviewing him at all.

The Foreign Office issued a statement to the BBC in response to the Fayed interview: 'As we have repeatedly made clear there is not a shred of truth in the allegation that the tragic accident in Paris on the 31 August 1997 was the result of a conspiracy. The implication that an agency of the British government might have had some involvement is baseless and is deeply upsetting for the Royal Family, the Princess's family and all those who wish to remember her life and achievements.'[7]

When I met Fayed's retired spokesman, Michael Cole, near the start of my own investigation, he regaled me with a list of 'unanswered questions' that Fayed thought the French investigation should address. After the investigation's conclusions were made public, Cole's replacement, Laurie Mayer, visited London's TV studios with a similar list of 'unanswered questions'. Most of these questions appeared to be designed to draw attention away from why Princess Diana died while she was in the care of the Fayed family. Mayer failed to practice the cardinal principle of Cole's post-crash stewardship of Fayed's PR – never allow Mohamed himself to be interviewed. Significantly, Cole had 'retired' the week after Fayed's 'it was no accident' interview in the *Mirror* which first breached this principle – the PR chief had known nothing about the interview until it was published. Two days after Fayed appeared as the main interviewee on ITV's *Diana – Secrets Behind the*

---

[6] *Today*, BBC Radio 4, 17 September 1999.
[7] *Today*, BBC Radio 4, 17 September 1999.

Crash debacle on 3 June 1998, Fayed blundered down the steps of the Palais de Justice in Paris to savage Princess Diana's mother as well as the photographers. His dénouement on the BBC *Today* programme confirmed that Fayed's credibility was shattered.

15. THE MASKS FALL

'As a police officer you don't start off with any theories, you go where the evidence takes you.'

Sir John Stevens, Metropolitan police commissioner,
Hard Talk, BBC, 24 January 2004

Michael Burgess, the coroner for the Queen's Household, did not open the inquests into Diana's and Dodi's deaths until 6 January 2004. Burgess is also the Surrey county coroner and, because Dodi Fayed was deemed to have resided at his father's home in Oxted, Surrey, the inquest into his death also comes under Burgess's authority. Announcing the inquests, Burgess explained that 'the complexity of the situation' had caused the delay.

The principal factor in the 'complexity' had been the prolonged legal attempts in the French courts by Fayed to challenge different aspects of Stéphan's investigation. Burgess had felt unable to commence the inquests while there was a possibility, admittedly remote, that Fayed would succeed in overturning elements of Stéphan's report or its findings or that one of his actions might succeed in France.

These legal attempts eventually expired in late 2003 after a six-year campaign, when a French court cleared three paparazzi of 'invading' Diana and Dodi's privacy by taking the last pictures of the couple alive as they drove away from the Ritz. In the pro-Fayed press, predictable headlines – 'FRENCH INSULT DIANA'[1] – appeared. Mohamed Fayed, once again, was 'infuriated' by the decision and vowed to appeal. 'I fail to see her [Judge Goetzman's] logic,' said Dodi's father. 'The paparazzi played a significant part in the tragedy and should be punished.'

However, the judge had ruled that 'anyone walking in the rue Cambon could have seen Diana and Dodi' and that they both 'knew they would be photographed . . . the couple was not unaware that they were exposing themselves to being photographed when leaving the hotel . . . the photographs were not taken clandestinely'.[2]

Fayed had already tried, unsuccessfully, in 2000 in the High Court in London, to force Burgess's predecessor as royal coroner, Dr John Burton, to hold a joint inquest into the deaths of his son and the Princess rather than separate ones, but Mr Justice Newman ruled that there was

---

[1] *Daily Express*, 29 November 2003.
[2] Ibid.

'nothing to demonstrate that Dr Burton's decision [to hold separate inquests] was unlawful'.[3]

When Burgess eventually opened Princess Diana's inquest at London's Queen Elizabeth Conference Centre in the morning of 6 January 2004 and Dodi's, in the afternoon, in Reigate in Surrey, they attracted worldwide media attention. The two bereaved families who had reacted so differently to the tragedy were both represented. Princess Diana's sister, Sarah McCorquodale, sat at the front of the large auditorium of the conference centre with her lawyers. Hundreds of journalists from across the world were seated silently behind them. On the opposite side, also at the front, sat Mohamed Fayed with a sizeable, besuited retinue that appeared to include lawyers, PR people and bodyguards. Michael Mansfield QC, who had acted for Fayed since he unsuccessfully challenged the coroner's decision to hold separate inquests into Dodi and Diana's deaths, continued to represent him. Now the QC sat with Dodi's father as they listened to Burgess opening Princess Diana's inquest.

The two families had not encountered each other since Diana's sister visited Mohamed Fayed at Harrods in the week after the crash, and the Egyptian had conveyed his theory about Diana's 'last words'. Fayed and his wife had also been present at Diana's funeral. The Egyptian's stock had fallen steadily in the Spencer family's eyes since then. At the end of 2003 he incurred their silent wrath when he announced, on US TV, that Diana had been pregnant by his son when she died. Asked by Patricia Cornwell in an ABC documentary how he knew this, Fayed replied, 'She told me on the phone.'[4]

The claim had become a central tenet of Fayed's 'conspiracy theory', providing motive for Diana's 'murder' by the forces of darkness, and which has, in my opinion, distracted attention from the Fayeds' own role in the crash. Fayed and his PR operation had alleged that the Princess was 'murdered' as the British royal family disliked foreigners. For the previous two years Fayed had been appearing on his own website describing Dodi as '. . . an Egyptian, naturally tanned, his daddy has curly hair, you know, and he has the same. It's just they would not accept that.'[5]

We have already seen (pp. 104–6) how appalled Diana's family, friends and doctor were by the suggestion she could have been pregnant

---

[3] BBC News Online, 18 July 2000.
[4] ABC News, 30 October 2003.
[5] 'Encounters With The Unexplained: Who Killed Princess Diana?', USA Pax TV, (Grizzly Adams Productions) 2 November 2001.

when it first emerged shortly after she died. With Dodi's father adding his authority to it, and by claiming to have spoken with Diana herself about it, the pain was intensified. Furthermore, with no apparent contact with the Fayed operation, the *Independent on Sunday* newspaper, citing 'a senior police source in France' reported that 'Diana, Princess of Wales, was pregnant at the time of her death'.[6] The report went on to allege that there had been a 'cover-up' about the pregnancy and hinted that 'medical reports' in Judge Stéphan's dossier demonstrate this.

Rosa Monckton was so incensed by Fayed's ABC claim, which she knew to be untrue, that she agreed to be interviewed for my 2004 'The Diana Conspiracy' documentary on Channel 4. This was Rosa's first and only British TV interview about the holiday she had spent with her friend in Greece immediately before Diana left for her last holiday with Dodi. 'I know for an absolute fact that she could not have been pregnant, because when we were on the boat, which was ten days before she died, she had her period, so she could not have been pregnant.'[7]

The Pitié-Salpêtrière hospital spokesman, Thierry Meresse, contradicted the *Independent on Sunday*'s claim to have seen French documents 'proving' Diana was pregnant when she died, saying that there were none. 'Our sole concern was not to discover whether she was pregnant, but to save her life. We didn't do any tests to see if she were pregnant, so no one can know whether she was or not.'[8]

Commander Mulès, who had been in charge of security in and around the Pitié-Salpêtrière hospital, added, 'Why [an autopsy] on Henri Paul and not Dodi and Diana? In France, we do not conduct an autopsy on the bodies of passengers. We do an autopsy on the body of the driver to find out if there are any signs of alcohol or other elements in his system. But legally, there is no logical reason to do an autopsy on the passengers' bodies.'[9]

So nobody in France could have known whether the Princess was pregnant when she died, but in England there was complete certainty in the mortuary on 31 August 1997, the day she died. The autopsies on both Diana and Dodi were conducted at the Fulham mortuary in South London – the mortuary is always on stand-by in case of a royal death. The duty manager was Robert Thompson, who had been in service for fifteen years, and an early morning message to his pager alerted him that

---

[6] *Independent on Sunday*, 21 December 2003.
[7] Author's interview with Rosa Monckton, 2003.
[8] Author's interview with Thierry Meresse, 2003.
[9] CBS Interview with Commander Mulès, 2004.

he would be required that afternoon. Also present at Princess Diana's autopsy were the then coroner of the Queen's Household, Dr John Burton, his then deputy, Michael Burgess, as well as Home Office pathologist Dr Robert Chapman. Robert Thompson managed both autopsies:

'Diana's body didn't arrive until eight o'clock in the evening, so it was a very long day. We simply finished Dodi's postmortem, cleaned down, disinfected the mortuary and prepared it for Diana's arrival.

'The internal examination proceeded much as they always do. The organs were removed in this case as they always are by the pathologist, Dr Chapman, with myself only providing assistance where necessary. Dr Chapman removed the organs, and then examined them on a dissecting bench very closely.'

Thompson described the defining moment: 'Dr Chapman and I were standing opposite each other over the body. Dr Chapman, in situ, divided the uterus, looked up and said, "Oh well, she wasn't pregnant," in a voice that was not just directed at me, but at the room in general.'[10]

This finding is contained in the Princess's postmortem report, which will be available to the inquest but which has not been made public. The day after Diana's inquest opened, the now retired Dr Burton reluctantly came forward to comment in public for the first time, 'I never wanted to go into the details of the postmortem examination.' Dr Burton said his motivation in doing so was the 'absurd' conspiracy theories.

'While I know she was not pregnant, 85 per cent of people will still believe she was. I feel so sorry for her sons that this is being brought up again. I kept my silence on this because I never wanted to inflict it upon them.' Dr Burton stated that he had examined Diana's womb during the autopsy while it was on the dissection bench and he confirmed that she was not pregnant. 'The most bizarre theories are going about. She had only met Dodi six weeks before. I mean, the story that she was obviously pregnant: even if she got pregnant the first time she met him, that she shook hands and [he] got her pregnant, the baby would only be six weeks old at the most. It doesn't stop everyone wanting to believe it.'[11]

In my opinion the evidence shows that Princess Diana was not pregnant by Dodi, or anybody else, when she died and the picture (see p. 104) of Diana that sparked the pregnancy speculation after her death was taken *before* she met Dodi Fayed in the South of France.

---

[10] Author's interview with Robert Thompson, 2003.
[11] Interview with Doctor Burton, *Evening Standard*, 7 January 2004.

Opening Princess Diana's inquest, Burgess read a prepared statement in which he outlined the scope of it. He stated that the purpose of the inquest was to establish how, when and where the 'cause of death arose . . . It is an inquisitorial process, a process of investigation, quite unlike a trial where the prosecutor accuses and the accused defends.' Burgess outlined the task of an inquest: 'Its single-minded aim is to find the answers to the questions: who the deceased person was, and how, when and where the cause of death arose.'[12]

The inquest will not be a 'rubber stamp' exercise, Burgess stressed, but undoubtedly the French investigation's dossier will make a substantial contribution in assisting the coroner to achieve his objectives. Burgess is a speed-reader, which should help him read and assimilate the 6,000 pages of the dossier. I managed to obtain a copy of the French dossier shortly after the inquest was opened, and was asked to review it by the *Daily Mail*.[13]

The dossier is crammed full of hundreds of pictures – from the arrival of Dodi Fayed's party at Le Bourget, to the aftermath of the crash in the Alma tunnel – that the photographers under investigation took of Princess Diana's last few days, especially the last day in Paris, reminding the reader of the objectives Judge Stéphan's investigation was commissioned to achieve – to judge the extent of the photographers' 'failure to assist a person in danger' and 'involuntary homicide'. Many of the pictures have never been seen before, but some of those taken during Diana and Dodi's last day in Paris will be familiar. A few shots by the SOLA picture agency of Diana swimming alone from the *Jonikal* in bright sunshine on 28 August start the sad chronology. On 30 August an unsmiling Princess is tracked through Paris from her arrival at Le Bourget. The only photos in the dossier of the couple together are of them disembarking from their plane at Le Bourget and the final ones which find them sitting in the Mercedes at the rear of the Ritz. Dodi looks tense and Diana's face is obscured.

The pictures show Henri Paul greeting the party from their plane and capture the couple hurrying in and out of limousines outside the Fayed apartment in the rue Arsène-Houssaye and then the Ritz. In none of the pictures in the dossier do either Diana or Dodi smile; sometimes they hold their hands up over their faces. In the last photo before the crash, of Henri Paul and Trevor Rees-Jones as the Mercedes prepares to leave the Ritz, the driver looks relaxed at the wheel as the bodyguard peers

---

[12] Coroner's statement at the opening of Princess Diana's inquest, 6 January 2004.
[13] *Daily Mail*, 24 January 2004.

though the windscreen. No pictures were taken of the couple or the Mercedes between the Ritz and the Alma tunnel, and the sad, final pictures are of the crumpled car in the Alma tunnel. Princess Diana lies dying in the back of the Mercedes, with her back to the driver's seat, in the twisted wreckage. She appears to be conscious, with no visible signs of injury. Shortly after these pictures were taken, Diana suffered her first heart attack. In other pictures Dodi's corpse is being carried away or medics appear to be engaged in their futile attempt to revive Henri Paul.

Stéphan could not rely upon one single witness who claimed to have seen the crash and it is clear from the scores of witness statements in the dossier why. The nearest witness to the crash was Algerian-born Mohamed Medjahdi, who was driving his girlfriend, Souad Moufakkir, through the Alma tunnel ahead of the Mercedes. Medjahdi claimed to have got a good view of the crash in his rear-view and side mirrors: 'It was a dreadful sound, like a bomb exploding, magnified and echoing around the underpass. The car exploded, disintegrated with pieces flying off in all directions.' Moufakkir said she turned and saw the Mercedes bouncing off a pillar and into the wall on the other side. But neither saw any other vehicles or motorbikes, and neither saw a 'flash'. The 'flash' was mentioned by the only other 'witness' to the crash itself, François Levi. Levi's statement also reveals that he was in touch with the press the day after the crash, before contacting the police. Indeed, he says in his statement that it was *Sunday Times* journalists who advised him to call the Ritz and only later did he contact the police. Reading his police statement it becomes obvious why Levi was discounted by Judge Stéphan. Levi claimed to have been travelling behind the Mercedes: 'To be precise I saw a white car between me and the convoy' (the convoy being the Mercedes and accompanying paparazzi on motorbikes).

However, the investigation established that the Mercedes crashed as it tried to overtake a white Fiat, and the paparazzi were not close to the Mercedes when it crashed. Thus the white Fiat that the French established was 'brushed' by the Mercedes was never between any car and the Mercedes.

Levi goes on to make his 'flash before the crash' claim. 'I distinctly saw a motorbike swerve in front of the car. There was a big white flash.' Levi acknowledges at the end of his statement: 'You tell me that my statements contradict statements by the other witnesses.'

It appears that, upon this line of testimony, a line that Jean-Claude Mulès dismissed as being without significance and unreliable and which was not mentioned in the summary of the Paris prosecutor's final report in September 1999, Fayed's PR operation built its 'conspiracy theory'.

Fayed's 2003/4 action in Scotland went further, using Levi's statement in a renewed but unsuccessful bid for a public inquiry. Fayed's QC put together Fayed's PR operation's 'unanswered questions' about the crash to argue that British secret-service agents posing as paparazzi had blinded Henri Paul and caused him to crash. Throwing out Fayed's action the judge, Lord Drummond-Young, said, 'I am of the opinion that the petition and the accompanying documentation do not disclose an arguable case for the inference that UK security services were implicated in any way in the death or surrounding events.'[14] In his judgement, the judge dismissed the action as 'speculative and irrelevant'. Thus the Scottish court and the French investigation came to essentially the same conclusions about Fayed's allegations and Levi's 'flash before the crash' claim.

During my several interviews with him, I showed Commander Mulès a tape of one of Levi's several TV appearances[15] in which he told viewers in 1998 about the 'flash before the crash'. Mulès had forgotten who Levi was, but as he watched, he said,

'It's staggering, it's someone's mind playing tricks, imagination run wild. In my opinion this is nonsense ... This is the job of the examinations that we do at the Criminal Brigade. We take everything through right to the end, and we see if the person, the witness, is credible or not. We have ways through questioning, to separate what is well grounded, from what is imagination and story-telling ...'[16]

There were witnesses near the Place de L'Alma who testify to hearing the crash, and M. et Mme Dauzonne (see pp. 119–20) said they saw the Fiat emerging from the tunnel.

A detailed diagram of the crash made by the Criminal Brigade is included in the dossier. It shows the final positions of the Mercedes after its collision with pillar 13 in the Alma tunnel, and also where the debris and fragments of glass were found that were later established to have come from the white Fiat. The forensic analyses at the IRCGN of the debris and the white-paint scratch found on the Mercedes are also incorporated in the dossier.

The complete history of the Mercedes was trawled through in meticulous detail. Garage bills to Etoile Limousine show the extensive repairs undertaken earlier in 1997 after the car had been stolen and damaged. A statement from Etoile chauffeur, Olivier Lafaye, the car's regular driver in the week before the crash, stated that he had had no

[14] BBC Online, 13 March 2004.
[15] 'Secrets Behind The Crash', ITV (Fulcrum Productions), June 1998.
[16] Author's interview with Mulès, 2003.

mechanical problems with the car during two journeys earlier on 30 August. He took clients on a short shopping trip and made another journey to Roissy airport. Lafaye reports that the brakes were working perfectly. He did, however, record his surprise that Paul had driven the Mercedes, 'I never saw M. Paul drive one of Etoile Limousine's cars. He was the acting head of Ritz security and not a chauffeur.'

Professor Murray Mackay studied the dossier's comprehensive documentation on the Mercedes, concluding that 'as far as the engineering side of the car is concerned there's no suggestion at all that there was anything wrong with it. There were no defects present, the brakes were in good condition. Everything seemed to be working as it should.'

Mackay dismissed media reports that the car's brakes might have been deficient. 'From what I've read of the examinations that have been done the investigation looked at all that. They looked at the brake systems, tested them individually and found nothing wrong. They were in good repair. Tyres were fine, they had plenty of tread. Those sorts of simple things all checked out.'[17]

Inevitably the most significant part of the dossier deals with Henri Paul, whose autopsy showed he was drunk when he died. This voluminous section of the dossier includes pictures of the labelled samples extracted, as well as the machines that were used to analyse them and the results of the analyses. Robert Forrest, professor of forensic toxicology at Sheffield University's Medico-Legal Centre, could find no significant fault with the French procedures or results. He was shown an English translation of Paul's autopsy and the subsequent expert reports. Prof. Forrest found 'nothing in the trail of evidence which suggests that there's anything "funny" about the way in which the samples have been taken. They do appear to have been taken from Henri Paul's body in the way in which these papers describe.'

The dossier's papers give a detailed description of the chemicals found in Henri Paul's blood, his organs and in the contents of his stomach. Quantities of fluoxetine, the active constituent of Prozac, were detected in Paul's blood, urine, liver, lungs, pancreas and kidneys. Professor Forrest was impressed. 'The way in which the toxicology has been done was state-of-the-art at the time the crash happened. The analytical data, the gas chromatographic tracings and all the serial numbers seem to match up . . . I think the alcohol levels relate to the samples which were taken at Henri Paul's postmortem examination.'[18]

---

[17] Murray Mackay interview, CBS 2004.
[18] Professor Robert Forrest interview, CBS 2004.

In Professor Forrest's view, the autopsy's findings that Paul was taking both Prozac and Tiapride were highly significant. 'The reason is that Prozac pushes your mood way up. You then combine that with the disinhibiting effect of alcohol, you can get behaviour that is inappropriate. Quite apart from the fact that alcohol slows your reactions and makes it difficult for you to take decisions appropriately when several things happen at once – typical of a situation which happens when a crash occurs. Quite apart from that, your ability to make appropriate judgements about the way you ought to drive and the "soft area" around driving impairment can be made quite a lot worse by a mixture of alcohol and a drug like fluoxetine.' These drugs are virtually only used in the treatment of problem drinkers. The fact that Tiapride is in Henri Paul's system means that, at some point, he had an alcohol problem.

Professor Forrest believes that Paul's alcoholism would have helped him to appear more sober than he actually was in the Ritz CCTV pictures of him parking his car, walking around the hotel and preparing for his final journey with Dodi and Princess Diana. Looking through the dossier's analysis, Prof. Forrest commented, 'What we've got here is an increased alcohol concentration. And people who are very heavy drinkers who have developed tolerance to alcohol can show less obvious behavioural change in association with intoxication which would render you and I clearly drunk.'

Every part of Henri Paul's personal and professional life also came under the Criminal Brigade's 'scanner' – his girlfriends, his neighbours, his Ritz colleagues, his address book, his phone calls from his mobile and his home. The investigation also retrieved Paul's bank accounts. One discovery was that one of his accounts had received regular payments of 40,000 francs in cash; the day before he died Paul received one such payment according to a Barclays bank statement in the dossier. This took the balance on that account to 119,748.28 francs (18,422.81 euros).

Within a year of the crash, Fayed's team had managed to persuade sections of the media that there might have been something fishy about Paul's numerous bank accounts, and that 'unexplained' deposits of 40,000 francs suggested he might have been working for either the British or French secret intelligence service. ITV's 1998 'Secrets Behind The Crash' first raised the issue in Britain. Presenter Nicholas Owen, while walking around Paris, stated: 'Henri Paul . . . was a man with some very big secrets indeed. Apart from two accounts in a bank outside Paris, he also had three accounts and a safety-deposit box here at the Banque Nationale de Paris in the Place Vendôme, just a few steps from the Ritz.

Just a short walk away, he had another three accounts here at Barclays in the Avenue de l'Opéra, but that's not all. He also had one current and four deposit accounts here in the Caisse d'Epargne just near the Louvre. In the eight months before the crash, 40,000 francs – that's about £4,000 – was paid into an account here on five separate occasions, each time in cash. In all, Henri Paul had just over 1.2 million francs in the bank, that's about £122,000. And no one can say where it came from.'[19] Richard Tomlinson would later suggest that Paul might have had links with British or French intelligence. Putting the two elements together, team Fayed would then suggest that Paul was paid by British intelligence to kill Diana and Dodi.

However, Commander Mulès states that the Criminal Brigade's 'bank investigation' of Paul's accounts was 'routine procedure' in such a case. 'We do what we call a "bank investigation". We do this to have information about the flow of money and the accounts of a person. It's completely normal. We check every little detail of the person's life completely. This is an essential part of an investigation and normal procedure. If, let's say, tomorrow you are involved in a case, even as an accomplice, every little detail of your life will be checked. Your bank accounts, your phone calls . . . everything will be checked. This is typical procedure at the Criminal Brigade.'

The five regular payments to Paul of 40,000 francs, the last two of which were paid in August 1997 around Princess Diana's two visits to Paris, were not deemed by Mulès to be significant. 'Forty thousand francs is not a lot of money considering the environment in which he lived. Henri Paul lived in an environment full with very rich people, very rich clients, who often don't have money on them. So Henri Paul sometimes lent money to these people. He was getting important tips from his client. He was a man of trust, a man who would accompany extremely rich people, and he was receiving tips, and I don't mean 50 francs, but 5,000 to 10,000 francs at a time. So he could very well have lent some money to his VIP clients.'[20] He continued, 'Paul's are all normal accounts. This was a man who took precautions. He had several bank accounts possibly because he had loans and some banks offered him better advantages than others. These are normal accounts, not Swiss accounts.'

The author and investigative journalist, Tom Bower, is a leading expert on Mohamed Fayed and also his unofficial biographer.[21] He told

[19] 'Secrets Behind The Crash', ITV (Fulcrum Productions), June 1998.
[20] Commander Mulès interview, CBS 2004.
[21] Bower, *Fayed: The Unauthorized Biography*, Macmillan, 1998.

CBS that he believed Fayed himself would know the source of his employee's funds.

'Henri Paul was quite an important man in the Fayed security organisation. Within the Ritz there were people who paid a lot of money for various bits of information. The Ritz has an elaborate bugging operation where they listened in to the telephone conversations . . . And that would give Henri Paul sources of money. You've got to remember Mohamed Fayed pays people in cash. He is a man who hands out, on his own admission, £100,000 a week sometimes in cash. So he would have paid Henri Paul in cash for favours and Paul wasn't a simple driver. Anyone who worked for Mohamed Fayed as the head of security was a man who had objectives other than just preventing thieves from coming into the Ritz. His job also was to look after the interests of Mohamed Fayed and that provided a lot of money.'

Bower added, 'Paul could have been an informant for the security services, too. But they don't pay much money. You don't get money from MI6 or the CIA for giving a bit of information – a few hundred dollars maybe. However, Paul would have got a lot of money from Mohamed Fayed for arranging favours for Mohamed Fayed because he paid people in cash.

'The Ritz Hotel was a meeting place for a lot of rich, important people. They paid Henri Paul money and cash for various favours. I mean, he was a man who could provide information to very rich people. And those people pay. So that would be the source of his cash. In France, taxes are high; Paul would have been much happier getting paid in cash than being paid through a cheque.'[22]

Commander Mulès made it clear that the investigation had limited interest in pursuing Henri Paul's financial standing further: 'That was not the goal of the investigation. The fact that he had 40,000 francs deposits did not bring anything new to the investigation. For us, it was just an indication, but the goal was not to investigate if there was any suspicious type of financial activity in Henri Paul's finances. If we had concentrated on this aspect we would have completely lost the focus of the investigation. The urgency at the time was to determine the conditions of the accident. We could not work on Dodi Al Fayed, on Henri Paul, by looking at things that have nothing to do with the accident. Some have insinuated that Henri Paul was doing something wrong. The press tried to kill Henri Paul a second time by bringing him down socially. We did not.'[23]

---

[22] Tom Bower interview, CBS 2004.
[23] Commander Mulès interview, CBS 2004.

The issue of Henri Paul's finances became one of the dividing lines between the two investigations into the crash – the official French investigation and Fayed's parallel effort. The French investigation saw no link between Paul's bank accounts and the crash, while team Fayed has highlighted 'unexplained payments' which 'the French investigation failed to pursue and/or take [into] account'.[24]

The point of such PR tactics, underpinned by extensive legal backup, might appear hard to grasp. However, attempting to disprove this as an issue, by proving a negative statement – e.g. Henri Paul did *not* work for MI6/the DGSE – is difficult if not impossible and helps to prolong, possibly indefinitely, the notion that Paul's funds or, indeed, secret intelligence agencies had made some mysterious contribution to the tragedy.

Michael Burgess acknowledged the widespread public doubts about the Princess's death which Fayed's campaign has played the principal role in creating. As part of his inquest, the coroner commissioned Britain's most senior police officer, Sir John Stevens, the Metropolitan police commissioner, to look into allegations that 'these deaths were not the result of a sad, but relatively straight forward, road traffic accident in Paris'.[25]

Some questioned whether the UK's top policeman should be devoting his time and resources to such a task at a time when the country was deemed to be under unprecedented threat from international terrorism. However, with opinion polls and surveys continuing to show a substantial proportion of British opinion confused about exactly how Princess Diana died, and many veering towards Fayed's theories, others believe that the nation is owed a rigorous and definitive explanation. Sir John's involvement should ensure this happens, and should also reduce Fayed's scope to press for judicial review of the inquest's verdict when it is delivered in 2005.

As Diana's and Dodi's separate inquests opened, Fayed was attempting to instil further doubts about the official French report into the crash with a new video, 'The Mystery of the Alma Tunnel'. Mohamed Fayed personally distributed the video to visiting TV teams and journalists from around the world.

Making the case are John Macnamara, now 68 and officially retired, who has led Fayed's parallel investigation since 1997; Richard Tomlinson appears, as does retired spokesman Michael Cole. EIR's Jeffrey Steinberg pops up and the Fayed video incorporates slabs of the

---

[24] Fayed lawyer's letter to Channel 4, 25 November 2003.
[25] Michael Burgess's statement at the opening of Princess Diana's Inquest, 6 January 2004.

sympathetic 1998 ITV documentary, 'Secrets Behind The Crash', including an interview with James Hewitt, one of Diana's former lovers. Appropriately, the ITV programme that many critics, including myself, had branded Fayed propaganda, and which ITV executives sprang to the defence of, has now *become* Fayed propaganda – extracts fitting seamlessly into 'The Mystery of the Alma Tunnel'.

One such excerpt features Nicholas Owen's exploration of the 'mystery' of Henri Paul's finances (see above). Another sequence, predictably, sees François Levi (pp. 114–17) repeating his account about the 'flash before the crash'. Appropriately, the commentary is inexpertly read by one of Fayed's long-standing PR advisors, Brian Basham, who has worked on and off for Fayed since the 1980s battle for Harrods. Basham became notorious in the early 1990s when his contract with British Airways was terminated after the airline conceded defeat, and paid British record libel damages, to Virgin Atlantic and its owner, Sir Richard Branson, over its 'dirty tricks' campaign.[26] Basham himself is a republican with little affection for the British royal family.

The evidence raised in the 2003 Fayed video includes a Basham-revoiced segment of a Channel 5 documentary about Prince Philip's past before he married Queen Elizabeth II. Fayed then appears to claim that Prince Philip's upbringing had apparently 'turned [him] into an arrogant racist who thinks he is above the law'.

Fayed appears again near the end of the video to announce that, 'As a father who has lost his beloved son, I have investigated every aspect of the car crash which killed my son, Dodi, Diana, Princess of Wales and their driver, Henri Paul. The evidence is clear: these three innocent people were murdered. New evidence continues to emerge that supports what I have been saying . . .

'During her last holiday, with me and my family in France, Diana told me her life was in danger. She had received direct death threats. She blamed Prince Philip and told me of the proof she had kept in case anything happened to her. On that terrible night when she died, her words came back to me, and I knew that Diana had been right. They had killed her and taken the life of my son as well. I am now certain that Prince Philip was behind the murder of my son.'

Fayed had been attempting to goad the royal family into some sort of legal action against him since 1999. During a libel action Fayed brought against the former Conservative minister, Neil Hamilton, he stood in the

---

[26] *Dirty Tricks – British Airways' Secret War Against Virgin Atlantic*, Martyn Gregory, Virgin Books 2000.

witness box of the High Court and invited the Duke of Edinburgh to sue him over his claim that he had been the 'mastermind' of the conspiracy to kill Dodi and Princess Diana.[27] Indeed, the most unintentionally amusing section of the Fayed video is entitled 'Prince Philip – The Finger Of Blame'. With unintentional echoes of Monty Python, Prince Philip and MI6 are compared to Henry II and his knights who killed Thomas à Becket. Intones Basham, 'Four days after Christmas in the year 1170, four knights loyal to the then King – Henry II – murdered the Archbishop of Canterbury, Thomas à Becket, in Canterbury Cathedral. They had been prompted to do so by the rash words of infuriated Henry II: "Will no one rid me of this turbulent priest?" Is Prince Philip a modern-day Henry II, with MI6 playing the role of the murderer knights? Prince Philip's hatred of Diana is well documented. Mohamed Al Fayed believes that MI6 murdered his son Dodi and Diana. He lays the blame firmly at Prince Philip's door.'

Fayed himself appears in vision to pledge, 'With God's help, I pledge my life to bring Prince Philip and his terrorist thugs to justice before the British people and the people of the world.'[28]

A haggard-looking Fayed makes this pledge in front of the shrine to Diana and Dodi in the basement of his Harrods store. The shrine consists of a grubby champagne glass which, members of the public are informed, was used by the couple in the Imperial Suite shortly before the crash. The Repossi ring, which Mohamed Fayed bought and Princess Diana never saw, is the centrepiece of the shrine – now described in Harrods as an 'engagement' ring.

My initial reaction to watching the video was that it was destined for cyberspace, and the www.alfayed.com website, and that it could never be broadcast by terrestrial TV stations. Fayed has regularly run similar videos on his website to promote his conspiracy theories. In 2001 a Los Angeles company, Grizzly Adams, produced a programme in the *Encounters with the Unexplained* series for Pax TV about the Paris crash. Subsequently the programme could be accessed on www.alfayed.com. However, large portions of this video had already been broadcast on terrestrial TV in the UK, and I learned from Japanese TV journalists in the winter of 2004 that it had already been shown in Asia.

In my opinion, the video will mislead uninformed members of the public about the dead couple's feelings for each other. Many throughout the world have been led to believe the couple died when on the

---

[27] BBC News, 22 November 1999.
[28] 'The Mystery of the Alma Tunnel', 2003.

threshold of marriage, though few outside the Fayed family or its entourage have ever supported this claim. Indeed, the section of the Fayed video that reports this unlikely outcome is subtitled 'The Announcement They Wanted To Stop'. Central to this sequence is the jeweller from whom Mohamed Fayed bought the ring, Alberto Repossi. This segment particularly fascinated me. In 1998, for my first documentary about the Paris crash, 'Diana – The Accident',[29] I had recorded an interview with Repossi in which he clearly refuted the idea that the ring was an engagement ring (See pp. 24–5). In the autumn of 2003, whilst in Paris preparing 'The Diana Conspiracy',[30] a follow-up documentary for Channel 4, I was surprised to read an interview in *Paris Match* about the ring. The headline quoted Repossi as saying, 'The day when . . . Diana and Dodi announced their engagement to me'[31] which was the opposite of what he had said to me six months after the crash, as I record on pages 99–100.

Furthermore, the *Paris Match* article featured four still pictures from the Repossi shop security video that Repossi had told me in 1998 had been destroyed. The stills showed Dodi entering Repossi's Paris shop on his last evening alive. The pictures apparently showed him collecting the ring that both Fayed (since 1998) and Repossi now describe as the 'engagement ring'.

Intrigued by this development, I returned to the Repossi shop in the Place Vendôme in Paris with a camera crew to quiz the jeweller about this puzzling change in his account. In 1998 Repossi had told me that he had never met Diana, and that he had had no idea if the ring was an engagement ring. Furthermore he said that he had travelled to Paris on 30 August 1997 in the hope of meeting Diana in person. He had also confessed to disappointment that Dodi had turned up alone to collect the ring and thus he had not met Diana.[32]

In November 2003, forgetting as we started our interview that I had spoken to him in 1998, he told me a completely different story. Repossi claimed that Diana and Dodi had, in fact, met him in secret in a hotel in Saint-Tropez on 22 August 1997 (the day after she arrived in the South of France to start her last holiday with Dodi). Repossi claimed that he had actually placed his ring on Diana's finger himself and had agreed to adjust it as it was slightly too big. This, he claimed, was the moment

[29] 'Diana – The Accident' Channel 4 June 1998.
[30] 'The Diana Conspiracy' Channel 4 February 2004.
[31] *Paris Match*, September 2003.
[32] Author's interview with Repossi, 1998.

when the couple 'announced their engagement' to him. According to Repossi, neither of the couple's bodyguards was present at the hotel rendezvous, and no paparazzi were either.

Thus much of what Repossi had told me in 1998 appeared to be contradicted by this new account. When I put this to him and showed him a transcript of our 1998 encounter, the Italian jeweller became flustered and his stilted English responses reverted to flustered French. He explained that he had not in fact destroyed the CCTV tape of Dodi's visit at all, as he had told me in 1998. He claimed that he had misled me about this to 'protect Diana's boys'; now that they were both men he felt able to reveal the 'truth'. Repossi did concede that he had rediscovered the CCTV tape (and apparently his memory) after receiving 'an injunction' from Fayed over the tape.[33] Repossi also claimed that Trevor Rees-Jones's book *The Bodyguard's Story*, published in 2000, had prompted him to come up with this new account. In his book the bodyguard identifies the significance of the ring.

> The ring, now on display as part of the memorial to Dodi and
> Diana at Harrods, became the incendiary spark for the global
> spread of conspiracy theories that fuelled political and racist
> passions, clouded the investigation and besmirched the innocent.[34]

Rees-Jones's account of the couple's movements (which were also tracked by a hoard of paparazzi and reporters) rules out the possibility of any meeting with Repossi in Saint-Tropez on 22 August 1997 or at any other time during the holiday.

> I was in charge of their security and it's more than courtesy, it's
> strictly required protocol, that security on the ground had to report
> any movements of our principals outside the family compound.
> It would have been a total violation of orders, a sackable offence.
> We were never informed. It is virtually impossible that it
> happened.[35]

Repossi claimed to me that Rees-Jones's book had prompted him to reveal his new version of events. However, Repossi's new story was incomplete and, as it contradicted all known accounts of Diana's and

---

[33] Author's interview with Repossi, 2003.
[34] *The Bodyguard's Story*, p. 63 (Little, Brown 2000).
[35] Ibid., p. 60.

Dodi's movements, it lacked credibility. I thought it significant he could not remember the name of the hotel where he claimed to have met Diana and Dodi in Saint-Tropez, and placed the ring on Diana's finger. I believe that Trevor Rees-Jones's account, which is supported by his fellow bodyguard, Kez Wingfield, is more reliable.

I further believe that the testimonies of Rosa Monckton, Paul Burrell and Richard Kay, all of whom spoke to the Princess shortly before her death, should define history's verdict upon Mohamed Fayed's 'engagement' theory and Diana's feelings towards his son. The three all enjoyed close but very different relationships with the Princess. They are united in their view that Diana had no intention of becoming engaged to Dodi. In August 1997 Diana told Rosa and her butler, Paul Burrell, that she knew Dodi would buy her a ring, having showered her with presents since their meeting a month earlier. Diana told Rosa Monckton, while boating in the Greek islands less than two weeks before her death, that it would go 'firmly on the fourth finger of my right hand'.

As the Fayed PR machine went into overdrive in 2003/4, and continued to claim that Diana and Dodi got engaged before they died, Rosa elaborated on the Greek holiday: 'She was relaxed. We had just lots of girl talk, you know, when there's two girls together you talk about things that matter. She talked about her new relationship with Dodi and she talked about other relationships and her family, and everything, we talked about everything. She was enjoying herself. In my view, and I actually put this to her, I said what you are doing is having your teenage years now. You're having fun, you're having a fling, and you're enjoying it, and so you should. But in my view, it was no more than that.'[36]

One subject the women did not talk about on their Greek holiday, which ended ten days before Diana died, was a marriage to Dodi. 'We didn't even discuss it, you know, we didn't even discuss the way the relationship could go, you know. It was very new. She was right at the beginning of it, and she was just enjoying herself. But there was no question at all that it was heading for an engagement . . . I don't see how they could have been. I think it's a complete fabrication.'

Rosa had her final conversation with Diana while she was on the *Jonikal* on 27 August 1997 on the Princess's mobile phone. 'She was looking forward, when I last spoke to her, which was on the Wednesday, she said, I can't wait to get back to London and get back to my boys and get back to the gym. She'd sort of had enough. She just wanted to get back into her old routine, she'd been away a long time.'

---

[36] Author's interview with Rosa Monckton, 2003.

Diana's butler, Paul Burrell, added interesting background to these exchanges in his 2003 book about his period serving the Princess, *A Royal Duty*. Burrell also spoke several times to Princess Diana on the *Jonikal*.

> In another call from the boat, she speculated about whether the next gift would be a ring. She was excited about the prospect, but was becoming increasingly worried about what it all meant. 'What would I do Paul, if it was a ring? I want another marriage like I need a bad rash,' she said.
>
> 'It's easy. You accept it graciously and slip it on the fourth finger of your right hand. Don't put it on the wrong finger if you don't want to send the wrong signals!' I warned light-heartedly.
>
> Fourth finger. Right hand. We kept saying it.
>
> 'That means it will become a friendship ring,' I said.
>
> 'What a clever idea. I will. I will,' she said.[37]

Diana's journalist friend, Richard Kay, spoke to the Princess on Saturday 30 August 1997, hours before her death. Kay was doing his weekend shopping in London when he received the call on his mobile phone. 'She was saying to the world, yes I have found someone, I'm very happy. But that's a completely different stage from, we're going to get engaged, we're going to be married. I didn't get that impression at all and this whole ring business, I've been very dubious about.'[38]

Ironically, Mohamed Fayed's own account immediately before the crash would appear to bear more relation to reality than his subsequent embellishments. Fayed told the *New York Times* immediately before the crash that his son's love for Diana was 'nothing really special . . . normal people fall in love. It's still just two people getting to know each other.'[39]

The Fayed theory that Diana was planning to settle down with Dodi in the villa Windsor outside Paris was dismantled on the first anniversary of the crash by bodyguard Ben Murrell (see pp. 107–9). Gregorio Martin was in Spain at the time of the visit (and spokesman Cole was in England) and we know, from Ben Murrell and the Fayed security video, that no 'decorator' was present, and Diana spent less than 28 minutes in the villa (see p. 109). About two hours after she left the villa Diana made her call to Richard Kay. 'She mentioned that during

---

[37] *A Royal Duty*, Paul Burrell, Michael Joseph, 2003.
[38] Author's interview with Richard Kay, 2003.
[39] *New York Times* interview quoted in the *Daily Express*, 29 August 1997.

the day they had been to Bois de Boulogne and been to the Windsor villa that the Duchess of Windsor had lived in. I asked her what was it like. She said it was full of old ghosts and I thought that was a very telling phrase. I asked her, "Not for you?" . . . And she said, "No, not for me." [40]

I do not believe that Diana's 'engagement' to Dodi, her 'pregnancy' by him, and the couple's plans to live together in Paris or anywhere else are supported by the facts. Nonetheless, millions around the world now believe some or all of these theories, as well as the more important ones Fayed's team has put forward about the fatal crash.

The distinguished royal historian, Robert Lacey, commented: 'I think the Fayed campaign has been brilliant in its achievement. One may dislike the methods, but the way in which over the years more and more people have come to believe Mr Fayed's explanation and theories about what happened that dark night to the extent of accusing Prince Philip . . . illustrates what had been called the dark arts of public relations and news manipulation and that much overused word, spin.' [41]

The investigation's dossier of over 6,000 pages reveals the 'brilliance' of Fayed's spin operation. There is not one page, or even one line, of evidence read in its proper context, which supports any of the wild allegations that Fayed's team has regaled the world with since the crash. The dossier shows how comprehensive the investigation was, and how unlikely it is that either Diana's or Dodi's inquests will arrive at conclusions that differ to any significant degree.

The dossier also stands as an ironic and inadvertent tribute to the ingenuity and imagination of the Fayed PR machine. But who devised and implemented the strategy? The Egyptian has used a combination of ex-BBC News reporters with no previous PR experience – Michael Cole, Laurie Mayer, Chris Morris – and professional PR operators, Max Clifford and Brian Basham among them. Only Fayed himself and his head of security, John Macnamara, have remained in situ since the crash. Once Michael Cole's 'golden rule' of denying the media direct access to Mohamed was breached in early 1998, his successors have struggled to deal with their boss's more outrageous claims.

The dossier provides reassurance for those who might have doubted French investigative and medical procedures. And it undermines totally Fayed's charge of incompetence or subterfuge by the French that had first started to rear its head on the eve of Diana's funeral in September 1997 (see pp. 85–6).

---

[40] Author's interview with Richard Kay, 2003.
[41] Author's interview with Robert Lacey, 2003.

In 2003 Fayed claimed on US TV, 'You see him [Henri Paul] on the video and see he's completely 100 per cent sober, fine, talking to everybody, giving instructions to everyone. They changed the blood of Henri Paul with somebody else.'[42]

The central evidence in the dossier contradicts this claim and in my opinion proves that Henri Paul was drunk. There was a second set of tests on Paul's corpse supervised by Judge Stéphan himself (see p. 72), which are documented in detail in the dossier. An unnamed clerk accompanied Judge Hervé Stéphan, and a team of medical experts and police, to the Institut Medico-Legal (IML) within 48 hours of Stéphan's appointment as head of the investigation. Professor Dominique Lecomte had performed an autopsy in the morning of 31 August 1997 and their mission was to re-examine Henri Paul's body. Two tests on Paul's blood, extracted at the autopsy and analysed independently, had shown that he was between three and four times over the legal drink-drive limit. 'Di's Driver Drunk as a Pig' raged one British headline when the French released the results of Henri Paul's autopsy. Before Diana's funeral, Mohamed Fayed's press operation had started its long-running challenge to the authenticity of the findings (see pp. 85–6) after his own expert, Professor Peter Vanezis, was refused permission to examine Henri Paul's samples.

Paul's parents had expressed their immediate shock to Judge Stéphan (see p. 72), as they knew their son to be a keen pilot and tennis player, and knew little of his drinking (which was, however, well known at the Ritz). Seizing on the Pauls' concern, Stéphan led a delegation to IML on the Thursday after the crash. Stéphan was accompanied by Dr Campana, who was tasked with extracting fresh samples of blood, urine and the 'other usual samples'. Dr Pépin immediately sealed the samples with wax and took them to his TOXLAB for analysis. Policemen Captain Le Jalle and Lieutenant Bourbois were joined by a local policeman, M. Boulet – this police delegation took pictures of Paul's corpse (number 2147), which are filed in the dossier. These photos show Paul's naked body with a long line of stitching from his neck to his groin area where the pathologist had removed for analysis and then replaced his organs in the conventional manner. In Mohamed Fayed's claim of seeing Princess Diana's corpse he said it looked 'beautiful' and 'serene'. Ironically, although the corpse of the man who drove the Princess and his son to their deaths would never be described as beautiful, it does, in a strange way, look serene. In death Paul appears to be at peace.

---

[42] 'The Belzer Connection: Diana Conspiracy', K2 Pictures, Sci-Fi Channel (USA), 25 August 2003.

Stéphan's clerk's note records that the party spent 45 minutes witnessing the fresh samples being extracted from Paul's corpse. Samples of Paul's femoral blood, muscle tissue and hair were taken and placed in bottles, which were numbered and then photographed. The blood and muscle tissue (samples 2 & 3) were given 'immediately' to TOXLAB's analyst, Dr Gilbert Pépin. The clerk signed the handwritten record and it was countersigned by Judge Stéphan at the mortuary at 17.45 on 4 September 1997.

The judge's dossier also includes interviews with Paul's doctor, and friend of twenty years, Dr Dominique Melo. He confirms he had been prescribing drugs to Paul to combat alcoholism and depression for more than a year before his death. The drugs included Prozac, Aotal and Tiapridal. The bottles in which such drugs are supplied warn users not to drink while taking them. Later, more detailed tests on the Stéphan-supervised samples revealed traces of both Prozac and Tiapridal. In his synthesis of the different toxicological reports on Henri Paul's corpse, Dr Pépin quotes the 1997 edition of the French medical bible, the Vidal dictionary, which warns of the effects that Prozac, which contains fluoxetine, can have, 'altering attention span and the capacity to react. Thus it is advisable to warn drivers of vehicles and machine operators of the risks.'[43]

At the beginning of 2004, more than six years after the crash, and after Diana's and Dodi's inquests had opened, Fayed's team still appeared to be trying to persuade the public that the bar bill from the Imperial suite did not contain alcoholic drinks.[44] John Macnamara, in a letter to the *Sunday Telegraph*, said he had examined the bill and objected to the paper's description of 'Mr Paul's lengthy bar bill'. In his letter Fayed's security chief listed everything the bill contained apart from the alcoholic drinks. The dossier confirms that it did contain alcohol – two Ricards, a brand of pastis, which cost 80 francs each (see also p. 74). Claude Roulet, the Ritz hotel's assistant president, confirms in his interview with the police that Bar Bill No. 4891 for 1,260 francs was the bill charged to the Imperial Suite. Roulet states that Henri Paul and the two bodyguards put their food and drinks on this bill before the fatal journey began and, in their statements to the investigation, the bodyguards confirmed that they did not drink the Ricard.

In his first statement, made the day after the crash, Roulet also appears to shed some light upon another 'mystery' – that of Paul's

---

[43] Synthesis of toxicological expertises by Dr Gilbert Pépin.
[44] Macnamara letter to *Sunday Telegraph*, 14 January 2004.

whereabouts during the evening of 30 August, after he left the Ritz at about 19.15 and before he returned, at Dodi's request, at 22.05. According to Roulet, Paul went to a bar very close to the Ritz. In a statement made the day after the crash Roulet says, 'It was about 19.30 that I saw him in a café, Le Bar de Bourgogne, rue des Petits Champs.'[45] Subsequent statements by Roulet, and bar staff from the Bar de Bourgogne, were less precise and appeared to contradict Roulet's initial account. The French investigation concluded that Roulet's claim to have seen Paul in the bar was not definitive. In the view of the Criminal Brigade, which failed to definitively solve this minor mystery, Paul most probably returned to his apartment before being summoned back to the Ritz. The analysis of Paul's blood showed a higher level of alcohol than two Ricards could have produced, even allowing for Ritz bar staff pouring generous measures for the hotel's acting head of security. It should not be forgotten that no one – including Henri Paul – had any idea he would be driving before Dodi asked him to after speaking to his father, Mohamed, on the phone in England at about midnight.

Roulet concludes his 1 September statement with the observation that 'It was not unusual, under pressure from the paparazzi, for Dodi to ask Philippe Dourneau to jump the lights to escape them.'[46] Paul, who was not a qualified chauffeur and had little, if any, experience of driving Dodi, jumped the last set of lights before the Alma tunnel in the Place de la Concorde to put distance between his Mercedes and the paparazzi.

Michael Burgess made his first trip to Paris at the beginning of February 2004 to meet senior French Ministry of Justice officials, headed by Jean-Claude Marin, the head of criminal affairs. The ministry is in the Place Vendôme, next door to the Ritz hotel from where Princess Diana and Dodi set off on their last journey. From all accounts it was a productive and cordial meeting. Burgess stressed that he hoped to build on the French investigation; he did not intend to knock it down. Arrangements were made for Sir John Stevens's team to work with the French police, with the coroner stressing that he saw co-operation between the Met and its French counterparts as being essential.

Sir John's team would soon find itself at the Criminal Brigade's imposing HQ at the Quai d'Orfèvres on the banks of the Seine, where Martine Monteil's detectives are based and where many witnesses were interviewed. Those who were quizzed by Commander Jean-Claude Mulès found that his office was decorated in a most unconventional

---

[45] Roulet statement, 1 September 1997.
[46] Ibid.

manner. The walls were covered in masks that amuse, intimidate and surprise visitors as they enter. When the well-known paparazzo, James Andanson, arrived to be interviewed by Mulès in February 1998, he asked the commander why he had chosen such decoration. 'The masks fall here,' replied the wiry Mulès with a twinkle in his eye. Andanson reached into his breast pocket, fished out a dictaphone, and recorded the remark.

Mulès had become aware of Andanson's formidable reputation as a paparazzo, and also of the unpopularity that his bullying and arrogant personality had caused. In the summer of 1997, Andanson had been one of the leading paparazzi, working for the SIPA agency, following Princess Diana and Dodi in the South of France. Indeed, Andanson brokered deals between the paparazzi and the Princess that produced some of the famous pictures of Diana on her last holiday with Dodi. Once the Andanson-engineered photo opportunities were over, the Princess had been allowed some peace to relax with Dodi as the photographers raced to send their latest pictures around the world. Mohamed Fayed could bask in further publicity – the world's most famous Princess relaxing on his yacht, with his son and secure within his multi-million-pound security.

After Princess Diana's death, Mulès discovered that Andanson's professional pre-eminence had, however, created many enemies who resented his manner and possibly his achievements. After it had been established that a white Fiat Uno had been involved in the Alma tunnel crash, the Crim had received calls from rival paparazzi who informed them that Andanson owned a white Fiat.

Mohamed Fayed's parallel investigation into the tragedy, led in France by Mulès's former Criminal Brigade boss, Pierre Ottavioli (see pp. 141–3), had alerted Judge Stéphan to Andanson's Fiat as well. John Macnamara claimed a triumph: 'It was our investigators, not the French police, who found the Fiat Uno. It was found in a garage in Paris and traced to a paparazzi named James Andanson.'[47]

While this was not wholly accurate – the Fiat was found in Lignière not Paris – the discovery that Andanson owned a white Fiat had caused the Criminal Brigade to descend upon Andanson's farm in Lignière, 160 miles south of Paris at the beginning of 1998 to inspect what was found to be a very old vehicle. Mulès recalls what his officers found: 'The car had 325,000 kilometres on the clock. When a car like this has done 325,000 or 400,000 kilometres, it's given up the ghost. He had placed

---

[47] Macnamara interview 'Diana – The Night She Died', Channel 5 (Psychology News) 2003.

it on bricks, it had no battery and he wasn't using it any more. I believe the car wasn't even insured.'[48]

Interviews by the Crim with Andanson's neighbours confirmed the photographer's claim that his Fiat had not moved anywhere for months. When Mulès interviewed Andanson the photographer explained his movements on the night of the crash. He had been at home in Lignière with his wife and daughter. He went to bed at 22.30 on 30 August and he rose early to drive to Orly airport outside Paris in his BMW and catch the 07.20 flight to Corsica, returning later the same day. Andanson produced a credit-card receipt for a motorway toll, his flight details, and a receipt for a Hertz car he had hired in Corsica. He told Mulès his mother-in-law had been using the Fiat for a while after he had ceased to use it in 1995 but that it had been standing on bricks outside his stable since October 1997.

Following the Crim's raid and Andanson's interview with Mulès, both the photographer and the vehicle were eliminated from the investigation into the Paris crash.[49] This should have marked the end of Andanson's contribution to the saga – this line of investigation had already expired before Fayed's PR seized the opportunity to turn it into a 'mask' of its own.

However, the 54-year-old Andanson's unexpected death, in apparently mysterious circumstances – the photographer was found burned to death in his estate car in May 2000 – reignited Mohamed Fayed's bid to place him in the Alma tunnel on the night of the crash. The French investigation's failure to find the white Fiat that had been clipped by the Mercedes gave Fayed's PR machine the chance to highlight and exploit this flaw. Fayed spokesman Michael Cole first characterised the white Fiat as 'the grassy knoll' of the crash (see p. 122) and his successors, working closely with John Macnamara, have lost few opportunities to exploit the notion. Thus Andanson and his Fiat are at the centre of Fayed's 2003 'Mystery of the Alma Tunnel' video, which is more reminiscent of *Groundhog Day* than *JFK* in that the same flawed themes recur endlessly rather than making a convincing case of a conspiracy. Andanson's name also appeared in Fayed's unsuccessful petition to the Scottish court in 2003 (see above).[50]

The inquest into Andanson's death was conducted by investigative judge, Natalie Martie. She found a trail of clues and evidence left by

---

[48] Author's interview with Commander Mulès, 2003.
[49] Ibid.
[50] Fayed petition to to the Scottish Court of Session, 2003.

Andanson that led her to record a verdict of suicide. She remarked sardonically that she wished that she had come across evidence suggesting a more exciting or unusual verdict, but she had not.[51]

However, in the UK, the *Daily Star* revived the story of Andanson's death at the end of 2003. Beneath a picture of Diana a headline proclaimed, 'Key witness burned to death in a locked car'. The article revealed: 'Andanson was the owner of the infamous white Fiat which clipped Di's chauffeur-driven Mercedes seconds before it crashed in Paris . . . Speculation grew that he was murdered by security service agents covering their tracks . . . What disturbed police most was the wrecked car had been locked with a key from the outside, then set alight with the photographer inside.'[52]

A similar version of the Andanson story had appeared in a Channel 5 documentary earlier in the year.[53] Unfortunately, circulation increases for media outlets when they feature Diana, even when recycling stale or false news. The editor of the *Daily Mirror*, Piers Morgan, whose paper effectively became Mohamed Fayed's house journal under his editorship, told me that he had never believed in any of the conspiracy theories; he thinks the evidence shows that the Paris car crash was an accident. However, the *Daily Mirror* has run more Fayed-inspired headlines than any other British newspaper and Morgan frankly conceded that the deceased Princess did sell his paper. 'In terms of impact on circulation, Diana is twice as big since she died as she was when she was alive, and twice as big as anything else that we've touched – really quite extraordinary.'[54]

From its investigation, the Criminal Brigade are certain that neither Andanson nor his Fiat played any role in the fatal crash. I believe that it is inconceivable that Mr Burgess's inquest will find the Fiat, or its driver, played a malign role in the accident as I have found no evidence in the dossier to lead to such a view. But none of the media that reported this story saw fit to include the Crim's findings.

On another level, however, in the court of public opinion, this tactic has worked well for Fayed, increasing public doubts about the French investigation into the crash, and reaffirming his own role as the bereaved father earnestly looking for answers. Such articles are often accompanied by the list of the 'unanswered questions' about the crash that has been

[51] Natalie Martie interview, CBS 2003.
[52] *Daily Star*, 22 October 2003.
[53] 'Diana – The Night She Died', Channel 5 2003.
[54] Author's interview with Piers Morgan, 2003.

the Fayed PR staple strategy since the crash and it leads people away from asking about what I believe were crucial lapses in the security he provided for the Princess. In October 2003, for example, the *Daily Star* posed '8 sinister questions' alongside its Andanson/Fiat story, all of which were either inaccurate or irrelevant. The *Star*'s list was typical of questions many British newspapers asked in the winter of 2003/4 when Diana's and Dodi's inquests opened. Such lists demonstrated how deep-seated the misinformation about the crash had become – admittedly in newspapers that know there are papers to be sold by putting the words 'Diana' and 'mystery' in the same headline. As the following analysis demonstrates, many of them can be traced to the Fayed PR machine.

THE *DAILY STAR* – THE CONSPIRACY THEORIES[55]

'In the seven years since Diana's death hundreds of conspiracy theories have evolved to support claims that the Princess and Dodi were victims of an establishment murder plot. Here are some of the most intriguing – and outlandish.'

- 'Driver Henry [sic] Paul was working for MI6 and inexplicably had £102,000 in 13 bank accounts.'

This particular canard had been doing the media rounds since the ITV programme first suggested in 1998 that Paul was a man with 'very big secrets' and reported that there was something suspicious about the dead driver's finances. Richard Tomlinson later added the 'MI6' element without ever producing any evidence that British intelligence was in touch with Paul or, if the agency was, how this influenced events on the night of 31 August 1997. The Criminal Brigade's unremarkable findings about Paul's finances (see above) are routinely ignored in such articles.

- 'A Fiat Uno deliberately clipped Diana's car as it entered the Alma tunnel. Its alleged driver, paparazzo James Andanson, died mysteriously two years later in a burned-out car.'

Forensic tests showed that the Mercedes 'brushed' the Fiat, not vice versa. Neither Andanson nor his Fiat were in Paris when the crash happened (see above) but this has not stopped John Macnamara

---

[55] *Daily Star*, 22 October 2003.

continuing to raise the role of the dead paparazzo and his Fiat (see below).

- 'A blinding flash from an anti-personnel stunning device lit up the tunnel immediately before the crash.'

Francois Levi's claims were supported by no other witness and were rejected by the French investigation.

- 'CCTV cameras in the tunnel were facing the wall, preventing crash footage. Trucks sprayed the area with disinfectant two hours later, destroying forensic evidence.'

The investigation's dossier reveals mundane reasons for the absence of 'crash footage'. Firstly, there are no cameras in the Alma tunnel at all, let alone facing the wall. Police Lieutenant Bernard Gisbert states in the dossier that no speed cameras had been installed on the Mercedes's route on 31 August 1997. Another document makes clear that the single traffic camera in the Place de L'Alma, above the tunnel, was not working properly. The official responsible for that camera reports that his team was unable to manipulate the camera properly that night, or use its zoom lens. The images the camera in the Place de L'Alma had been producing were 'unusable' and 'blurred', thus the traffic-control team could not use it to monitor the scene before or after the crash.

According to Commander Mulès, no 'forensic evidence' was destroyed. Municipal cleaning vehicles were only allowed to spray the tunnel after the Criminal Brigade was satisfied it had collected all necessary evidence. 'The scene was preserved immediately after the accident . . . When I arrived, I continued preserving the scene, but once my work was done, there was no reason to keep it closed. I wasn't going to seal off the tunnel and stop the traffic. It's unthinkable. The procedures which I put into effect were very, very precise. Nothing was left to chance. We combed the tunnel millimetre by millimetre. No other element significant to the investigation could have been discovered. I had no reason, once the Mercedes had been taken away, to block the scene. I wasn't going to turn it into a shrine.'[56]

Mulès describes his detective work in the Alma tunnel as being like a 'photographer with a pen' – every detail found was

---

[56] Author's interview with Commander Mulès, 2003.

meticulously recorded by his team. The Crim's photographers also took pictures of the scene in the tunnel from the wrecked Mercedes to the car's point of impact with the pillar and the kerb, as well as the shards of glass and debris that were scattered around.

Professor Murray Mackay has a clear view of Mulès's decision to open the tunnel, which team Fayed tried to spin into a controversy to the detriment of the French investigation: 'Well, I can't see that there was anything lost in, for example, the time that was spent at the scene and then when you've finished, as is typical with any even fatal road accidents, you know the scene is cleared, it's time to get traffic moving. You record the evidence photographically, you take measurements, you collect components, debris at the scene. I can't think that there was anything more that would have been achieved had they kept the tunnel closed for another twenty-four hours.'[57]

- 'Diana was embalmed within hours to destroy medical evidence that she was carrying Dodi's baby.'

Untrue according to those present at Diana's autopsy in Fulham, including the former royal coroner who was there (see above). Though Diana had been partially embalmed by the French, this limited procedure had not affected the organs, including the womb, that they routinely analysed during the postmortem.

- 'Henri Paul's blood sample was switched with one from someone else who died that night. That's why the tests found such high levels of carbon monoxide.'

Impossible according to Professor Dominique Lecomte, who performed Paul's autopsy, and Commander Mulès, who witnessed her work. The investigation's dossier demonstrates with photographs and text that the samples were taken from the correct body and were properly tested. Judge Stéphan's visit on 4 September with police and senior medics copper-bottomed the initial autopsy's findings. The 'high levels' of carbon monoxide were not judged to be of any significance by the French investigation (see pp. 124–9).

- 'Armed secret agents raided the Paris and London offices of photo agencies and stole crash images.'

---

[57] Author's interview with Murray Mackay, 2003.

This 'mystery' comes straight from Fayed's team via UK tabloids. In 'The Mystery of the Alma Tunnel' the commentary informs viewers, 'Then the plot (sic) took another startling twist . . . three masked men broke in to Andanson's office in Paris and shot the security guard.'

Cue the head of Fayed's parallel investigation, John Macnamara, who said in the video: 'The burglars spent three hours ransacking his [Andanson's] office and, despite frantic phone calls from people in the office, the Paris police never attended. In fact, some people in the photo agency actually felt the burglars were from the French security services.' Basham's video commentary rounds off this segment: 'Undoubtedly, the security services were looking for photographs taken before, at the time and after the crash which would show the presence of British MI6 officers there.'

'Some people' in SIPA might have felt French secret services were involved (although the SIPA employees in question are not identified in the Fayed video). However, SIPA's owners are not amongst them. The Turkish founder and owner of the SIPA agency, Gorskin Sipahiojlu, and his American wife Phyllis Springer both knew Andanson well and were amongst the last to see him alive, in their Paris office two days before he died. Both find it difficult to believe that those who broke in to their offices were 'secret agents', or that the intrusion had anything to do with the crash or with Andanson.

Says Sipahiojlu, 'The thieves just stole cameras and things, which you can sell very easily. And the big computer, they left. Andanson's computer was in the office, in his room, because he left it there. It was in his office and nobody touched it.'[58] The armed thieves' modus operandi also did not suggest professional secret service agents; they managed to shoot a security guard in the foot.

Phyllis Springer says, 'I am 100 per cent sure he [Andanson] committed suicide. I think tabloid journalism has picked up the murder conspiracy idea. It helps to sell newspapers. But I don't think it has any foundation for it.' When Mohamed Fayed's theory, that James Andanson was murdered because he was somehow involved with Princess Diana's death, is put to Gorskin Sipahiojlu his response is curt: 'It is bullshit.'[59]

---

[58] All SIPA quotes from CBS interviews with Gorskin Sipahiojlu and Phyllis Springer, 2004.
[59] Ibid.

- 'Ambulance men inexplicably took nearly 90 minutes to get Diana to hospital, ignoring two clinics that could have treated her.'

The reason for the delay was that the Princess suffered a heart attack whilst being transferred from the Mercedes to the ambulance (see pp. 58–9). According to the President of SAMU, Dr Marc Giroud, authorised to speak on behalf of those who tried so hard to save Princess Diana's life, everything possible was done to save her. It is worth examining this last 'unanswered question' in detail, as Fayed's PR operation has obtained considerable mileage from the episode. In early 1998 the Fayed-influenced *Death of a Princess* book was published. US medics, none of whom had had a chance to see the Princess's medical records or speak to the medics involved in trying to save her, were quoted heavily criticising the French efforts.

Six years later Fayed still sees criticism of the emergency service as a point of advantage. His video 'The Mystery of the Alma Tunnel' identifies the care the French failed to provide for Diana as a sub-mystery – 'The Mystery of the Ambulance Journey'. The commentary runs: 'Meanwhile, early that morning, amid all the frantic activity back at the Alma tunnel, the fate of the most famous woman in the world lay in the hands of French emergency workers. According to media reports, Diana was semi-conscious but had signs of internal bleeding, low blood pressure and difficulty breathing. Yet, for some unexplained reason, it took 1 hour and 43 minutes to deliver Diana to a hospital that was only 3.8 miles away. Why?'

The Fayed video commentary cites 'media reports' about this 'fatal' delay, yet Fayed and his lawyers have had access to the dossier since the investigation started in 1997/8. Fayed's former spokesman, Michael Cole, despite having retired in 1998, launched another fierce attack on Diana's medical treatment on the BBC on the day the inquest opened in 2004.[60]

The medics accused by team Fayed are prohibited by French law from speaking publicly. However, minister Kouchner (see p. 87) supported their actions, and had Fayed's team asked SAMU's Dr Marc Giroud, he would have told them why there was a delay. 'It took very long, because Princess Diana was in a hospital mobile

---

[60] The Jeremy Vine programme, BBC Radio 2, 6 January 2004.

intensive care unit. She was not on the street. She was in a medical environment. At the very beginning of her situation, she had a heart attack, and she had to be treated before going to the hospital, otherwise she would have died on the scene. She was resuscitated the moment she had this heart attack. But after that she had blood pressure problems, and when you do not have a good blood pressure, you have to be very, very prudent, very slow driving to transport a patient in this condition. And they also had to treat the patient during the transfer. So it is the way we do it in France.'

However, an 'expert' interviewee continues in Fayed's propaganda video: 'Things are slightly different in France to what they are in the United Kingdom. But it is rather strange that she was treated for so long at the roadside, as it were, because, really, if someone is that seriously ill, the sooner they're got – they're taken to a centre of excellence, a casualty department with intensive care, the better.'[61]

And then Basham's commentary picks up, 'And the French authorities have also offered no explanation as to why the ambulance took fifteen minutes to reach the crash scene on a quiet night.'

The dossier records that ambulances arrived within six minutes of the crash. The makers of the Fayed documentary are as aware of this as their boss who has had access to the dossier for over five years. However, in the Fayed video, a British doctor described as 'a former casualty officer' appears to comment: 'It is strange. I would have expected an ambulance to be there within five minutes, that is what you would normally expect if you had a crash in Oxford Street.'

Basham's commentary then alleges, 'There has also been no explanation as to why the ambulance stopped for ten minutes when they were just 800 metres from the hospital.'

The 'former casualty officer' then reappears to say, 'It's a very, very odd thing to do. No ambulance would ever do that in this country, and I believe that no ambulance anywhere in the world would ever do that, unless there was a conspiracy.'

Having introduced the crucial 'C' word, and ignored the evidence that the reason for this pause was that Diana's blood level had dropped to a dangerously low level (see p. 58), the commentary observes, '. . . and the ambulance drove past several

---

[61] 'The Mystery of the Alma Tunnel', 2003.

other hospitals that were closer to the crash site, on its way to the Pitié-Salpêtrière.'

Dr Marc Giroud explains why. 'Princess Diana received the treatment which was the most appropriate available in Paris at that moment. She was looked after by a very good medical team, very, very experienced in emergency and in very hard emergency situations. She was transported directly to the best hospital. But, unfortunately, she suffered from an injury which was impossible to treat efficiently.'[62]

The Fayed video, however, comes to another conclusion. 'Time was of the essence, but there were tremendous delays. Is it possible that Diana could have lived, had she been taken to hospital more quickly? No one knows. And the French authorities refuse to co-operate by releasing Diana's medical records.'

The French medical team's view that Diana could not have survived (see pp. 59–60) and French law ensures that her medical records remain private, as the records of any citizen would be in identical circumstances. The dossier contains details of the strenuous efforts to save the Princess's life but not the intimate details – France's strict medical secrecy laws prevent this. However, after more than six years of rebutting inaccurate stories from the Fayed camp, which started with the lies that Fayed saw Princess Diana's body and received her last words, spokesman Thierry Meresse was prepared to vent the hospital's feelings about the Egyptian's campaign:

'If you're selling papers, you're going to sell more if you say that the situation was a bit "mysterious". Mohamed Al Fayed has supplied all of it. There is evidence that he himself was responsible for the personal security at the Ritz, and he controls what goes on in his own establishment. He cannot admit that one of his chauffeurs was involved in the death of his son, and also Princess Diana. Fayed has manipulated the press, which often lets itself be manipulated very easily.'

While still bound by strict medical secrecy, the hospital staff took to describing Fayed's team's activities as 'L'affaire Fayed'. As noted earlier, Fayed had caused deep offence by placing his own bodyguards in the hospital during Trevor Rees-Jones's recuperation. However, according to Meresse, when the bodyguard left the hospital Fayed promised to make a significant donation.

---

[62] Author's interview with Dr Marc Giroud, 2003.

'It's true that Mr Fayed made many declarations saying that he would give something to the hospital. And today we are still awaiting this gift. Fortunately we do not rely on Mr Fayed's gifts to make the hospital work! By contrast, the Rees-Jones family, who are of modest means, made no declarations. They were very satisfied with the way we had looked after their son, Trevor. They made out a cheque before leaving which allowed us to improve the reception area in the building where Trevor was hospitalised. Today, when you go into this area you can see a painting of a goldfish, and it's due to the kindness of Trevor and his family that it is there – that was their gift.'[63]

For their part, in addition to often criticising the quality of the care Princess Diana received, Fayed's lawyers now describe the French investigation as 'partial, secretive and deeply flawed'.[64]

Yes, it was partial in that it stuck to its brief investigating only those matters it was commissioned to do, and yes, it was secretive as French law requires it to be, but I do not believe that it was 'deeply flawed'. The investigation's inability to find the white Fiat was its only failure of any significance.

Fayed publicly professed faith in Stéphan's investigation while it was in progress[65] before spending over four years in the French courts challenging its findings when, inevitably, the evidence did not lead it to the conclusions desired. Fayed currently professes faith in the coroner's inquest but has given no indication he will accept its findings if Michael Burgess finds no evidence of a 'conspiracy'.

Near the end of 2003, shortly before Diana's and Dodi's inquests started, Fayed leaped on the sensational revelation by Paul Burrell of a letter, allegedly written by Diana in 1996, in which she wrote that, '[They're] planning "an accident" in my car so Charles can marry again ... I will suffer brake failure and serious head injuries.'[66] 'They' had been blanked out in the original headline, but later the *Mirror* revealed that the blank had been obscuring the words 'my husband'. The letter caused a sensation in the British press and reignited interest in Princess Diana's death. Snap opinion polls showed that more than 75 per cent of British respondents believed Diana was 'murdered'. As the shock of

---

[63] Author's interview with Thierry Meresse, 2003.
[64] Letter from Fayed's lawyer to the *Daily Mail*, 2 February 2004.
[65] 'Al Fayed pledges his support for crash inquiry', *The Times*, 13 March 1998.
[66] *Daily Mirror*, 20 October 2003.

the letter wore off, however, questions were raised about its authenticity, and why Diana had not worn a safety belt if she was, indeed, worried about a serious car accident. Others wondered why Burrell had taken more than six years to reveal the letter, and why he had denied the French investigation access to it. The serialisation by the *Daily Mirror* of Burrell's book about his time serving the Princess offered a tempting explanation. The Royal Family has wisely refused to be goaded by Fayed's allegations about Prince Philip 'masterminding' Princess Diana's murder, and the Spencer family has retained a dignified silence. Both families know that the media circus will return in force when Diana's inquest is reconvened in 2005, and they will have to brace themselves accordingly.

I happened to be in Paris for a meeting with Jean-Claude Mulès when the Burrell letter was published. The seasoned French detective told me that the Criminal Brigade had been aware of Princess Diana's well-chronicled fears for her own safety during their investigation, and that, in itself, the letter would not have altered their approach, even if the letter's authenticity could be have been verified.[67] In the *Sunday Telegraph*, Rosa Monckton wrote that she had received four letters from the Princess in the same month as Burrell claimed Diana gave the letter to him, October 1996, and none of them reflected the tone or the content of her alleged letter to Burrell. (The Burrell letter was undated and addressed simply to 'Paul'.) At the beginning of 2004, Sir John Stevens made it clear that he would interview Prince Charles, as part of his inquiry on behalf of the royal coroner, if he thought it necessary, 'As a police officer you don't start off with any theories, you go where the evidence takes you'[68]

I have frequently been asked since I started investigating the Paris crash if I have even the smallest doubt that it was an accident. I reply, with growing conviction, that the more I look at the evidence the fewer reasons I find to doubt the French investigation's findings. As I made my 2004 documentary on the crash, 'The Diana Conspiracy', for Channel 4, I entertained the hope that the evidence in it of Fayed's conspiracy against the truth of what really happened in Paris might help dispel the audience's doubts about Princess Diana's death.

The heart of the film was a reconstruction of the phone call around midnight on 30 August 1997 between Mohamed and Dodi Fayed,

---

[67] Author's interview with Commander Mulès 2003.

[68] Interview with Sir John Stevens, *Hard Talk*, BBC, 22 January 2004.

during which Henri Paul was authorised to drive Princess Diana away from the Ritz (see pp. 49–50). This decision meant that Diana left Fayed's hotel with a Fayed bodyguard for a Fayed apartment with his specific authority. She was with Fayed's son, in a car driven by Fayed's unqualified and alcoholic 'head of hotel security', speeding at nearly three times the speed limit through the most dangerous tunnel in Paris. The film tried to show how Fayed's subsequent lies, distortions and embellishments have served to divert attention away from that fatal phone call. Reviews of the documentary were kind. *The Times* wrote: 'The writer-director-narrator Martyn Gregory went through every moving part in the conspiracy machine proving one or both of two things: A) it emanated from the office of Mohamed Al Fayed and B) it wasn't actually true.'[69] The *Independent* commented: 'The film did a decent job of debunking the mistakes, the confusions and the downright lies behind the conspiracy theories around the deaths of Di and Dodi . . . cheering for fans of sanity in public discourse.'[70]

However, any thought that the film might have convinced those who have come to believe that the crash was the result of a conspiracy were dashed by a Channel 4 poll taken after transmission. This found that 78 per cent of the 9,000 viewers who voted still believed that the crash was 'not an accident'. A disappointing result, but one that served to redouble my determination to update this book. I fervently hope readers do not come to a similar conclusion, and will realise that all the evidence in this book shows that the sad deaths of both Princess Diana and Dodi Fayed were accidental. The memories of both are besmirched by the 'conspiracy theories' of their deaths.

At the end of April 2004 Michael Burgess's decision to commission Sir John Stevens to investigate the conspiracy theories surrounding the Paris crash made headlines again. The two men made a well-publicised visit to Paris where they spent time at the Ritz hotel, visiting the Imperial Suite in which Diana and Dodi spent their final hours. Sir John also inspected the revolving doors through which the couple entered the Ritz and spoke to senior hotel staff. The party drove twice through the Alma tunnel (once in daylight and again at night). In the afternoon the tunnel was closed to traffic for the main part of the visit. Gendarmes cordoned off the site as the coroner and the commissioner, together with Martine Monteil and the detectives Sir John has entrusted to lead his probe,

---

[69] *The Times*, 6 Feb 2004.
[70] *Independent*, 6 Feb 2004.

Deputy Assistant Commissioner Alan Brown and Detective Superintendent Dave Douglas, representing the team of a dozen Scotland Yard detectives working on Sir John's inquiry, made their way through over a hundred TV, radio and newspaper journalists, predominantly from the British media. The party spent nearly half an hour inspecting the tunnel on foot in the middle of a brilliantly sunny spring afternoon. Apart from some fresh graffiti, little appeared to have changed since the crash. The party studied the only visible evidence of the crash – the mark on pillar 13 caused by the Mercedes.

Monteil described to the British delegation what the French investigation had established and showed them how the French believe Princess Diana, Dodi Fayed and Henri Paul died. Speaking at the mouth of the tunnel after his visit, Sir John curtly dismissed suggestions that his visit was a publicity stunt – 'I don't have time for PR stunts' – and stressed the importance of visiting the scene of the crash: 'no proper investigation could happen without coming here'. Sir John also revealed that had found the tunnel 'narrower' and 'not as long' as he had gathered from watching video pictures and studying photos of it. The commissioner also found that there was 'more of a slope' leading into the tunnel than he had imagined.[71]

Sir John stressed that his duty was to have an open mind, and he re-emphasised that he would be led by the evidence in preparing his report for the coroner. Strategically Michael Burgess's objective must be to attempt to head off, or at least reduce the scope for, a legal challenge from Mohamed Fayed after his inquests into Diana's and Dodi's deaths conclude in 2005. I would be very surprised if the coroner's conclusion were to differ significantly from that of the French investigation. However, in stressing the open-minded nature of his probe, Sir John pledged to leave 'no stone unturned' and that he would 'report on every aspect of the conspiracy theories and either prove or disprove those theories'.

Michael Burgess's inquests have, as their priority, the aim of 'separating fact from fiction'. As there are no facts to support any conspiracy theory, I believe that it is inconceivable that the inquest will establish that there was any form of plot to murder Diana and Dodi. Those involved in Mohamed Fayed's campaign estimate that the Egyptian has already spent over five million pounds on the project. It has brought him little joy in the French, American, Scottish or English courts, but it has helped him to hold sway in the court of public opinion

---

[71] Sir John Stevens, speaking at the Alma tunnel, 26 April 2004.

around the world. However, it is almost inconceivable to me that Fayed will accept its findings. I believe he will challenge any finding that confirms that the crash was an accident as part of his self-proclaimed quest for 'justice'. He might do this in the courts or by continuing to seek an audience in cyberspace. The world wide web does not require as much evidence as the terrestrial courts, and Fayed would be playing to a receptive audience. Princess Diana's friend, Rosa Monckton, summarised the situation aptly: 'She was such an extraordinary woman that people find it very difficult to accept she could have died such an ordinary death. I think that's the problem that people have.'[72]

One reason that Princess Diana was the most popular member of the Royal Family of recent times was because she survived her unhappy marriage into Britain's Royal Family. That she failed to survive her encounter with the Fayed clan is part of her tragedy. Another tragedy is that her love for the man who might have changed her life, and those of her two sons for good and for ever, Dr Hasnat Khan, was not publicly or fully reciprocated. As Diana struggled to come to terms with the end of that relationship, she accepted the fateful invitation to pass the summer with the Fayeds, and she became smitten with Mohamed's feckless son. She perished as a result, and her immediate legacy is being tainted by her lover's father's energetic and lavishly funded attempts to rewrite her history in his own interests. This book is an attempt to ensure those efforts do not succeed, and to liberate some of the truth about the last days of Diana, Princess of Wales.

---

[72] Author's interview with Rosa Monckton, 2003.

APPENDIX

FINAL REPORT BY THE PARIS PROSECUTOR'S OFFICE
[This translation was first published in *The Times*, London, on 4 September 1999.]

Examining Magistrate:
Mr Hervé STEPHAN
Ms Christine DEVIDAL

Prosecutor:
Ms Maud COUJARD

COURT OF THE FIRST INSTANCE

PUBLIC PROSECUTOR'S LEGALLY BINDING JUDGEMENT OF NO GROUNDS FOR PROSECUTION
The Public Prosecutor of the French Republic, at the court of the First Instance, having examined the following enquiry against:

[the following eight were charged on 2 September 1997]
(1) ARNAL Serge
     D.O.B. 10th August 1961 in PARIS 12th district
     Freelance Photographer
     Placed in custody: 02/09/97 to 21/10/97

(2) ARSOV Nikola
     D.O.B. 20th April 1959 in SKOPJE (Yugoslavia)
     Photographer

(3) DARMON Stéphane
     D.O.B. 27th May 1965 in PARIS 1st district
     Messenger
     Placed in custody: 02/09/97 to 21/10/97

(4) LANGEVIN Jacques
     D.O.B. 21st September 1953 in LAVAL (Mayenne)
     Freelance photographer
     Placed in custody: 02/09/97 to 13/10/97

(5) MARTINEZ Christian
     D.O.B. 15th May 1954 in PARIS 12th district
     Press photographer
     FREE SUBJECT TO LEGAL RESTRICTIONS PENDING TRIAL

(6) RAT Romuald
   D.O.B. 17th September 1971 in LE RAINCY (Seine Saint Denis)
   Photographer
   FREE SUBJECT TO LEGAL RESTRICTIONS PENDING TRIAL

(7) VERES Laslo
   D.O.B. 1st December 1943 in BECEJ (Yugoslavia)
   Photographer

(8) ODEKERKEN David
   D.O.B. 8th March 1971 in CRETEUIL (94)
   Freelance photographer
   FREE SUBJECT TO LEGAL RESTRICTIONS PENDING TRIAL

   [the following were charged on 5 September 1997]
(9) CHASSERY Fabrice
   D.O.B. 16th March 1967 in PARIS 12th district
   Freelance photographer
   FREE SUBJECT TO LEGAL RESTRICTIONS PENDING TRIAL

(10) BENAMOU Serge
   D.O.B. 15th September 1953 in SAIDA (Algeria)
   Photo-journalist
   Placed in custody: 05/09/97 to 22/10/97

The above are under investigation charged with:
   failing to assist people in danger
   involuntary homicide involuntary injury
   ITT [temporary interruption of work] of more than three months

PLAINTIFFS
Mr Jean PAUL
Mrs Jean PAUL
represented by: Mr Jean Pierre BRIZAY

Mr Mohammed AL FAYED
represented by: Mr Bernard DARTEVELLE and Mr Georges KIEJMAN

Mrs Francis SHAND-KYDD
Mrs Sarah MC CORQUODALE
represented by: Mr Alain TOUCAS

Mr Trevor REES JONES
represented by: Mr Christian CURTIL

THE ENQUIRY HAS ESTABLISHED THE FOLLOWING FACTS:

Initial findings

At 0.26hrs on August 31, 1997, the switchboard at Paris fire brigade headquarters received a code-18 emergency call informing them of a serious traffic accident in the Pont d'Alma tunnel in Paris's 8th arrondissement.

A few minutes later, a police patrol on Cours Albert 1er consisting of officers Lino GAGLIADORNE and Sebastian DORZEE, patrolling Cours Albert 1er, was told of the accident by passers by and made their way to the scene.

The first Paris fire brigade crew arrived at the scene at 0.32hrs.

Inside the tunnel, in the Concorde-Boulogne lane, police and rescue services discovered a black Mercedes vehicle, type S280, registration number 680 LTV75. The vehicle was badly damaged and had come to rest against the outer wall of the tunnel, facing in the opposite direction to the normal flow of traffic.

Four people were found inside the vehicle
– Lady Diana SPENCER, who had been sitting in the rear right passenger seat, was still conscious and crouched on the floor of the vehicle with her back to the road.

– At her side, stretched out on the rear seat, was Emad AL FAYED, who had been sitting in the rear left passenger seat and appeared to be dead. Nevertheless, fire officers were still trying – in vain – to resuscitate him when he was pronounced dead by a doctor at 1.30hrs.

– In the front of the vehicle was the driver, Henri PAUL, the deputy security manager at the Ritz hotel, who had been killed immediately and was declared dead on removal from the wreckage.

– The front passenger was Trevor REES JONES, a body guard in the employment of the AL FAYED family, who was still conscious and had suffered serious multiple injuries to the face.

The two forward passengers' airbags had functioned normally.

Three people attended to the casualties: Dr Frédéric MAILLEZ, a doctor with 'SOS Médécin', and two volunteer fire officers, Dominique DALBY and a second who is unnamed. All three had been driving in the opposite direction, and on seeing the wrecked car, had stopped to go spontaneously to the aid of its occupants.

In the tunnel, among the onlookers who had gathered around the vehicle, several photographers were in action.

The two police officers, GAGLIARDONE and DORZEE, had trouble keeping the onlookers at bay in order to secure the scene and all the first witnesses reported that the photographers, who had arrived at the scene almost immediately, had pushed around the vehicle for the sole purpose of taking pictures of the casualties.

Autopsy conclusions

Autopsy examination concluded that Henri PAUL and Emad AL FAYED had both suffered a rupture in the isthmus of the aorta and a fractured spine, with, in the case of Henri PAUL, a medullar section in the dorsal region and in the case of Emad AL FAYED a medullar section in the cervical region.

Lady Diana SPENCER received pre-hospital intensive care treatment, both while she was trapped in the wreckage, from which she was finally released at 1 a.m., and during her transfer by ambulance, until her arrival at Pitie Salpetriere hospital at 2.06hrs.

However, despite intensive surgical intervention, doctors had no option but to declare her dead at 4 a.m.

The report submitted by professors Dominique LECOMTE and Andre LIENHART concluded that the cause of death was a wound to the upper left pulmonary vein, together with a rupture to the pericardium. The experts believed that it was exceptional for a patient who had suffered such serious intra-thoracic lesions to reach hospital alive, resuscitation had been in accordance with pre-hospitalisation regulations. According to the experts, the surgical team was beyond reproach, and no other surgical, anaesthetic or resuscitation strategy could have prevented deterioration in the condition of the patient.

The same experts pointed to the obviously traumatic origin of the injuries to the three victims, stating that those suffered by the first two were frequently observed in severe crash cases, head-on with extreme deceleration, while those to Lady Diana SPENCER were more unusual and could probably be explained by the victim's sideways position at the moment of impact.

The opening of the enquiry:

The Paris Prosecution Department, which immediately sent a representative to the scene, entrusted the enquiry of the case to the Paris police crime squad. It is in these conditions that several press photographers: Christian MARTINEZ, from the Angely Agency, Romuald RAT from the Gamma Agency, Stéphane DARMON, his companion, Jacques LAN-GEVIN, from the Sygma Agency, Serge ARNAL, from the Steels Press Agency, Laslo VERES, independent photographer and Nikola ARSOV, from the Sipa Presse, were taken in for questioning because of their attitude at the scene.

By Public Prosecutor's charge dated 2nd September 1997, the Paris Prosecution Department asked for an enquiry to be opened against the above named for failing to give assistance to persons in danger and, against an unnamed person, for homicide and involuntary injury.

However the examining magistrate named to lead these proceeding put under investigation all the people who were brought before him for all the charges listed in the initial charge.

As three photographers had left the scene before the police arrived, Fabrice CHASSERY, David ODEKERKEN and Serge BENAMOU, all independent photographers, reported to the crime squad offices on 4th September 1997 and, on 5th September 1997, were put under investigation for the same charges by the investigating magistrate.

The paths explored by the enquiry:

– The enquiry, which was finally entrusted to two examining magistrates by the Presiding Judge of the Court of Paris, because of the extent and complexity of the investigations to be carried out, was going to clarify the context in which the photographers had followed the Mercedes in which the couple were travelling and the effect of their presence on the behaviour of the driver of the vehicle immediately before the accident.

– In addition, the preliminary investigation file had to identify and examine the attitude adopted by these same photographers in the moments which immediately preceded the accident.

– The enquiry was also going to look into the conditions in which Henri PAUL had taken the wheel of the Mercedes carrying the couple on the evening of 31st August 1997.

On this particular point, numerous experts' reports examined following the autopsy on the body of Henri PAUL rapidly showed the presence of a level of pure alcohol per litre of blood of between 1.73 and 1.75 grams, which is far superior, in all cases, than the legal level.

Similarly, these analyses revealed as those carried out on samples of the hair and bone marrow of the deceased, that he regularly consumed Prozac and Tiapridal, both medicines which are not recommended for drivers, as they provoke a change in the ability to be vigilant, particularly when they are taken in combination with alcohol.

Finally, the amount of transferrin in the blood showed a level of 32 UI/l, compatible, according to the experts with a chronic alcoholism over the course of at least a week.

The investigations which were carried out both at the scene and on the vehicle itself, allowed for the hypothesis of a possible collision with another vehicle.

The Mercedes S280, in which the passengers were found, belonged to the company Etoile Limousine and had been hired by this company to the Ritz hotel, its only client. It was examined by the experts from the Institut de Recherche Criminelle de la Gendarmerie Nationale (I.R.C.G.N.), then by Mr NIBODEAU-FRINDEL and Mr AMOUROUX, the experts commissioned by the examining magistrates, who all concluded that it had a low mileage, and was in perfect mechanical and working order.

Jean-François MUSA, manager of Etoile Limousine, confirmed that, on 31st August, it did not have any trace of accidental damage or scratches.

The investigations showed traces of whitish colour both on the front right wing and on the body of the right wing mirror, found further on in the tunnel.

The additional research carried out by I.R.C.G.N. showed traces, both on the front right wing and on the body of the wing mirror, which came from the same vehicle, whose technical characteristics corresponded to a vehicle make Fiat "Uno', white in colour, built in Italy in the period 1983 to the end of August 1987.

In addition, some red and white optical debris found on the right hand lane, 7 or 8 metres from the entrance to the Alma tunnel were described as also coming from a rear light of a vehicle make Fiat "Uno', built in Italy in the period May 1983 to September 1989.

The arrival in Paris of the couple Diana Spencer and Emad Al Fayed
The arrival of the couple in Paris and their movements during the day of 30th August 1997 mobilised a growing number of press photographers.

Lady Diana SPENCER, Princess of Wales, and her friend, Emad AL FAYED, had landed at Le Bourget airport in the morning of the 30th August 1997 from Sardinia, at the end of a Mediterranean cruise, where they had been followed by a great number of the world's press.

The couple were accompanied by two English bodyguards, employed by the private security of the AL FAYED family, Trevor REES JONES and Alexander WINGFIELD.

Two vehicles were waiting for them, a Range Rover which was driven by Henri PAUL, deputy security manager of the Ritz hotel, owned by the father of Emad AL FAYED, Mohammed AL FAYED, and a Mercedes 600, driven by Philippe DOURNEAU, Mohammed AL FAYED's official driver when he was in France.

The Princess had not advised the British Embassy of her presence in France and had not requested any particular protection from the French authorities.

The press was present from their arrival. At the airport were: Fabrice CHASSERY, at the wheel of a charcoal grey Peugeot 205, registration no. 5816 WJ 92, David ODEKERKEN was driving a beige Mitsubishi 'Pajero' 4/4, registration no. 520 LPZ75, Romuald RAT and his driver, Stéphane DARMON, on a dark blue Honda motorcycle, registration no. 302 LXT75 and Alain GUIZARD, from the Angely Agency, was in a grey-blue Peugeot 205, registration no. 3904 ZR 92, accompanied by three press motorcyclists from the same agency.

After a detour to one of the residences of the AL FAYED family, the Windsor villa, situated on the Bois de Boulogne, Lady Diana SPENCER and Emad AL FAYED went to the Ritz hotel.

During the different journeys, the photographers ended up losing sight of the vehicles and only Alexander WINGFIELD recalled the dangerous behaviour of some of them on the road. Trevor REES JONES and Philippe DOURNEAU, on the other hand, testified that the photographers had always remained behind the Range Rover.

At about 18.00hrs the couple, still in the Mercedes driven by Philippe DOURNEAU, returned to the AL FAYED family hotel, rue Arsène Houssaye, very close to the Arc de Triomphe, while Jean-François MUSA replaced Henri PAUL at the wheel of the Range Rover.

Numerous photographers had again started to follow them at that moment, and, according to Trevor REES JONES, he had asked them not to take photos during the journey, a request which they respected.

However there were still more of them as the couple's car turned into rue Arsène Houssaye, and there was then a jostling, followed by an incident between Romuald RAT and the security personnel, an incident which was quickly resolved by the intervention of Trevor REES JONES and Alexander WINGFIELD.

As well as the photographers who had been present since Le Bourget, there were in front of the building in the rue Arsène Houssaye, Serge BENAMOU and Laslo VERES, who were both riding their scooters, as well as Christian MARTINEZ and Serge ARNAL, who had come in the latter's car, a Fiat black 'UNO', registration no. 444 JNB 75.

During this time Henri PAUL, who was not on duty that evening, had left the Ritz hotel at about 19.00hrs, telling the security guard, François TENDIL, that he could always be reached on his mobile telephone.

Claude ROULET, the assistant of Franck Klein, the manager of the Ritz hotel, who was not in Paris at that time, had, at the request of Emad AL FAYED, reserved a table for the couple in a restaurant in the capital, where he had gone to wait for them.

He cancelled this reservation at about 21.00, as Emad AL FAYED informed him that, because of the crowds of journalists they were dining at the Ritz, in the hope of getting some more peace.

Despite these precautions, when the Mercedes and the Range Rover arrived at Place Vendôme, the photographers had followed them from the rue Arsène Houssaye, and in front of the hotel there was a big crowds of curious onlookers and journalists.

As the couple left their vehicle belatedly there was a crush at the moment when they entered the hotel.

This situation annoyed Emad AL FAYED, as testified by Trevor REES JONES and Alexander WINGFIELD, who added that, not being made aware of the change of programme until the journey to the Ritz, they were unable to anticipate the difficulties.

Trevor REES JONES even stated: 'Dodi took an active part in security arrangements, he was the boss and in addition we did not know the programme in advance, only he knew the programme.'

Henri PAUL was informed of the incident by François TENDIL, then took the initiative to return to the hotel, where he reported at 22.07hrs, as seen by the hotel surveillance camera.

Then he joined the two English body guards at the bar where he consumed two glasses of 'Ricard'.

The change in the programme: The diversionary tactics decided by Emad Al Fayed

As soon as he arrived at the Ritz, Emad AL FAYED, for his part, called Thierry ROCHER, the night manager of the hotel to inform him of the situation.

Learning from the latter that Henri PAUL had returned, he asked him to tell him that they needed a third vehicle, placed in rue Cambon, at the back of the building, to return to rue Arsène Houssaye, and that the two vehicles used by the couple during the day would stay in Place Vendôme to create a diversion.

Trevor REES JONES and Alexander WINGFIELD confirmed that the decision to use a third vehicle had been taken by Emad AL FAYED and that it was he who had asked Henri PAUL to drive it.

Emad AL FAYED had in addition stipulated that Trevor REES JONES should accompany them.

The two bodyguards explained that they had expressed their disagreement with these arrangements, but only in as far as they were to separate.

None of them, however expressed any reservations about the capability of Henri PAUL to drive. They stated that nothing in his behaviour led them to think that he was drunk and they claimed that they had not seen the types of drinks that he had consumed.

In fact, of the four employees in charge of the bar that evening, only Alain WILLAUMEZ noted that Henri PAUL was drunk; Thierry ROCHER, who went to tell Henri PAUL the instructions from Emad AL FAYED found that his behaviour was completely normal.

He stated that Henri PAUL had replied that 'he was going to finish his "Ricard" with the English'.

The results of the analyses, notably of the amount of transferrin, showed the existence of a certain amount of chronic alcoholism and the testimony of one of his closest friends, Dr Dominique MELO revealed that it was not an isolated problem, as the latter had consulted him a year and a half previously about the matter.

The enquiry was not able to establish formally if the employers of Henri PAUL were in a position to know about this aspect of his personality: apart from the testimony of Alain WILLAUMEZ, none of the other professional colleagues of Henri PAUL had heard anything about this subject. He did have the reputation of being someone who 'enjoyed life'.

He had been employed at the Ritz since 1985 and was well liked by the management.

On a private level his best friends, his ex girlfriend, his neighbours, all painted a portrait of a man who was both 'shy' and at the same time 'enjoyed life'. No one seemed to have noticed the existence of a problem linked to alcohol.

In fact, if the appointment of Henri PAUL as the driver poses a problem about the awareness of his state on the evening in question and his intemperance, it should also lead to an examination of the conditions in which it had been decided to resort to a vehicle from the company Etoile Limousine, whose fleet was made up of high powered cars, necessitating to drive them, the possession of a special licence, which Mr Henri PAUL did not possess.

On this point the versions of the Ritz management and Jean François MUSA, the manager of Etoile Limousine, diverge: Jean François MUSA claimed that he had expressed reticence when he heard that Henri PAUL would drive the car, notably because he did not have an ad hoc licence, but no witness confirms this point.

Jean François MUSA, who however admitted still allowing the use of the vehicle, despite knowing that Henri PAUL was to drive it, justified this by reason of the fact that he could not refuse what was asked of him.

Examining the nature of the commercial links which united the Ritz – Jean-François MUSA used to drive for the Ritz – to the Etoile Limousine company, one can see the total dependence of the Etoile Limousine company on the Ritz, its only client, which put it in competition with another company offering identical services – the MURDOCH company.

Finally, it is worth remembering that during the day Jean-François MUSA had been used to drive the Range Rover for Emad AL FAYED and that the same Jean-François MUSA, who did not belong officially to the staff of the Ritz, had been used on different occasions in the same conditions, as if he were still an employee of the hotel.

From a general point of view, even if Emad AL FAYED and the Princess had not gone down to the Ritz, the management and the staff of the institution as a whole were put at their entire disposal from their arrival in Paris and Emad AL FAYED had, as a last resort, the power to decide all matters.

While the diversionary manoeuvre was being prepared, the photographers were still waiting in front of the hotel, in the Place Vendôme, and several more arrived: notably Alain GUIZARD, Jacques LANGEVIN, who arrived in a grey Golf registration no. 3765PL94, and Nikola ARSOV, driving a white BMW motorbike registration 448 BNE 91.

Towards midnight, Philippe DOURNEAU and Jean-François MUSA simulated a fake departure, driving around the Place Vendôme in the Mercedes 600 and the Range Rover.

Several journalists noticed that Henri PAUL was behaving unusually towards them that evening, coming to see them, and announcing the departure of the couple as imminent. Several described him as 'laughing, particularly jovial'.

Frederic LUCARD, the young valet in charge of driving the Mercedes S280 to the Rue Cambon, confirmed the 'jovial' discussions between Henri PAUL and the journalists and even added – although he alone described it – that when Henri PAUL took the wheel of the Mercedes in the Rue Cambon, he heard him say to the journalists present: 'Don't try to follow us, you'll never catch us.'

Anticipating the possibility of the couple's exit by the rear of the building, Serge BENAMOU, Jacques LANGEVIN, Fabrice CHASSERY and Alain GUIZARD went to the Rue Cambon and watched both the arrival of the Mercedes S280 and the departure of the couple.

They then warned Romuald RAT, Christian MARTINEZ, Serge ARNAL and David ODEKERKEN, who had stayed in front of the hotel.

Jacques LANGEVIN, Fabrice CHASSERY and Serge BENAMOU took a few pictures of the couple, then the Mercedes left at speed.

It was then 12.20 a.m. on the hotel's surveillance camera clock in the Rue Cambon.

The drive from The Ritz to Alma
Among those under investigation, several confirmed they had followed the same path as the Mercedes.

Romuald RAT, Stéphane DARMON, Serge ARNAL and Christian MARTINEZ claimed that after a red light in the Place de la Concorde, the Mercedes accelerated to a very high speed along the river, and that they rapidly lost sight of it.

They had then slowed down at the exit of the first tunnel, thinking that the Mercedes might have turned off, but they continued along the road, only seeing the Mercedes again, this time involved in the accident, as they approached the Alma tunnel.

Serge BENAMOU had also followed the river, but rapidly left behind, he had taken the first tunnel exit and arrived at the Place de l'Alma.

Jacques LANGEVIN meanwhile explained that his car had been parked in the Rue Cambon, and after a detour through the Place Vendôme, he had decided to go to meet friends for dinner. It was by chance, and some time later, that he followed the same road as the Mercedes.

David ODEKERKEN found himself behind the Mercedes until the Concorde red traffic light. He claimed he had then decided not to follow further. He saw the Mercedes depart in a whirlwind, followed by Serge ARNAL's vehicle, and he was then overtaken by Romuald RAT and Stéphane DARMON. He explained that to get to his home he had also by chance followed the Mercedes' route.

Consequently, none of the photographers admits that they 'chased' the car carrying the couple, nor that they had impeded his progress or taken pictures en route. None of the negatives seized from the photographers shows pictures taken on the journey. Nor did any of them admit to having been close enough to the Mercedes to have witnessed the actual accident.

There were three photographers under investigation who claimed not even to have tried to follow the Mercedes:

– Laslo VERES stayed in front of the Ritz and only learned of the accident later in a phone call from Serge BENAMOU. His story was confirmed by the Ritz surveillance cameras, which established that at 12.26 a.m. he was still in front of the hotel.

– Fabrice CHASSERY declared that, in agreement with David ODEKER-KEN, he had decided to not follow the car and that from the Place de la Concorde he had taken the Champs Elysées, where a call from David ODEKERKEN informed him of the accident.

– Finally Nicola ARSOV had stayed in front of the Ritz with some other photographers, including Pierre HOUNSFIELD, and had finally followed the Range Rover and the Mercedes 600 until the Champs Elysées, then avenue Wilson, where he had left these two vehicles and turned into Cours Albert 1er to arrive at the Place de l'Alma.

In fact the critical examination of the accounts of the persons questioned does not allow them to be radically called into question:

– As regards first of all Romuald RAT and Stéphane DARMON, the experts' reports comparing the speed of the different vehicles established that over 1400 metres, or the distance between the Avenue Champs Elysées and the Pont de l'Alma, their motorcycle was slower than the Mercedes.

– As for Serge BENAMOU, who was driving a scooter, the question did not arise, and the same can be said for Serge ARNAL, whose Fiat 'Uno' could not be compared with the Mercedes.

The moment's hesitation mentioned by Romuald RAT, Stéphane DARMON, Christian MARTINEZ and Serge ARNAL at the exit of the first tunnel seems logical, in as far as the exit towards the Place de l'Alma allowed access to the Avenue Marceau and to thus follow directly on to the Rue de Presbourg and the Rue Arsène Houssaye. This was moreover the route, which Philippe DOURNEAU was taking in his Mercedes 600.

In addition, if some witnesses noted the presence of motorcycles behind the Mercedes, or even their annoying behaviour during the journey between the Place de la Concorde and the Alma tunnel, they did not state either the number or the type.

Finally the witnesses situated, at the moment of the accident, opposite the entrance to the tunnel, definitely noticed a motorcycle, but whereas according to some of them it was following the Mercedes closely, according to others, it did not arrive until after the accident. Above all they proved incapable of describing it with a minimum of details.

– The explanations of David ODEKERKEN and Fabrice CHASSERY were not totally convincing as Romuald RAT, Stéphane DARMON, Serge ARNAL, Christian MARTINEZ and Serge BENAMOU confirmed having seen them behind the Mercedes at the red traffic light at la Concorde.

Furthermore it is difficult to understand why professionals reputed to be 'persistent' and who had already waited for hours would have given up in this manner.

But, there again, the presence of the David ODEKERKEN quite distinctive vehicle was, however, neither noticed by the witnesses to the journey nor by the witnesses to the accident.

In addition, on the list of telephone calls made, a call by David ODEKERKEN to Fabrice CHASSERY at 00.24:05, or at a time which corresponds to minutes after the accident, is identified, which would tend to confirm that they had separated, perhaps in order to better 'cover' all the possible routes.

– If the statements made by Nikola ARSOV do not correspond to the route described by Philippe DOURNEAU, as being the one that he would have followed, one cannot deduce with certainty that he had set off in pursuit of the Mercedes.

On the one hand the testimony of Pierre HOUNSFIELD, another reporter present in front of the Ritz, confirmed that Nikola ARSOV had left the Place Vendôme too late to be found immediately behind the Mercedes and, on the other hand, if a witness, Jean-Louis BONNIN, stated that he had been overtaken on the right bank [of the Seine] by a motorcycle with a number plate '91', like that of Nikola ARSOV, he described two people on the motorcycle, when it has been established that Nikola ARSOV was driving alone.

– As for Jacques LANGEVIN, his position was only called into question by Alain GUIZARD, who, in his first statement, had explained that he had seen Jacques LANGEVIN's Golf in the group of vehicles behind the Mercedes at the traffic light on the Place de la Concorde, but, when confronted, had not confirmed this statement.

– Finally, the only survivor of the accident, Trevor REES JONES, suffering from amnesia, had no memory of the part of the journey between the Ritz and the Alma tunnel, and was not able to supply precise information on the progress of the journey.

The only thing he could confirm was the presence behind them leaving the Rue Cambon of a scooter and a small light coloured car as well as, at the stop at the traffic lights on Place de la Concorde, the presence of a motorcycle at their sides, before the Mercedes sped off quickly in first gear.

In conclusion, it is not possible to determine exactly which of the people under examination who followed the Mercedes for the whole of the journey right up to the place of the accident, as a doubt exists on this point with regard to Fabrice CHASSERY and Nikola ARSOV.

As for those who had taken the same route as the Mercedes, neither their behaviour on the road nor their exact speed is known precisely.

And even if it is undeniable that they arrived in the tunnel a very short time after the accident, one cannot estimate with any certainty what distance they were away from the Mercedes at the moment when the latter sped into the tunnel.

Finally, taking account of the technical findings of the I.R.C.G.N. experts, one can state that none of the vehicles used by the people under examination corresponds to the Fiat 'Uno' which is likely to have been in collision with the Mercedes.

The analysis of the causes and the liability with regard to the crimes of homicide and voluntary (sic) injury
First of all, as far as the possible role played in the accident by a Fiat 'Uno', the existence of which was revealed by the traces found on the Mercedes, the experts' reports have underlined that, in every hypothesis, its role could only have been a passive one.

The driver of this Fiat 'Uno' has not been able to be identified, despite extremely long and detailed investigations which have been lead by the enquiry team. It only had, to direct its research, the witness statements of a couple of drivers, who, at approximately the time which could correspond to the accident, told of the abnormal behaviour of the driver of a Fiat 'Uno' crossing the Place de l'Alma in the direction of Boulogne.

Interrogated about the circumstances of the collision between this unknown Fiat 'Uno' and the Mercedes S280, the I.R.C.G.N. experts indicated that it was a collision 'three quarters behind', and that at the moment of contact between the two vehicles the speed of the Mercedes was faster than that of the Fiat 'Uno'.

The experts NIBODEAU-FRINDEL and AMOUROUX, for their part, concluded that the contact between the Mercedes and the Fiat 'Uno' only consisted of a simple scrape, which had not led to a significant reduction in speed by the Mercedes.

The speed at which the Mercedes was travelling was described as very fast by all the witnesses, both during the journey along the banks [of the Seine] and at the moment when it entered the tunnel.

Mr NIBODEAU-FRINDEL and Mr AMOUROUX estimated the speed of the Mercedes, before the collision at a total of between a maximum of 155 km/hour and a minimum of 118 km/hour and the speed, at the moment of the crash on the thirteenth pillar of the Alma tunnel was between 95 and 109 km/hour with a margin of error of more or less 10 per cent.

They attributed the direct causes of the accident to this excessive speed which, taking account of the particular profile of the road, had rendered the vehicle difficult to control, all the more so because of the presence of the Fiat 'Uno' at the entrance of the tunnel and the fact that the driver of the Mercedes had very poor control of his vehicle.

They finally stated that Emad AL FAYED and Lady Diana SPENCER would have survived if they had fastened their safety belts.

Consequently, from all of the investigation's leads and from the different expert reports it transpires that the direct cause of the accident is the presence, at the wheel of the Mercedes S280, of a driver who had consumed a considerable amount of alcohol, combined with the fact that he had recently taken medication, driving at a speed not only faster than the maximum speed limit in built up areas, but excessive when taking account of the layout of the places and the predictable obstacles, notably the presence on his right of a vehicle moving at a slower pace.

Therefore the loss of control of the vehicle by the driver in the Alma tunnel constitutes the main cause of the accident.

Now, any possibility of pursuing this case is extinguished by the very fact of its previous demise by the setting in motion of the public action.

Therefore, in these conditions it remains that the criminal liability of those persons under examination for homicide and involuntary injuries can only be considered in terms of indirect cause, since the direct cause of the accident has thus been established.

In other words, the question is knowing whether the fact that a certain number of photographers had undertaken to follow the vehicle carrying Diana SPENCER and Emad AL FAYED played a contributory role, and a clear contributory role, by creating psychological conditions whereby the driver felt constrained to drive at an excessive speed.

This supposes first of all, therefore, that the photographers had 'pursued' the vehicle.

Now it is observed that, for the duration of the day, if the growing presence of the photographers did legitimately irritate the Princess and her companion, it was not unexpected, given the extreme media coverage of their relationship, nor, given the amount of means and personnel at their disposal, an event which had left them completely helpless.

The presence of these photographers during the day, although undesirable, had not manifested itself in dangerous practices, nor in recourse to ruses or subterfuges, all the photos taken showing clearly scenes in public.

Taking account of these elements, it is not possible to support the view that this general context constitutes a hounding of the couple by the photographers.

Secondly, this supposes researching how many photographers had followed the couple, their number being able to play an important role in the creation of a psychological effect on the driver, and who from among the photographers had been able to play this role.

In this regard, a rigorous assessment of the charges against each of the people under examination led to eliminating Laslo VERES from any responsibility, as it has been established that he had not followed the Mercedes and to not uphold that of Fabrice CHASSERY and Nikola ARSOV for whom there remains some doubt on this point.

Finally, with regard to Romuald RAT, Stéphane DARMON, Serge ARNAL, Christian MARTINEZ, Serge BENAMOU, David ODEKERKEN and Jacques LANGEVIN, it is necessary to determine with certainty if, at the moment when the driver lost control of the vehicle, they were within sight of the Mercedes.

The enquiry not having being able to establish this, one cannot therefore state that their presence provoked such a stress in the driver that it definitely explains the speed taken.

In fact, in the hypothesis of a slower speed, or 118 km/hour, it is rather rash to allude to a 'fleeing' behaviour.

The speed adopted by the driver can also clearly be attributed to the presence of alcohol in his blood, the effect of which was increased by the medicines, and thereby characterise the psychological effect of a driver who was totally uninhibited at the wheel of a powerful car and sure of having [out]distanced the photographers.

Consequently, it was not shown that at the moment when the driver lost control of his vehicle, he found himself having to drive at speed, rendering the accident inevitable.

One can only state that there is no clear underlying link between the speed of the vehicle and the presence of photographers following the vehicle.

Therefore the charges of homicide and involuntary injury will be judged as no grounds for prosecution with respect to Romuald RAT, Christian

MARTINEZ, Stéphane DARMON, Jacques LANGEVIN, Serge ARNAL, Laslo VERES, Nikola ARSOV, Fabrice CHASSERY, David ODEKERKEN and Serge BENAMOU.

The establishment of an incidental civil claim for damages by Trevor Rees Jones
On 23rd September 1998, alongside the preliminary investigation of the case opened on 2nd September 1997, Trevor REES JONES' counsel lodged a claim for damages against X for having put in danger the life of another person, by reason of the fact that, by putting at the Ritz' disposal a powerful car without a driver who held a licence as required by the regulations, the managers of the Etoile Limousine company had directly exposed Trevor REES JONES to the risk of death, mutilation or permanent disability.

This claim was followed on 2nd November 1998 by the opening of an enquiry and, by reason of the connection with the enquiry opened 2nd September 1997, a joinder order was made on 30th November 1998.

This claim could not go ahead, in as far as, on the one hand the crime of having endangered the life of another person is only constituted in the absence of harmful result, which is not the case of Trevor REES JONES, as he showed numerous traumatic lesions following the accident of 31st August 1997 and the experts commissioned to evaluate the gravity [of his injuries] and determine the resulting ITT, concluded on 2nd October 1997 that the initial ITT was still in course and would not be less than six months.

On the other hand, in order to establish the crime, it is necessary to show that the manifestly deliberate violation of a particular safety or cautionary obligation imposed by law or regulations has directly exposed another person to an immediate risk of death, mutilation or permanent disability.

One cannot sustain in the matter of the non-respect of the provisions of the decree of the 15th July 1955 and the decree of 18th April 1966, which impose for the driving of high powered vehicles, the possession of a special licence, has directly exposed the plaintiff to an immediate risk of death, mutilation or permanent disability, it being a matter of carrying out a relatively short journey in town, i.e. in a secure road environment and on board a vehicle, certainly high powered, but technically accessible to the holders of a Category B driving licence.

Consequently the claim will be judged as there being no grounds for prosecution.

After the accident: liability with regard to the crime of failing to come to the aid of people in danger

In order to come to a decision regarding each of the persons under examination on the imputability of the facts with regard to not coming to the aid of people in danger, first of all requires the establishment, with utmost exactitude, of the time sequence of events after the accident occurred, in order to define the exact period during which they can be legitimately charged with voluntary failure.

Taking account of the multiplicity of sources of information, which cannot be synchronised with certainty, the sequence of the events has been established based on several factors:

The first source comes from the recording of the security cameras at the Ritz hotel, where the internal clock indicated the departure of the Mercedes from the Rue Cambon at 00.20.

Then come the telephone switchboards of the emergency services:

– at the number '18', the number of the main Fire Station, the first call was received at 00.26, the call from Dr. MAILLEZ who arrived on the scene at almost the same period of time.

– at the number '17', emergency number for the police, the first call was recorded at 00.29:59.

Thirdly, numerous pieces of information were obtained from the listings, supplied by the mobile telephone operators Itinéris and SFR, of all the calls made from a portable telephone on 30th and 31st August 1997, between midnight and one o'clock in the morning, in the Concorde/Vendôme/Alma areas.

Thus one finds a first call to '18' at 00.23:43, from Paul CARRIL's mobile, who declared having called as soon as he heard the crash.

This first call was followed by a number of others both to '18' and to '112', the emergency number which is common to Itinéris and SFR.

In addition the listing mentions, at 00.23, a call from Serge ARNAL's mobile to '12'.

Finally the emergency services themselves constitute the last source of information, as the police commander having received the call from the

GAGLIARDONE/DORZEE patrol indicated that it was then 00.30, while the report established by the fireman mentioned that the first crew arrived at 00.32.

In spite of an inevitable margin of error, it is accepted therefore that a short time passed between the departure from the Rue Cambon and the occurrence of the accident, as well as the existence, in very quick succession of a large number of calls to the emergency services then the rapid arrival of these services.

Equally one notes that the call from Dr MAILLEZ to the firemen happened a very short time after the accident, which is to be emphasized, as from the moment when the doctor was at the location and took charge of things, the legal obligation to personally act is no longer imposed with the same force for any non specialists present at the scene.

In fact it transpires from the time sequence of the different calls and from the testimony of Mark BUTT, who accompanied Dr MAILLEZ, that when Dr MAILLEZ left his vehicle, which was stopped on the opposite carriageway, to assist the injured, the first policemen had not yet arrived.

It is consequently in the few minutes preceding Dr MAILLEZ's arrival that the attitude of the different people under examination can be usefully considered by piecing together their statements, the analysis of the photos which they took and the statements of the witnesses most directly involved.

In fact, the enquiry was able to piece together the existence of a small group of witnesses present at the scene before the arrival of Dr MAILLEZ, knowing that other onlookers had equally appeared very quickly on the scene, as seen on the photographs, but without being able to be identified.

– Belkacem BOUZID and Abdelatif REDJIL, walking in the Place de la Reine Astrid, explained that they rushed into the tunnel as soon as they heard the crash.

Belkacem BOUZID stated that he then saw four photographers in action, among whom he identified Romuald RAT, while Abdelatif REDJIL claimed that they had been the first on the scene, even before a first photographer, who got off a motorcycle and whom he identified as being Romuald RAT.

It is worth noting that Adelatif REDJIL could only be heard rather belatedly.

However they are both identifiable on different photos, Belkacem BOUZID, dressed in a mustard coloured jacket and Abdelatif REDJIL in blue jeans and a green jacket.

– Two young people had left a car travelling in the opposite direction to go to the vehicle involved in the accident: Damien DALBY, a voluntary fireman, and his brother Sébastien PENNEQUIN.

They explained that at least four photographers were already there, and they identified Romuald RAT, whom they described as kneeling in front of the open back right door, the scene which was found on a photograph by Christian MARTINEZ.

They heard him shout in the direction of another photographer who was moving away: 'she is alive', then saw him push back the other photographers.

After having gone round the car to estimate the state of the injured, Damien DALBY had then seen Dr MAILLEZ, who was taking charge of Lady Diana SPENCER and he himself, together with another unidentified fireman, therefore dealt with Trevor REES JONES, Damien DALBY being dressed in blue jeans and a blue T-shirt and the other volunteer fireman in blue jeans and a blue-grey T-shirt.

Sébastien PENNEQUIN stated that he had helped a man to describe the state of the injured, as this man had the firemen on line, thanks to a mobile phone. This man was James HUTH, who was in a flat in Cours Albert 1er, and who explained that he went into the tunnel as soon as he heard the crash.

On photo D470, Sébastien PENNEQUIN appears in a black jacket and black jeans.

– Finally Clifford GOOROOVADOO, a limousine driver, who was waiting for his clients at the Place de l'Alma when he heard the crash caused by the accident, stated that at the time he arrived near the vehicle involved in the accident four or five people, of whom three were taking photographs, were near the Mercedes.

He recognised Romuald RAT, whom he described as particularly agitated: 'Romuald RAT was everywhere around the car (. . .), he was moving around in all directions'.

He also said he had seen him argue with Christian MARTINEZ.

He spoke in English to the injured to reassure them and, indeed, he also appears on several photographs.

In addition, during the course of the enquiry, Stéphane DARMON, Serge ARNAL, Christian MARTINEZ, Romuald RAT and Serge BENAMOU admitted that they arrived at the scene of the accident before the arrival of Dr MAILLEZ.

– Stéphane DARMON stated that he was the first to enter the tunnel where he had parked his motorcycle about ten metres in front of the Mercedes, Romuald RAT had got off the machine and had gone towards the car when Serge BENAMOU and Serge ARNAL arrived.

Serge ARNAL informed him that he had called the emergency services.

Stéphane DARMON had moved his motorcycle, then he remained apart [from the others], quite distressed, according to his statement.

– Romuald RAT admitted that, as soon as he got off his motorcycle, he had run towards the Mercedes and taken three photographs. Then he had opened the back right door, taken the princess's pulse and had said to her, as well as to Trevor REES JONES, that 'the doctor was on his way'. He stated that he had not started to take pictures again until after the arrival of the police. He added that at the moment when he saw the injured and realised the severity of their state, he had heard someone shout: 'I have called the emergency services'.

On a total of 19 photos taken by Romuald RAT in the tunnel there are certainly three photographs which depict just the Mercedes, it must be added that a non-identified individual is in the shot in two of the photographs and a man who could be Mr BENAMOU on the third.

Finally, there is a fourth photo, which did not show either Dr MAILLEZ or the policemen, but already a number of onlookers.

According to the expert DEWOLF, Romuald RAT was the second to take photographs of the Mercedes alone, and he never put his camera less than 5 metres from the subjects.

– Serge ARNAL stated that he had parked his vehicle in the direction of the exit of the tunnel then had immediately called the emergency services, dialling '112' on his mobile phone. He had a contact on line and, despite a very bad reception, had provided the first pieces of information.

He explained that he had then gone down into the tunnel, where Romuald RAT, Christian MARTINEZ, David ODEKERKEN and Serge BENAMOU were already, and he had taken photos of the Mercedes.

He took 16 photographs in the tunnel, of which 8 featured the Mercedes completely alone.

According to the expert the photo D226 was certainly, of all the photos seized, the first to be taken immediately after the accident, as the smoke coming from the car can be made out, the lights were on and the driver's air bag was still inflated. The seven photographs after that had been taken by going around the vehicle, from the back to the front.

At the time of taking the following photos, Serge ARNAL had never approached the injured closer than 1.5 metres.

– Christian MARTINEZ stated that he had left the vehicle of Serge ARNAL with his camera, having seen Romuald RAT at the place and heard someone say 'I can't get 12'. He thought it was Serge ARNAL.

He had taken some photographs before going, with Serge ARNAL, to move the vehicle of Serge ARNAL, then came back and took more photos.

He was the one who had taken the most, 31 in total, and the expert identified him as the one who had come the closest [to the victims], less than 1.5 metres from Lady Diana SPENCER, notably at the moment when Dr MAILLEZ was attending to her.

On four of these photos Dr MAILLEZ did not appear.

– Serge BENAMOU stated that, when he entered the tunnel, in the opposite direction to the traffic, as he was coming from the Place de l'Alma, and that Romuald RAT, Christian MARTINEZ and Serge ARNAL were already near the Mercedes, Serge Arnal told him that he had called the emergency services.

Both Dr MAILLEZ and the firemen appear on all the photos belonging to him, which were seized belatedly, as he was not questioned that evening.

– For his part, David ODEKERKEN stated that he had not parked in the tunnel, when he passed by the car, he had seen the first four photographers and, going towards the exit of the tunnel, had passed Stéphane DARMON. Then he called Fabrice CHASSERY and explained that he had not called the emergency services at that moment as he had heard people say that they had already been called.

– Finally Jacques LANGEVIN, Fabrice CHASSERY, Nikola ARSOV and Laslo VERES stated they arrived on the scene much later than the arrival of the emergency services.

It is noted that, policemen and firemen appear on all the photos taken by Fabrice CHASSERY, Jacques LANGEVIN and David ODEKERKEN.

As for Nikola ARSOV, he said that he took some photographs, when the emergency services were present, but his flash did not work.

In addition, no witness mentioned their presence before the arrival of the emergency services.

Consequently, since there are no facts which establish the presence of David ODEKERKEN, Jacques LANGEVIN, Fabrice CHASSERY, Nikola ARSOV and Laslo VERES at the scene during the period of time preceding the arrival of the police and the emergency services, and a fortiori that of Dr MAILLEZ, one cannot claim that they failed to offer assistance at the scene.

One must wonder then about the credit that can be accorded to the statements by Serge ARNAL concerning the telephone call to the emergency services, in as far as he explained that he had dialled '112' when, on the listings of calls passed on from the mobile telephones, the call that he made at 0.23 had been to '12', the number for telephone information.

During his detention by the crime squad, the investigating officers had ascertained the last 10 numbers dialled in his mobile telephone memory. They found the '112' just before a call to his Chief Editor, Franck KLEIN, this last communication being found, in the same order, on the listing of mobile calls.

Consequently, the inconsistency existing between the reading of his calls in his mobile and that of the general listing cannot constitute an offence [there being none].

Serge ARNAL, having acted to call the emergency services, cannot be held in custody.

Then with regard to Stéphane DARMON, Christian MARTINEZ, Serge BENAMOU and Romuald RAT, one must note that, if the law requires you to offer to people in danger immediate and personal assistance, or to call for assistance, that which each of them was able to do, as they all had a mobile telephone, it remains that the offence cannot be said to have occurred in the absence of intent.

This can be deduced from the establishment of the facts, consequently it is not proved that Stéphane DARMON, Serge BENAMOU and Christian MARTINEZ, who were informed by Serge ARNAL that he had made a call to the emergency services, had, by refraining from making a call themselves, the intention of not proffering assistance to the passengers of the vehicle involved in the accident.

Finally, with regard to Romuald RAT, the few seconds that he took to take three photos, before approaching the vehicle involved in the accident, do not appear in themselves likely to represent criminal intent.

On the one hand, he also maintained that he had heard someone shout that the emergency services had been informed, an assertion which is not improbable, given the telephone call by Serge ARNAL. On the other hand, it emerges from the different testimonies, and the photos seized, that he had stopped taking photos as soon as he had reached the vehicle, and was able to ascertain the state of the injured, and did not resume until after the arrival of Dr MAILLEZ.

The conduct which he adopted in this period of time, crouching down in front of the back passenger door, calling another photographer to tell him that the Princess was alive, then arguing with the other photographers, was liable to several interpretations, favourable or not according to whether you considered that, in the panic of the moment, he had tried to intervene, albeit clumsily, or whether he was acting as a professional cynic, calling his colleagues for a 'scoop', then pushing them away to organise his own room for manoeuvre.

In these conditions, it does not appear that the constituent elements of the crime of not assisting a person in danger were identified, the charges weighing on the various aspects of the case under examination being insufficient to justify their referral to a tribunal entertaining jurisdiction.

The critical view which could be brought on the manner in which the various people under examination have, during the course of the night in question, exerted their professional activity can only be recorded within the circumstances of the moral appreciation or the code of ethics which govern the profession of journalist or photo-journalist.

CLAIMS OF NO GROUNDS FOR PROSECUTION

Whereas, within the terms of the enquiry, there are insufficient charges against the following: ARNAL Serge, ARSOV Nikola, DARMON Stéphane, LANGEVIN Jacques, MARTINEZ Christian, RAT Romuald, VERES Laslo, ODEKERKEN David, CHASSERY Fabrice and BENAMOU Serge of having committed the crimes of involuntary manslaughter, involuntary injury, having incurred an ITT of more than 3 months, and of failing to assist people in danger, of which they are charged, neither against all other charges of homicide or involuntary injury, having incurred an ITT of more than 3 months.

Whereas there are also insufficient charges against any of having committed the crime of endangering the life of another person:

In accordance with articles 175, 176 and 177 of the Code of Penal Procedure; the examining magistrates find that there is no case to answer in the case of the state versus the above named of the charges of involuntary homicide, involuntary injury incurring an ITT of more than 3 months, and of failing to assist a person in danger and against any of the charges of involuntary homicide and injury which have incurred an ITT of more than 3 months and of endangering the life of another person.

Signed by the Public Prosecutor

ACKNOWLEDGEMENTS

I have still not encountered a journalist who is better informed about the crash that killed Princess Diana than Sylvie Deroche. She worked with distinction for French and British media since the day of the Alma tunnel crash. I met Sylvie on my first day of investigation in Paris and without her brilliance, her commitment and her encouragement, this book would not have been written. I decided I wanted to write it during a conversation with her in the garden of the Rodin museum in Paris in the summer of 1998 when we realised that there was so much we would be unable to include in our 40-minute *Dispatches* film. She was my key researcher on that investigation, and she worked loyally and immensely hard. I am enormously indebted to Kirsty Lang for introducing me to her.

Happily, Sylvie is now the mother of young Anouk and lives in Washington with her husband, Tony Allen-Mills. At Sylvie's suggestion I worked with journalist and author Stephanie Marteau in Paris as I made my 2004 film *The Diana Conspiracy* for Channel 4. I can pay Stephanie no higher compliment than to say that she slipped comfortably into Sylvie's shoes. The multilingual Bianca Roccelli who, with fellow researcher Adam Macqueen, made such an important contribution to the first edition of this book, has developed into an accomplished TV producer who worked diligently to help bring *The Diana Conspiracy* to fruition. I thank Dorothy Byrne for commissioning both my Channel 4 films on the Paris crash. I enjoyed helping to produce two editions, in 1998 and 2004, of *48 Hours Investigates* for CBS with producers Doug Longhini and Joe Halderman. The penetrating interviews that Erin Morriati conducted for CBS in 2004 enrich Chapter 15.

I have written for several national newspapers on the Paris crash and no editor has been more supportive than Dominic Lawson, the editor of the *Sunday Telegraph*. Dominic has encouraged me and been extremely supportive of my work, giving it generous space in his newspaper.

My parents, John and Aurea, and the rest of my now happily extended family, have been enormously supportive, as they have been throughout my life.

Martyn Gregory
May 2004

CAST OF CHARACTERS

Diana, Princess of Wales.
Dr Hasnat Khan, Princess Diana's 'Mr Wonderful', 1995–7.
Earl Spencer, Charles, Diana's brother.
Lady Sarah McCorquodale, Lady Jane Fellowes, Diana's sisters.
Frances Shand Kydd, Diana's mother.
Earl Spencer, Johnnie, Diana's father.
Raine Spencer, Diana's stepmother.

Mohamed Fayed, owner of Harrods and the Paris Ritz.
Dodi Fayed, eldest son of Mohamed Fayed and Samira Khashoggi.
Kelly Fisher, Dodi Fayed's girlfriend, 1996–7.
Adnan Khashoggi, arms dealer, former brother-in-law to Mohamed; Dodi's uncle.

Michael Cole, Director of Public Affairs, Harrods, until February 1998.
Laurie Mayer, Cole's successor.
Max Clifford, publicity agent and unofficial advisor to the Fayed family.

Trevor Rees-Jones, Fayed bodyguard.
Alexander 'Kez' Wingfield, Fayed bodyguard.
Ben Murrell, Head of Security at villa Windsor, Paris.
John Macnamara, Fayed's Director of Security.
Paul Handley-Greaves, Director of Personal Security.
Bob Loftus, Director of Security at Harrods until 1996.
Brian Dodd, Founder of Fayed's personal protection.

Pierre Ottavioli, Head of Fayed's parallel investigation into the crash in Paris.
Georges Kiejman, Fayed's chief French lawyer.
Bernard Dartevelle, Kiejman's number two.

Alberto Repossi, master jeweller.

Henri Paul, acting Head of Security at the Paris Ritz.
Frank Klein, President of the Paris Ritz.
Claude Roulet, Assistant to the President of the Paris Ritz.

François Tendil, Night Security Officer on the night of 30/31 August 1997.
Frédéric Lucard, Ritz 'vehicle jockey' on 30/31 August 1997.

Philippe 'Niels' Siegel, Director of Etoile Limousine.
Jean-François Musa, Director of Etoile Limousine.

Philippe Dourneau, Dodi's personal chauffeur.
René Delorm, Dodi's butler.
Gregorio Martin, caretaker at villa Windsor, Paris.

Hervé Stéphan, *Juge d'instruction* (investigating magistrate).
Marie-Christine Devidal, *Juge d'instruction*.
Martine Monteil, Head of French Criminal Brigade.
Jean-Claude Mulès, Head of the Criminal Brigade's investigation into the Alma tunnel crash.
Patrick Riou, director of Paris judiciary police.
Maud Coujard, Paris prosecutor in charge of the Alma tunnel investigation.
Gabriel Bestard, Chief Paris prosecutor.
Philippe Massoni, Paris police chief.
Jean-Pierre Chevènement, French Interior Minister.
Sami Naïr, Technical Advisor to Chevènement.
Sir Michael Jay, British Ambassador in Paris.

Professeurs Riou and Pavie, doctors who treated Diana at Pitié-Salpêtrière hospital.
Dr Frédéric Mailliez, off-duty doctor who treated Princess Diana in the Alma tunnel.
Professeur Dominique Lecomte, conducted Henri Paul's autopsy.
Dr Gilbert Pépin, independent analyst of Paul's autopsy results.
Michel Nibodeau-Frindel and Bernard Amouroux, commissioned to produce the definitive technical report on the accident.

Professor Peter Vanezis, Regius professor of Forensic Medicine and Science, Glasgow University.
Dr Murray Mackay, professor emeritus of Transport Safety, Birmingham University.

The Accused Paparazzi:
Romuald Rat, Gamma agency.

Christian Martinez, Angeli agency.
Serge Arnal, Stills agency.
Nikola Arsov, Sipa agency.
Jacques Langevin, Sygma agency.
Laszlo Veres.
David Oderkerken or **Ker**.
Fabrice Chassery.
Serge Benamou.

Stéphane Darmon, motorcyclist working for Gamma.

Laurent Sola Diffusion agency, which tried to sell pictures of the crash.

Christian Curtil, French lawyer for Trevor Rees-Jones.
David Crawford, British lawyer for Trevor Rees-Jones.

Thomas Sancton and Scott MacLeod, *Time* magazine journalists and authors of *Death of a Princess*.
Richard Belfield, Producer of *Diana – Secrets Behind The Crash*, broadcast on ITV, 3 June 1998.
Nicholas Owen, ITN Royal Correspondent and presenter of the above documentary.
François Levi/Levistre, Rouen *mythomane*.
Piers Morgan, editor, the *Mirror*.
Lyndon Larouche, founder, Executive Intelligence Review (EIR).
Jeffrey Steinberg, director, EIR.
Richard Tomlinson, renegade British spy.

Dominic Lawson, editor, *Sunday Telegraph*.
Rosa Monckton, wife of Dominic Lawson and close friend of Diana.
Simone Simmons, Diana's faith healer and author of *Diana: The Secret Years*.
Lana Marks, designer and friend of Diana's.
Dr Lily, practitioner of Chinese medicine.

CHRONOLOGY

1997

June 3	Diana accepts Mohamed Fayed's holiday invitation.
June 4	Fayed buys luxury yacht, *Jonikal*.

July 11–20	Saint-Tropez holiday with Princes William and Harry.
July 14	Dodi Fayed arrives in Saint-Tropez.
July 25–27	Diana and Dodi on 'secret weekend' in Paris.
July 31	Diana and Dodi begin six-day cruise on the *Jonikal*.

August 7	DI'S NEW MAN IS AL FAYED'S SON exclusive in the *Mirror*.
August 8–11	Diana in Bosnia for anti-landmine campaign.
August 10	'THE KISS' picture appears in British press.
August 15–20	Diana in Greece with Rosa Monckton.
August 21	Diana and Dodi start their last Mediterranean holiday.
August 30	Diana and Dodi fly to Paris from Sardinia.
August 31	00.26: crash in the Alma tunnel, Paris. Dodi Fayed and Henri Paul die instantly.
	04.00: Princess Diana dies in the Pitié-Salpêtrière hospital.

September 1	Results of first blood tests on Henri Paul show he was over the French legal drink-drive limit when he died.
September 2	Judges Stéphan and Devidal appointed to lead the French investigation into the crash.
	Paparazzi arrested at scene are released on bail.
	Kez Wingfield interviewed by the investigation.
September 5	Harrods' press conference given by Michael Cole.
September 6	Funeral of Diana, Princess of Wales.
September 10	Second set of blood test results on Henri Paul confirm he was drunk. Traces of prescribed drugs were also found.
September 19	Trevor Rees-Jones interviewed by Judge Stéphan.

October 2	IRCGN police laboratories announce that forensic tests showed that a Fiat Uno was involved in the accident.
October 3	Trevor Rees-Jones discharged from hospital.

December 19	Trevor Rees-Jones returns to Paris to speak to the investigation.

1998

February 12	Mohamed Fayed claims IT WAS NO ACCIDENT in the *Mirror*.
February 20	Michael Cole retires as Mohamed Fayed's spokesman.
February 28	Trevor Rees-Jones interview in the *Mirror*.
March 2	Mohamed Fayed arrested over break-in to a safety deposit box at Harrods.
April 21	Trevor Rees-Jones leaves his Fayed job.
June 2	Kez Wingfield leaves his Fayed job.
June 3	ITV broadcasts *Diana – Secrets Behind the Crash*.
June 4	Channel 4 broadcasts *Dispatches*: 'The Accident'.
June 5	*Grande Confrontation* of witnesses to the crash. Outside, Fayed launches verbal attack on Diana's mother.
June 12	On behalf of Trevor Rees-Jones, Christian Curtil asks Judge Stéphan to broaden his investigation.
July 3	Kez Wingfield interviewed again by the French investigation.
August 23	Fayed blames Rees-Jones and Wingfield for the crash.
August 28	Richard Tomlinson, former British spy, heard by Judge Stéphan, at his own request.
September 2	The *Sun* publishes footage from Ben Murrell illustrating that Diana and Dodi spent only 28 minutes at the villa Windsor. Murrell had quit his Fayed job the previous month.
September 3	Princes William and Harry request that their mother be allowed to 'rest in peace'.
September 23	Rees-Jones registers as a plaintiff against the Ritz and Etoile Limousine for 'placing his life in danger'.

1999

February 19	Judge Stéphan delivers his 6,800-page report to prosecutor Maud Coujard.
May 21	Fayed and Paul families lodge complaints about Stéphan's investigation to the French Court of appeal.

July 2   Court of appeal rejects the above complaints.

August 17   Prosecutor Coujard recommends to judges Stéphan
                        and Devidal that none of those under investigation
                        should be charged.

September 3   The judges announce that none of the photographers
                        arrested after the crash is to be charged.
                        Mohamed Fayed announces he will appeal against the
                        decision not to prosecute any of the photographers.
                        For the next four years, he launches a series of actions
                        against the French investigation – none is successful.

2000
July 18   High Court in London rejects Fayed's legal bid to
                        hold joint inquests into Diana's and Dodi's deaths.

2002
March   *The Bodyguard's Story* by Trevor Rees-Jones published.

April 14   The French Supreme Court of Appeal ends the
                        French investigation into the crash and upholds the
                        dismissal of the manslaughter charges against the
                        paparazzi.

2003
March 28   Fayed leaves Britain to live in Switzerland.

August 29   Royal coroner, Michael Burgess, announces inquests
                        into Diana's and Dodi's deaths will proceed.

November 28   Paparazzi cleared of 'invading Diana and Dodi's
                        privacy' in Paris.

2004
January 6   Inquests into Princess Diana's and Dodi Fayed's
                        deaths opened and adjourned by coroner, Michael
                        Burgess, in London and Reigate. Burgess will recon-
                        vene the inquests in 2005.

March 13   Fayed's legal action to hold a public enquiry into the
                        Paris crash in Scotland fails.

April 26   Metropolitan police commissioner, Sir John Stevens,
                  and coroner Burgess visit the Alma tunnel with
                  Martine Monteil as part of the inquests into Diana's
                  and Dodi's deaths.

INDEX

ODENT